Global Legal History

This collection brings together a group of international legal historians to further scholarship in different areas of comparative and regional legal history. Authors are drawn from Europe, Asia, and the Americas to produce new insights into the relationship between law and society across time and space. The book is divided into three parts: legal history and legal culture across borders, constitutional experiences in global perspective, and the history of judicial experiences. The three themes, and the chapters corresponding to each, provide a balance between public law and private law topics, and reflect a variety of methodologies, both empirical and theoretical. The volume highlights the gains that may be made by comparing the development of law in different countries and different time periods.

The book will be of interest to an international readership in Legal History, Comparative Law, Law and Society, and History.

Joshua C. Tate is Professor of Law at Southern Methodist University, Dedman School of Law (Dallas, Texas, USA). He has been a visiting faculty member at the University of Pennsylvania Law School (Spring 2008), a Lloyd M. Robbins Senior Research Fellow at the University of California at Berkeley (Fall 2012), and a visiting scholar at the University of Alaska Fairbanks (Summer 2018). His research and teaching focus on legal history, property, and trusts and estates. From 2013 to 2015, he gave a series of more than sixty lectures in North and South America, Africa, Asia, and Europe in commemoration of the 800th anniversary of Magna Carta. He is currently engaged in a study of the development of property rights and remedies in medieval England, focusing on the issues of jurisdictional conflict with regard to rights of presentation to churches.

José Reinaldo de Lima Lopes is Professor of Law at the Law School of the Universidade de São Paulo, Brazil, where he teaches jurisprudence, legal theory, and legal history. His publications include a history of Brazilian legal culture (*Naturalismo jurídico no pensamento brasileiro* [*Legal naturalism in Brazilian legal thought*], São Paulo, Saraiva, 2014) and of the Brazilian Council of State in the XIXth century (*O Oráculo de Delfos* [*The Oracle of Delphi*], São Paulo, Saraiva, 2010). He also contributed to the *Oxford International Encyclopedia of Legal*

History, with the entries on Brazil and Portuguese colonial law. He has been a visiting professor at several universities abroad, including Bogotá, Colombia (2001); Munich, Germany (2002); Toulouse, France (2016); and Bordeaux, France (2018). He was also awarded the prize of best legal book of the year in 2006 by the Câmara Brasileira do Livro.

Andrés Botero-Bernal is Professor of Philosophy at the Philosophy School of the Universidad Industrial de Santander (Bucaramanga, Colombia), where he teaches and researches legal philosophy and legal history. His latest books are about the history and the basis of the oath given by witnesses in a judicial process and the history of legal positivism, with both texts to be published by the Universidad Industrial de Santander.

Global Legal History

A Comparative Law Perspective

Edited by Joshua C. Tate, José Reinaldo de Lima Lopes, and Andrés Botero-Bernal

Routledge
Taylor & Francis Group
LONDON AND NEW YORK

First published 2019 by Routledge

2 Park Square, Milton Park, Abingdon, Oxfordshire OX14 4RN
52 Vanderbilt Avenue, New York, NY 10017

Routledge is an imprint of the Taylor & Francis Group, an informa business

First issued in paperback 2020

British Library Cataloguing-in-Publication Data
A catalogue record for this book is available from the British Library

Library of Congress Cataloging-in-Publication Data
Names: Tate, Joshua C., editor. | Lopes, José Reinaldo de Lima, editor. | Botero Bernal, Andrés, editor.
Title: Global legal history: a comparative law perspective / edited by Joshua C. Tate, José Reinaldo de Lima Lopes, and Andrés Botero-Bernal.
Description: Abingdon, Oxon; New York, NY: Routledge, 2019. | Includes bibliographical references and index.
Identifiers: LCCN 2018042291
Subjects: LCSH: Law—History.
Classification: LCC K160 .G56 2019 | DDC 340.09—dc23
LC record available at https://lccn.loc.gov/2018042291

ISBN: 978-1-138-47849-7 (hbk)
ISBN: 978-0-367-53420-2 (pbk)

Typeset in Galliard
by codeMantra

Contents

List of figures vii
List of tables ix
List of contributors xi

Global comparative legal history: An introduction 1
JOSHUA C. TATE, JOSÉ REINALDO DE LIMA LOPES, AND ANDRÉS BOTERO-BERNAL

PART I
Legal history and legal culture across borders 19

1 **Sincerity-based proper relationship: Socrates and Confucius** 21
CHI-SHING CHEN

2 **Legal development from a comparative perspective: English contract law in the nineteenth century** 37
CATHARINE MACMILLAN

3 **Legal history and comparative perspective: A study of the Cuban experience** 53
FABRICIO MULET MARTÍNEZ

4 **Bar associations and the circulation of legal knowledge: Argentina and Brazil, 1917–1943** 67
MARIANA DE MORAES SILVEIRA

PART II
Constitutional experiences in global perspective 85

5 Lessons from the history of courts on the review of constitutional amendments in Colombia 87
MARIO ALBERTO CAJAS-SARRIA

6 The revolutionary constitution of 1917 in Mexico: From individual guarantees to social rights, 1917–1928 106
HUMBERTO MORALES MORENO

7 Presidential impeachments in Brazil: Lessons from the past and challenges for the future 122
RAFAEL MAFEI RABELO QUEIROZ

PART III
History of judicial experiences 141

8 Exclusion and inclusion of the French law on neighboring plots of land in the civil codes of francophone Switzerland, Louisiana, and Quebec: Reflections on the relation between law and society 143
ASYA OSTROUKH

9 A legal-historical chronicle of Rule-of-Law narratives in Hong Kong 158
ANDRA LE ROUX-KEMP

10 Justice in the Ibero-American world in the Enlightenment Era 176
ANDRÉA SLEMIAN

11 Family courts and violence against women in Guatemala, 1964–1996 187
JOHN W. WERTHEIMER

Index 203

List of figures

9.1 References to "Rule of Law" in the South China Morning Post and its affiliate publications, 1930–1999 163
9.2 References to "Rule of Law" in the South China Morning Post and its affiliate publications, 2000–2017 165

List of tables

6.1 Labor matter litigation in SCJN from 1921 to 1924: amparos (private and public companies) 114

6.2 Labor matter litigation of the SCJN 1921–1924: *amparos* (individuals, small family companies, and trade unions) 114

6.3 Litigation in labor matter of the SCJN 1925–1928: *Amparos* (companies) 115

6.4 Litigation in labor matters of the SCJN 1925–1928: *amparos* (individuals, small family companies, civil associations, and labor unions) 116

6.5 Labor matter files addressed to the full plenary of SCJN in the period 1925–1928 116

List of contributors

Andrés Botero-Bernal is Professor of Philosophy at the Philosophy School of the Universidad Industrial de Santander (Bucaramanga, Colombia), where he teaches and researches legal philosophy and legal history. His latest books are about the history and the basis of the oath given by witnesses in a judicial process and the history of legal positivism, with both texts to be published by the Universidad Industrial de Santander.

Mario Alberto Cajas-Sarria is Associate Professor and Head of the Legal Studies Department at Universidad Icesi, Colombia. His research interests are in Colombian Legal History and Constitutional Law. His publications include the two volumes of *La historia de la Corte Suprema de Justicia de Colombia, 1886–1991* [*The History of the Supreme Court of Colombia, 1886–1991*] (Universidad de los Andes, 2015).

Chi-Shing Chen is Professor at the College of Law of National ChengChi University in Taiwan. He has published several articles on theories of justice and law in ancient Greece, as well as articles on modern law. His recent publications include "Reason and Passion in Plato's Laws" and "Justice and Law in the *Republic* and Mencius."

José Reinaldo de Lima Lopes is Professor of Law at the Law School of the Universidade de São Paulo, Brazil, where he teaches jurisprudence, legal theory, and legal history. His publications include a history of Brazilian legal culture (*Naturalismo jurídico no pensamento brasileiro* [*Legal naturalism in Brazilian legal thought*], São Paulo, Saraiva, 2014) and of the Brazilian Council of State in the XIXth century (*O Oráculo de Delfos* [*The Oracle of Delphi*], São Paulo, Saraiva, 2010). He also contributed to the *Oxford International Encyclopedia of Legal History*, with the entries on Brazil and Portuguese colonial law. He has been a visiting professor at several universities abroad, including Bogotá, Colombia (2001); Munich, Germany (2002); Toulouse, France (2016); and Bordeaux, France (2018). He was also awarded the prize of best legal book of the year in 2006 by the Câmara Brasileira do Livro.

Catharine MacMillan is Professor of Private Law at the Dickson Poon School of Law, King's College London. Her research focuses on legal history in the common law world from 1750 to 1950 and contemporary private law. She has written widely on the historical development of private law, legal institutions, and individuals.

Humberto Morales Moreno is Head of the Economic and Social History Center at the Instituto de Ciencias de Gobierno y Desarrollo Estratégico of the Autonomous University of Puebla. He also serves as the Academic Secretary of the Latin American Institute of History of Law. His main research lines are as follows: Legal Law and Social Impact in Mexico (XIX–XX centuries) and Justice Administration and Legal Institutions in Mexico: 1821–1940. His recent books include *Pastor Rouaix y su influencia en el constitucionalismo social mexicano* (SCJN, México, 2016) and (editor) *Derecho y Justicia en la Revolución Mexicana: 1910–1940* (SCJN/FDCS/BUAP, México, 2016). He is a member of the international seminar Histoire du Droit of the Centre d'Etudes d'Histoire Judiciaire de l'Université de Lille2 (France) and UNAM (Mexico), and of the Mexican Seminar of History of Law and Judicial Culture at UNAM-Colegio de México and Escuela Libre de Derecho de México.

Fabricio Mulet Martínez is a PhD candidate at Huelva University in Spain. He was previously Professor of Legal History at Havana University, Cuba, where he graduated in Law and obtained a master's degree in Constitutional and Administrative Law. His research focuses on Cuban Constitutional History, Cuban Legal Culture, Legal Historiography, and the History of Commercial Law in Cuba and Spain. He is the author of various articles published in Europe, the United States, and Latin America.

Asya Ostroukh is a Senior Lecturer at the Cave Hill Campus of the University of the West Indies in Barbados, where she teaches Jurisprudence, Comparative Law, and the Law of Real Property (Common Law). She received her first doctoral degree in law from the Institute for State and Law of the Russian Academy of Sciences, for research on Jeremy Bentham's legal philosophy, and her second PhD from the University of Edinburgh, Scotland, with a thesis on "Reception of the French Civil Code in Quebec, Louisiana and Francophone Switzerland: a Socio-Legal Study." She also undertook postdoctoral research in the history of Quebec civil law at Université Laval, Quebec, Canada. Dr. Ostroukh's research interests include the reception of the French Code in francophone countries and territories and the history of property law in the civil law tradition. Dr. Ostroukh is the author of more than thirty publications and a holder of numerous fellowships, awards, and grants, including the prestigious Government of Canada Award, the Scholarship of the Swiss Confederation, and a Fulbright Scholarship.

Rafael Mafei Rabelo Queiroz is Assistant Professor at the Department of Legal Theory and Legal Sociology, University of São Paulo Faculty of Law. He holds LLB (2002), LLM (2006), and JSD (2009) degrees from the Faculty of Law of the University of São Paulo. He has been a fellow of the German

Academic Exchange Service (DAAD), a JSD researcher at the Max Planck Institute for Criminal Law in Freiburg, Germany (2008), and a Fapesp research fellow at the Center for Latin American and Latino Studies at American University in Washington, DC (2017). His main research fields include the history and sociology of Brazilian legal culture and institutions and methods for legal research and legal reasoning.

Andra le Roux-Kemp is an Assistant Professor at the School of Law, City University of Hong Kong (HKSAR). Her scholarship centers on the situatedness of law and explores the theoretical and practical dynamics of legal change in its various spatial and temporal localities. She was awarded a Y-rating as a Promising Young Researcher by the National Research Foundation of South Africa in 2016, and is, at the time of this publication, finalizing a transdisciplinary and mixed-method study on the recognition of remorse in law, as part of a research project funded by the Hong Kong Research Grants Council.

Mariana de Moraes Silveira is Associate Professor of Theory of History and History of Historiography at the Federal University of Minas Gerais (Belo Horizonte, Brazil), where she also contributes regularly to Studium Iuris – Research group on the History of Legal Culture. She was a visiting researcher at the Max Planck Institute for European Legal History (Frankfurt am Main, Germany) and is coeditor of the journal *Lingua Franca*, sponsored by SHARP – the Society for the History of Authorship, Reading and Publishing. Her research interests include the legal history of Latin America, especially during the first half of the twentieth century, intellectual history, comparative law, nonnational approaches to history, as well as the cross-border circulation of books and ideas.

Andréa Slemian is Associate Professor at the Department of History, Federal University of São Paulo, where she has taught Colonial History since 2011. Her research interests are in the judicial culture of Latin America between the eighteenth and nineteenth centuries, with a comparative emphasis on courts and legal proceedings. She has also written about the process of independence and state-building in America, particularly in Brazil.

Joshua C. Tate is Professor of Law at Southern Methodist University, Dedman School of Law (Dallas, Texas, USA). He has been a visiting faculty member at the University of Pennsylvania Law School (Spring 2008), a Lloyd M. Robbins Senior Research Fellow at the University of California at Berkeley (Fall 2012), and a visiting scholar at the University of Alaska Fairbanks (Summer 2018). His research and teaching focus on legal history, property, and trusts and estates. From 2013 to 2015, he gave a series of more than sixty lectures in North and South America, Africa, Asia, and Europe in commemoration of the 800th anniversary of Magna Carta. He is currently engaged in a study of the development of property rights and remedies in medieval England, focusing on the issues of jurisdictional conflict with regard to rights of presentation to churches.

John W. Wertheimer is the William R. Kenan, Jr., Professor of History at Davidson College. His publications include *Law and Society in the South: A History of North Carolina Court Cases* (New Directions in Southern History Series, University Press of Kentucky, 2009). His research focuses primarily on the legal history of the United States South and secondarily on the legal history of Latin America. Currently, he is working on two book projects: one about the history of race and the law in South Carolina and the other about the history of violence against women and the law in Guatemala.

Global comparative legal history

An introduction

Joshua C. Tate, José Reinaldo de Lima Lopes, and Andrés Botero-Bernal

Legal history

Globalization has been with us for some time now, but law schools for the most part still teach law as if it were a national phenomenon. Efforts to teach it differently are restricted to certain fields or left to specialized seminars, or to jurisprudence and comparative law courses, when they exist in particular law schools' curricula. Legal doctrine works as the supranational aspect of law in general, but it is usually put to the service of national law. Law professors do not usually care much about the fact that legal doctrines and institutions have been the contingent response to contingent situations in the past. Sometimes, those doctrines and institutions are taken for their face value. In short, even if we are living in a global context, law is still for the most part taken as a local, specifically a *national* phenomenon.

Social scientists of all kinds, from anthropologists to economists, are aware of the deep changes that globalization has brought to our world. It compresses time and space; it changes the way classes interact and struggle over scarce resources, including natural resources; it creates a new world of images and imagination that affects people's beliefs; and it puts in everyone's agenda, directly or indirectly, a series of universal or global issues: climate change and environmental crisis; refugees in foreign territories; international and universal consequences of localized conflicts in which world powers play their hidden cards in geopolitical games; human rights crises; the virtual space of virtual reality, and so on. Legislatures, courts, and law schools tend to treat all these phenomena as specific areas into which the legal system (and legal doctrines) can be divided or accommodated.

And yet if one pays close attention to legal history, it all makes sense. Legal history contributes to a deeper understanding of what is going on because law has been part and parcel of the institutionalized form of social life for a long time—if not forever, if we believe that *ubi societas, ibi ius* (taking it with all necessary *granum salis*). It also helps us understand the present. In fact, since the groundbreaking work of H.L.A. Hart, *The Concept of Law*—the long-standing form of positivism dedicated to not only giving legal theory a "scientific" epistemological bend but also taking legal rules as its central object of concern—is slowly replaced by a new approach toward legal and practical reasoning, argumentation, and interpretation.[1]

Thus, an attempt to put together several researchers to write about legal history from a global perspective gives us the opportunity for both developing some general thoughts on legal history itself and gaining a deeper and more detailed view of particular historical processes in a wide range of localized systems.

Legal history and its place in legal scholarship

Global legal history can be either a field or an approach in which legal history, comparative law, and more recently a global perspective converge. In a broad sense, comparative law and legal history have been the object of lawyers' concern for a long time. They have also been taught as autonomous disciplines and have become part of the law curriculum in some places. Many instances of comparison among legal systems appeared in Roman law, where names of certain institutions were even borrowed from the Greek, as the word *synallagma* (συνάλλαγμα) shows in contractual relations. The Romans distinguished between their own, particular laws, the *ius civile,* with its traditional relation to the *ius quiritium,* and the more general *ius gentium,* as the common normative practices of the known world especially of the Mediterranean area, their *mare nostrum.* This sort of common law was a field of common practice, common to all peoples at least of the Mediterranean basin.

The role of history has been a prominent one for lawyers in different times. In fact, when law became an autonomous discipline in the European Middle Ages, it was part of a larger cultural heritage: the heritage of the classics, which included not only the law books (the Digest, the Codex, the Institutes, and the Novellas) but also philosophy (Roman and Greek authors also used by the Islamic world of the time) and theology (the Scriptures, the *Sacra Pagina*). Historical texts, to be used in the present.[2] Ever since then, it has been very difficult to imagine and to understand a legal system without any appeal to history. Their law books also came from a certain tradition; they came from the past. You do not need to know the history of your washing machine to put it to work: you just follow the rules set forth in the user's manual. But this is not so in terms of law, which is a cultural, historical artifact: a reservoir of meanings, not of technical prescriptions.[3] Modern legal history and comparative law have developed as specialized disciplines for almost two centuries now. And it is against this historical background that contemporary efforts toward global legal history must be understood.

One can trace legal history back to the humanists of the sixteenth century (Kelley 1966; Pocock 1967; Halpérin 2014). However, it was mostly in the eighteenth century that historical courses and textbooks started to appear as important tools for the teaching and learning of national law in European universities. Along with books on the history of the Roman law, sometimes under the name of *Antiquitates,* several legal scholars started to write the history of their own, national systems. Legal history started to go national. In Germany, this eventually led to the rise of the Historical School (*Historische Rechtsschule*). In the absence of a German nation-state, Roman law worked as the culturally unifying element of lawyers' tradition, and so they started to cultivate the history of Roman law as part of German history as well. Of course, the most conspicuous example of such development is Friedrich Karl von Savigny. Once it was connected to the law of the nation-state, legal history served different purposes, including that of justifying and legitimizing national law, eventually functioning as an instrument of national identity for building a national narrative (Cherfouh 2014).

Global legal history and the nation-state: denationalizing legal history

Global legal history assumes a denationalization of its perspective. Nation-states are a comparatively recent creation, and positive national law emerged with them. Of course, positive local law has always been taken for granted by lawyers. For that reason, lawyers in the late Middle Ages and the early modern period had to deal constantly with the relationship between the general, universal or common law (*ius commune*) and local law (*ius patrium*). *Lex* was by definition Roman and Canon law, which lawyers would learn at the university. By contrast, *statuta* or positive local law—*ius patrium*—was learned in practice (at the courts, at the different corporations, by the notaries in charge of laying down contracts and testaments, etc.). Was this a situation of globalization, *mundialization*, or transnationalization of the legal culture? According to Halpérin, the answer is no: the so-called premodern legal world was not global because between the twelfth and the eighteenth centuries, there were no nations in Europe, at least not in the modern sense. Lawyers were not attached to nation-states: they had their own idiom and their own language (Halpérin 2018). It was only later, beginning in the seventeenth century, that some legal scholars started to write in their mother tongues, but most of the more theoretical works were still written in Latin up through the eighteenth century. Royal legislation and local law (*ius patrium*) were issued in the vernacular languages, but commentaries on local law were written in Latin, except for the most practical matters concerning civil or criminal procedure (usually called *Praticas*).[4]

The modern insistence on the sovereignty first of the monarchs and then of the nation-state may have given the impression that law should be contained in a "container society" (Beck 1999). Just as societies are contained in the state, law would be a manifestation of the state itself. Legal historians have already criticized both the idea that statutory provisions contain the law, and the idea that statutes can provide for every field of social life.[5]

More recently, the same criticism appears more frequently in different and renewed forms. Audren argues that a global legal history must first denationalize its point of departure. The case of France, to which he refers, is not the only one in which a militant comparatism took hold of national scholarly imagination. Audren claims that legal history served the purpose of constructing a national legal identity. Legal historians were skillful comparatists, but comparison in their hands worked as a powerful instrument to promote the nation-state. Legal history should now take a different turn. Following Serge Dauchay's lead, it should conceive its work of comparison in a more porous way, paying attention to the reciprocal exchange among legal systems and to the survival and coexistence of different influences in different cultural traditions or heritages (Audren 2018).

Thus, global legal history puts the nation-state into brackets, something other disciplines in the social sciences have already done for the last two decades, beginning with the work of anthropologists. Below the national level, in smaller communities, institutions are created and put to work. Ferguson (1994) and Escobar (1995) have put the impact of "development politics" into a more general context, indicating how social and political communities smaller than the nation-state have resisted or adapted national and international interventions into their local ways of life. Above and beyond the nation-state, political entities may develop a transnational identity. Holston and Appadurai (1999) have shown that some cities are actually global cities, supporting forms of political organization and life that transcend national borders. Legal history is trying to do the same, taking into consideration both the larger, worldwide context of legal thought, doctrines, and institutions, and the smaller, local settings from which some of these forms arise or in which some of them are introduced.

Two notable transnational trends have developed in legal history in recent decades. First, with respect to Europe, scholars now talk more frequently about a European legal tradition, and national narratives are now adopting wider perspectives. After World War II, the slow rebuilding of a European cultural unity around more democratic political ideals provided an environment favorable to the transcending of national boundaries. Several scholars, such as Duve (2014) and Conte (2009), have noticed this. As Conte explains it, as early as 1952, Eric Genzner suggested that Roman law, following in the steps of Savigny, would play a leading role in this development. Roman law and traditional legal history should play the role of strengthening legality, rule of law, human dignity, and so on. Such an approach, in Conte's account, would nonetheless miss the important contribution made by scholars like Francesco Calasso, who, without denying the importance of the Roman Law tradition, paid detailed attention to the transformation that Roman doctrines experienced in the hands of medieval legal scholars. Contrary to Genzner's view, Calasso had already made a lasting contribution to legal history in his Italian homeland, not by going back to Savigny's sort of *Dogmengeschichte*: he favored a much more historical, less doctrinal approach to legal institutions. Calasso feared that Genzner's ideas were too idealistic and eventually nonhistorical. It was understandable that in the context of European reconstruction after the disaster of World War II and the Nazi regime, lawyers would appeal to a long tradition of civilized coexistence—to a "civil condition," in Oakeshott's words (Oakeshott 1975)—and would once again turn to Roman law, against the macabre appeal to national, racial, and ethnically exclusivist views of legal systems. But they should not minimize the role of local practice.

One generation later, Franz Wieacker and Helmut Coing contributed to this European, supranational history of law by creating the Max Planck Institute for

European Legal History in Frankfurt. Nonetheless, a contemporary reading of their lasting contribution clearly detects the centrality of the German tradition and their difficulty in overcoming a national perspective in their background assumptions. In fact, their work does not read as a history of private law in general, as the title of Wieacker's *magnum opus* suggests, but a history of private law in Germany. But it is to their credit that they show how German law would not be what it is (or was) without the early contribution of a cosmopolitan tradition, that of the Roman law of the Middle Ages (the *ius commune* or *droit savant*). Of course, the contribution of Wieacker and Coing consists in telling this detailed history by explaining how this national tradition is indebted to mixed influences from all over Europe. In the 1970s, another European initiative was taking root in Florence, under the leadership of Paolo Grossi, whose first years were already dedicated to a transnational agenda: suffice it to remember the early meetings organized by his institute on the European, transnational importance of the *Salamanca school*, or the work of Savigny. In later years, the Florentine center continued to invite foreign contributors to an ever-expanding effort to denationalize legal history, focusing on themes of general interest referring to large supranational movements of ideas (such as systematic legal thought, democracy, fascism and authoritarian law, and transnational legal culture).

The other strand to have an impact on legal history comes from postcolonial studies. Edward Said's works, from *Orientalism* through *Culture and imperialism* (Said 1994), display one of the many possible ways into the field of global studies, as he directly connects the dominant discourse of imperial powers in different social fields to their relations with their colonial parts. Although these relations have usually been seen as one-directional, radiating out from the center to the periphery, Said showed that no empire could exist without being dependent on the cultures with which it was being contrasted. Such discourse and cultural production are, after all, inherently dialectical, as they are constituted in contrast to the other parts of the empire. In short, empires were hierarchical, but we can tell their story also from the point of view of their parts and so have a different view of the whole. The importance of the East is then clearer. The Islamic world shows a remarkable example of different possibilities for legal history, as mentioned in Sakrani's review of the legal history of Islamic influences on the European West (Sakrani 2014).

Serge Gruzinski, working at first on the history of Hispanic America (Mexico and Brazil) suggested that it is time for historians like himself to take a new approach toward cultural history (Gruzinski 1999). Instead of rearranging and filtering their source material to isolate its "elementary" parts, they should take reality as it is, "global and mixed." For Gruzinski, one of the important traits of contemporary cultural life is that people do not have to choose one culture, but tend to live simultaneously in more than one, if one defines cultures by their separate elements or identities. It is the historian's (disciplinary) point of view that tends to see incompatibilities and ambiguities, where the agents themselves just take the whole of their living world and proceed to act within it. Historians, Gruzinski says, should see the world as it is. The *metissage* is the result of *mondialization*, and is present everywhere, but it has been with us for much longer than the word *globalization* may suggest.[6] Culture is not a senseless patchwork, and syncretism is nothing new. Even the *Conquista* of the largest part of the Americas in the sixteenth century was more than a clash between two peoples: both within the Spanish side and on the side of the indigenous people there were several distinctions, several local identities in opposition. In short, a good cultural history should find its object in a mixed world and should be aware of the distant but real relations between different societies: it should seriously consider that different societies living in the same time span or period may share surprising connections. In a later book, Gruzinski explores what he calls the *mondialization* of the sixteenth century conducted by the Portuguese and Spanish empires when Western Europe finally put the Americas (the *Eagle*) and the Far East (the *Dragon*) in contact (Gruzinski 2012). Once again, as a historian, he suggests that the better way to tell and understand the history of this European adventure is to put it in global perspective. As McCarty puts it, the past was also complex, interconnected, and globalized (McCarty 2015: 287).

Different areas of the globe have also been seen with new perspectives. Take the case of the Americas. In the first decades of the twentieth century, the Association of American Law Schools sponsored the publication of a series of translations of European authors. The generation of Cardozo and Pound was well aware of their importance. In his *The nature of the judicial process*, Cardozo quotes François Gény seventeen times, and Eugen Ehrlich twelve times—the two most quoted authors in the short book! Recently, Rabban (2013) has shown how the generations of American legal scholars of the end of the nineteenth century were also in frequent and direct contact with their English and German colleagues. In South America, contacts between legal scholars and their European colleagues were also frequent, but in the last few decades legal historians have also been more aware of the specificity of their condition. In the years following the independence of their countries, they were in charge of putting up their own nation-states and followed the lead of the codification and constitutional movements. The general atmosphere was one of "catching up" with Europe. In the second half of the twentieth century, things changed and the "catching up" ideology has been under close scrutiny. Legal history helps in showing that what matters is not just a matter of catching up but of acknowledging deep structural differences in social life. The state and the law have different configurations in different societies, as had already been noticed by legal historians elsewhere.[7]

Do these developments in cultural studies and history have anything to say to legal history? Of course—even if, as we will try to show, a global perspective in legal history is even easier to consider. In fact, it should not take too much effort for lawyers to remember that, before the late eighteenth century, legal scholarship in Europe was essentially a cosmopolitan discipline, with one common language (Latin) and one common literary basis (the *Corpus Iuris Civilis* and the *Corpus Iuris Canonici*). The fact that England had developed a rather peculiar system should not deceive us: as early as the treatise on the laws of England called *Bracton*, references to the continental idea of law and citations of Roman law were not infrequent.[8]

Global legal history and comparative law

Global legal history shares features of comparative law, once it tackles its objects from a nonnational perspective.

Comparative law is perhaps more recent than legal history as a discipline. Its development depended on the establishment of law as a national, domestic matter throughout the late eighteenth and nineteenth centuries. It was only in the second half of the 1700s that most law schools in the European tradition included *ius patrium* in their curricula.[9] The first modern attempts to study comparative law were made by Carl Anton Joseph Mittermeier (1787–1867) and Karl S. Zachariae (1769–1843), who founded in 1829 a specialized journal on the subject (*Kritische Zeitschrift für Rechtswissenschaft und Gesetzgebung des Auslandes*) (Ascarelli 1949). In the first half of the nineteenth century, one also finds Sumner Maine's works, which had some impact all over Europe in the following years, and whose investigation concerned non-European societies as well. Lambert is well known for his efforts in the field. However, these efforts were at the time still made within the same cultural world, the world of the Western legal tradition.

Globalization acquired a new meaning with the availability of present-day tools of communication, which have altered our perception of the world. Even if the Western tradition continues to play an important role, it is no longer acceptable to take it as the only standard of law or even as a *natural* standard of the way law develops in history. Comparative law feels the impact of such globalization. Certain authors begin to criticize a long-accepted division of legal families in civil law and common law traditions, suggesting that a better way of arranging law throughout the world would be more sensitive to the relations between legal systems and other social systems, rather than to formal, structural features internal to Western law.

It was once usual to compare "families" of law, such as the civil law and the common law.[10] Comparatists also studied different institutions, frequently describing their formal aspects. Today, the historicity of law is taken for granted by most, if not all, comparative law scholars, even if they do so in different ways. Transplants (Watson) or formants (Sacco) are some among many of the conceptual tools designed to understand how legal ideas and institutions travel around the world, and this can only happen in time, that is, historically (Watson 1978: 313–336; Watson 1983: 1121–1157; Sacco 1991: 2–34).[11] Some historians have begun to make explicit social comparisons. One case in hand is Raoul van *Caenegen's Judges, Legislators & Professors*, where history is told by comparing which social group dominates the production of legal discourse (Caenegem 1987). Ugo Mattei (1997) proposed that comparison should take into account not only the formal aspect of legal systems and institutions, or their explicit historical affiliations or traditions but also the place law holds in social structures. Thus, he advanced the idea that we classify legal systems into rule of professional law, rule of political law, and rule of traditional law.

Global legal history, therefore, takes law as a general normative practice, varying across time and space, drawing comparisons among experiences in different times and places, and searching for the existence of ideas, rules, and institutions common to different societies. Its interest lies in commonalities and particularities beyond the nation-state and beyond traditional legal families. To do so, it takes an interest in all kinds of practices related to the legal system: legal education, law enforcement, courts, litigation, conflict resolution, private, daily business practices, etc. It puts the North Atlantic model of law and politics in brackets in order to avoid using it as a standard against which the long history of political and normative experiments of mankind could or should be measured. It considers that influences happen in a multidirectional way so that it is not just the "central," "imperial," or "developed" system that imposes changes on "the other." Ideas that were born in a certain place are incorporated into a different cultural, institutional, social, political background, and work differently, resulting in a new idea, institution, or practice. Institutions are complementary to each other, as Karl Renner taught us long ago, and "transplanted" ideas will, therefore, give rise to original practices (Renner 1949).

Several examples in history show that the most obvious and best-documented ones are those between the Spanish and Portuguese empires and their mirror states or colonies in the Americas. The existence of a "*derecho indiano*" in the case of the American "*Reynos*," or the Portuguese legal exceptions for the territories of present-day Brazil, is a conspicuous example of how imperial law had to adapt in a different cultural and political setting. The colonial context included a "multidirectional exchange" process, as acknowledged by many (McCarty 2015; Hespanha 2006). The 1812 experiment in constitutional design conducted by the Spanish *Cortes* gathered in Cadiz is another clear case: their constitutional experiment could not be the same as the French, among other reasons because the representatives of the American subjects of the *monarquia* had to be taken into account. The idea of a *nación* was not the same as the French idea of *nation* or *peuple*. The political arrangement in France—where the *Ancien Régime* had already laid the basis for a unified *nation*, as Tocqueville was so keen to notice in his *L'Ancien régime et la revolution*—would not hold for a totally different space. The mere presence of the American subjects in the *Cortes* of Cadiz forced a redefinition of terms such as nation, national, citizen, or subject. In this sense, even if we may continue to use concepts such as "transplants" (Watson 1978) or "formants" (Sacco 1991), a global perspective tends to stress the multidirectional, reciprocal influences of social and legal systems. Later, American codification was the result of several overlapping models and exchange of ideas: Andrés Bello's first successful effort (the Chilean Civil Code) was studied, analyzed, and criticized, but also used, by Teixeira de Freitas in Brazil, and Freitas' unsuccessful model (the *Esboço* or *Draft of the Civil Code*) was later used in parts by Vélez Sarsfield. They all believed in codification and systematic legislation, but at the same time believed in the preservation of local customs and traditions so that eventually their work resulted in original texts.

Finally, by considering that practices do not exist without meanings, global comparative legal history takes a keen interest also in the history of ideas, intellectual history, history of discourses, and conceptual history.

How global legal history is different from national legal histories

Law, therefore, has increasingly become a global phenomenon, perpetually in motion, rather than national and hermetically closed. Indeed, the very idea of "national law" was the product of a nationalist history of law introduced in the nineteenth and early twentieth centuries. The law was never constructed in a closed or autopoietic way, as some have believed, because even in those centuries cross-pollination between the national legal systems was too extensive, as the examples above illustrate. One might add that, since World War I, the belief in a national law—based, in turn, on a nationalist history of law and on a history of national law—began to erode quickly with the end of the nation-state myth and the loss of legitimacy of representative democracy. At the end of the twentieth century, thanks to radical changes in communications, markets, and politics (which we commonly call "globalization"), scholars and jurists finally began to reject the false yet powerful belief that law was both self-creating and limited by national borders.

The time, then, is right to propose a new way of doing legal history, a method that will move beyond the history of national law and the nationalist history of law. Two legal disciplines, united at the beginning but later separated epistemologically, must now be reunited: legal history and comparative law.

Here, we should make some observations on the development of both disciplines. The first is that, prior to the emergence of modern states in the strict sense, law was fundamentally a historical discipline and, especially as taught in universities, a comparative exercise involving different governing legal systems: natural law, canon law, civil/Roman law (*ius commune*), international law, national law, and feudal law. Faced with this methodological fusion in the legal studies of the old regime between comparative law and history, the nineteenth-century reaction involved the establishment of a new mythology: the nation-state and national law (Grossi 2004).

The emergence of the State and its expropriation of law, establishing national law as the main (and perhaps only) valid legal source, caused jurists to believe that the law was coextensive with the political will of the State, an entity demarcated geographically between national borders. If what mattered was the will of the state and nothing more, then "history" became synonymous with mere erudition, a way of imparting moral lessons (since history provides many of them) or simply a rhetorical device.[12] Likewise, comparative work lost its significance when the only law that mattered was that of one's own country. Of course, in the context of nineteenth-century colonialism, jurists did engage in a kind of comparative exercise. However, the colonizers viewed the legal systems of the colonized with prejudice and disdain, and attributed differences to the lack of development of the colonized peoples and the imagined superiority of European civilization. From the biased perspective of European and Latin American jurists, divergent patterns in the Global South were a sign of malfunction.

The myth of the State required a belief that law was made and reproduced in a system that was geographically and politically closed. If history was needed at all, it was to serve the State's purpose: hence, a nationalist history of national law. The desire to nationalize history, both as an ideological matter and regarding its object of study, contributed significantly, at least in Latin America, to the idea of a unique nation, one that differs from its neighbors despite many features in common. History—including legal history—had a clear political valence. This nationalist history continued to make comparisons, but in this case, between a hated pre-statist past and the beloved statist present. In Latin America, the latter was viewed as modern and civilized in comparison to the past, but still under construction when compared to the global North. On the other hand, the past was regarded with disdain, but it was also an object of fascination since it held the cultural roots of a supposed national people.

We now recognize that this nationalist belief was a fantasy. As we have already seen, the construction of national legal systems was never accomplished in a closed, autopoietic way. Rather, the law developed through a constant exchange of ideas, institutions, and juridical norms that will be explored in this book's chapters. Nevertheless, this very broad circulation of ideas, institutions, and norms was always permeated by a political discourse that wanted to see national law as a consolidated and hermetic system: different from other legal systems, including those of neighboring countries.

During the crisis of legitimacy of the liberal state, representative democracy and the law appeared to be the best guarantors for the rights of the citizen. Anti-formalists, especially in France and Germany, came forward to offer new proposals to empower the law in the late nineteenth and early twentieth centuries. One such proposal, led by Édouard Lambert (1866–1947) among others, was to revitalize the study of comparative law, but with a new aim: to look for alternatives to the crisis of national law by analyzing foreign legal institutions (Petit 2001). The transmission of legal knowledge across borders became an object of mainstream investigation. Comparative law acquired a privileged status as a discipline, and although it was not formally linked with history, understanding a foreign legal system requires some knowledge of history, and doing legal history necessarily involves comparison.

By the end of the twentieth century, the crisis of the State assumed a new form. Economic, political, and cultural globalization implied a greater erosion of the State and thus of its law. As a result, knowledge of supranational legal systems has become increasingly important. At the same time, due to greater exchange of goods, services, and ideas, it has become increasingly urgent to arrive at a satisfactory resolution of legal problems that the national system has failed to solve. Into this category, we may place such developments as the growing influence of the Common Law, in its American incarnation, on the Latin American legal systems (which have increasingly diverged from the family of continental Roman or civil law), and the strengthening of private international law and the *lex mercatoria*. These changes are incongruent with the belief in a closed, hermetic, and complete national law.

As a result of these developments, comparative law has spread beyond its initial home in the academy and has become a fundamental tool for professional practice (especially in large law firms), for the State (in the setting of its international policy), and for the economy. But the opportunities brought by globalization for the history of law and comparative law have not been exhausted.

In the academic field, the scope of both legal disciplines has significantly broadened. For example, in order to understand cross-pollination between legal systems, it is not enough to be familiar with the positive law of each system under comparison: one must have an appreciation for the culture surrounding those positive laws (the traditional domain of legal anthropology) and of the history that is essential to understanding the cultural framework that surrounds positive law. This points toward a new rapprochement between the history of law and comparative law, and it explains why the academic revitalization of comparative law, at least in Latin America, has gone hand in hand with a renewal of interest in legal history.

Thanks to the erosion of the modern mythology of the State, legal history has ceased to be ideologically nationalistic, and it no longer focuses exclusively on national law; thus, we have a history of law that seeks out possible connections between systems, rather than trying to deny or reject them.

At this crossroads for legal history and comparative law, we propose a new global history of law, which would have at least six distinct characteristics. First, it is a history that shares the goals of comparative law, seeking to discover and explain points of connection between systems as well as their differences. Second, it does not hesitate to cross epistemic frontiers, both within the law and between the social sciences and the humanities because the law and the culture that surrounds it are not the heritage of a single science. Third, it focuses on making connections between different legal systems visible, which is both a comparative exercise and a historical one because the similarities and differences are known through comparison and are explained historically. Fourth, in making connections, it does not ignore the nuances, so as not to fall into the error of the nationalist history of national law by believing that generalities were universal. Fifth, it attempts to be global, in that it recognizes that connections are not confined by artificial political borders, and to become stronger as international communications and economic and political relations intensify. However, it does not pretend to be global, if by that one means a total history of law in the world, for such a task would be better suited to the great storage systems of artificial intelligence than the critical work of the historian of global law. In other words, "global" is not synonymous with "total"; rather, it is more a change of lens, or a transformation in the attitude one takes in assuming the academic and professional task. As the saying goes: think globally, act locally.

Sixth, and finally, global legal history also reinforces research done at different levels of legal practice. It is a history of legal practice, so it includes the history of professional and nonprofessional agents who deal with the law. It is a history of legal ideas and legal doctrines that shape attitudes toward the law and its institutions, so it stresses the fact, and a well-known fact, that legal scholars are frequently familiar with what is happening in other places. Legal ideas have always been global: John Austin read Friedrich Karl von Savigny, and von Savigny read the French, just like Hugo Grotius had read the Spanish scholars, and years later Samuel Pufendorf read Grotius. Globalization has compressed time and space, but law had been global long before our age. Contemporary legal history is also an institutional history so that we can compare institutions beyond what is written in books: for example, comparing conflict-resolution experiences, regulation, statute-drafting, the use of analogical reasoning, and many other instances of institutional history. In other words, global history is also the history of law in action, not only of law in books. It is also a history of books: if books and periodicals are instruments or supports for conveying ideas, we can engage in this history of books, papers, periodicals that travel around the world.

Approaches to global legal history

The chapters in this book represent a variety of approaches to global legal history. The first four chapters, by Chi-Shing Chen, Catharine MacMillan, Fabricio Mulet Martínez, and Mariana de Moraes Silveira, shed light on how specific theories, doctrines, concepts, and institutions have transcended or crossed cultural boundaries. First, Chi-Shing Chen explains the centrality of "sincerity-based proper relationship" in the philosophy of Socrates (as set out by his student Plato) and that of Confucius. Although neither philosopher focused specifically on law, both had an important influence on the subsequent development of legal philosophy. Both philosophers stressed the importance of sincerity and proper relationships, including relationships with others, which were the source of justice.

MacMillan focuses in her chapter on how the life and work of one individual who followed a reverse path of immigration in the nineteenth century—from New Orleans to England—had an impact on the development of the law. Judah Benjamin, who had been a preeminent lawyer in Louisiana prior to the Civil War and a leader of the Confederate government, fled to England after the Confederacy collapsed. He then practiced law in England between 1866 and 1883, which was a period of change in English law. Benjamin made important contributions to the development of English contract law and constitutional law by introducing concepts from the civil law of Louisiana and American constitutional law.

In his chapter, Mulet examines the development of comparative legal methods in the history of Cuban jurisprudence. Comparative jurisprudence gained currency in Cuba at the end of the nineteenth century due to the influence of legal positivism, a European import. At the beginning of the twentieth century, Cuba achieved its independence from the Spanish colonial regime, and the new national state needed a new legal science and a national legal historiography. However, Cuba's immediate legal past was inextricable from the colonial experience, and anti-Spanish feeling was commonplace among Cuban intellectuals. Thus, there was a tendency to search for wider frameworks in legal historiography, far beyond traditional national boundaries.

Silveira's chapter discusses the role that institutions representing legal professions played in promoting exchanges between Brazil and Argentina. By looking at three key moments—early initiatives in the late 1910s, often connected to the actions of diplomats and politicians; the development of more articulate efforts for improving dialogues throughout the 1920s and 1930s; and the founding of the Inter-American Bar Association in 1940 and the first activities it sponsored—Silveira sheds light on why and how these important interchanges of ideas came to be ignored by both official discourses and historiography, in spite of their vitality and the high hopes that surrounded them.

The next three chapters, by Mario Alberto Cajas-Sarria, Humberto Morales Moreno, and Rafael Mafei Rabelo Queiroz, focus on constitutional experiences in Colombia, Mexico, and Brazil, noting developments that have generally been overlooked in the United States and Europe. First, Cajas-Sarria critically examines the history of how constitutional amendments have been reviewed by the courts in Colombia, beginning with the path toward the establishment of the Public Action of Unconstitutionality in 1910, which allows any citizen to directly challenge laws before the Supreme Court. Cajas considers the evolving role of the Supreme Court and the development of its "constitutional replacement doctrine," which limits the ability of Congress to change the constitution.

In his chapter, Morales highlights the evolution of individual rights, classified as "constitutional guarantees," within a wider reform that the Mexican revolutionaries in 1917 called "social guarantees." The paradigm of the Mexican revolutionary constitution of 1917 outlined two main streams of social rights in the Americas: social property rights and social labor organization, especially in the period from 1917 to 1928. Morales cites data from the Mexican Supreme Court of Justice during this period to show that the transition between individual and social rights stemmed not from the limited experience of the new members of the revolutionary Supreme Court, but from the fact that many magistrates disagreed with the interpretation of the *constituyentes* in 1917.

Turning further south, Queiroz describes the origins and developments of the process of presidential impeachment in Brazil. He argues that the authority for presidential impeachment trials, given to the Senate, presupposed several factors that have been mitigated over time. Moreover, according to Queiroz, Brazil's current constitution (1988), with the interpretation it has received from the countries' paramount court (Supremo Tribunal Federal) in the trials of presidents Collor (tried in 1992) and Rousseff (tried and removed in 2016), has widened this gap and made things worse by leaving the House with too little power and the Senate with too much. Queiroz proposes legal and constitutional reforms to (1) restore the lower house's sole power to accuse and (2) to grant the upper house the sole power to try impeachment accusations in the specific terms formulated by the lower house of Congress.

The final three chapters of this book, by Asya Ostroukh, Andra le Roux-Kemp, Andréa Slemian, and John Wertheimer, compare the history of judicial experiences in the Americas and in Hong Kong. Ostroukh examines the reception of the provisions of the French Civil Code of 1804 on the so-called law of neighborhood in Francophone Switzerland, Quebec, and Louisiana in the nineteenth century, noting how the provisions of the French Code were amended (or rejected) in accordance with the needs of respective societies. French provisions were often rejected in favor of provisions from ancient customary law of the respective territories, or from civil codes of other territories. At times, completely new provisions had to be formulated and incorporated into a civil code. Whenever the legislators in the respective territories rejected or amended provisions of French law, they did so because the French provisions did not match the local geography, agriculture, lifestyle, customs, or practices.

Returning to the continent of Asia, Le Roux-Kemp considers the seemingly existential crisis of the concept of "Rule of Law" in the context of the Hong Kong Special Administrative Region. Le Roux-Kemp explains that an exclusively legal, positivist analysis of the Rule of Law precludes a proper understanding of how the law in Hong Kong and its subjects participate in the (legal) fabrication and contestation of the concept and its discourse across time and space. Le Roux-Kemp argues that a more pluralistic conceptualization of the Rule of Law in Hong Kong would counter its current constitutive ideology and rhetoric, and dissolve its exclusive and binary stance.

Slemian takes the discussion back to South America, suggesting how the judicial system implemented in Iberian America should be understood as a common process, taking into account the different rhythms of the colonization of territories in Portuguese and Spanish America from the sixteenth century. The chapter argues that illustrated reforms put into practice at the end of the eighteenth century are a privileged observation point of their approaches and specificities. She argues that, although the so-called enlightened processes reformed what was already in place in the territory, the new policies did not drastically change the logic of the justice system. Although they were evidently different, the measures of both colonial powers responded to the specific needs of their territories. The existence of a common juridical tradition allowed the Americans to distinguish themselves from others inhabiting the territory.

In the final chapter, Wertheimer discusses the history of domestic violence courts in Guatemala. A widely overlooked first step toward the recent legal response to domestic violence was Guatemala's Family Court Act of 1964, which established dedicated courts to handle all family-related legal matters. Although these new tribunals were blind to the widespread problem of violence against women, they enabled officials to penetrate the domestic sphere as never before, impinging, at least to some extent, on traditional patriarchal prerogatives. They also accustomed family members to suing each other in court, a vital precursor to later attempts to combat domestic violence. From the start, women were, by a huge margin, the most frequent and effective family court litigants. Wertheimer explains how the feminization of litigation that began in family courts soon influenced litigation patterns throughout the nation's court system.

The origins of this book trace back to the International Research Collaborative in Comparative Legal History of the Law and Society Association, which sponsored panels at the Association's meetings in New Orleans (2016) and Mexico City (2017). Partial funding for these panels was provided by the U.S. National Science Foundation. We are grateful to the Law and Society Association and its past-president Valerie Hans for supporting this project. We appreciate the support of our home institutions—SMU Dedman School of Law, the University of São Paulo, and the Industrial University of Santander—as well as the University of Alaska-Fairbanks and its Rasmuson Library. In addition, we wish to thank Laura Beck Varela, Lyndsay Campbell, Signa Daum Shanks, Jiang Dong, Lisa Hasday, Greg Ivy, Mia Korpiola, Yasutomo Morigiwa, José Ramón Narváez, Polly Price, Noah Rosenblum, Katharina Isabel Schmidt, and Todd Sherman for their support.

Notes

1 For two paradigmatic accounts of the change, see MacCormick (1983: 1) and Atienza (1997). Even a self-declared positivist like Joseph Raz is concerned with legal reasoning (Raz 1990).

2 This is why Augustine, in his *De doctrina Christiana*, set the basis for what would be called the historical method of interpretation. In order to understand the Scriptures, Augustine said, its interpreters had to know where the stories and examples were coming from. Cf. Augustine, *A doutrina cristã*, 3a. ed., trad. Nair de A. Oliveira (São Paulo: Paulus, 2011). Engl. transl. by R. P. H. Green, Oxford University Press, 1995.

3 Non-lawyers tend to think of legal rules as akin to users' manuals. It is a simplistic image of the system, based on a misconception of what a legal rule is. This is probably why professionals in other areas tend to be much more "formalistic" when using legal rules (as when they are in management and have to apply the internal rules of their agency or corporation, for example). For an attempt to distinguish their various forms of norms or rules, see Von Wright (1963).

4 The *Practice* of Antonio Vanguerve Cabral (1730) was written in Portuguese, but the most popular commentary on the Portuguese *Ordenações* (issued in Portuguese in 1603) was written in Latin (Pegas 1729). Some years later, an introductory textbook used by law students at the University of Coimbra was still written in Latin (Freire 1789).

5 Paolo Grossi (1998, 2004) has repeatedly insisted that premodern statutory law, positive law, or ordinances issued by the prince (sovereign) applied in limited fields of social life. A large part of social interactions depended on private law, which meant not only the contractual field of business transactions but also law made by the private citizens or subjects of the realm, especially through daily customs and practices.

6 Here, it is important to distinguish *mondialization* from *globalization*. *Mondialization* refers to the processes that are shared or connected between various cultures, but are transformed by each of them. On the other hand, *globalization* indicates shared processes that are transformed little—or not at all—by each culture to adapt them to their own processes, with the risk of generating the homogeneity of behaviors.

7 Tarello (1976) shows that French, German, and Neapolitan enlightenment were rather different among themselves, due to the different social structure of those societies.

8 For the connections between Roman law, the humanist tradition and English law see, e.g. Pocock (1967).

9 France first introduced national law (*ius patrium*) in 1649, but most other nations only did so in the 1700s: Portugal in 1772, Spain during the so-called Bourbonis reforms, and different Italian universities in about the same period. For a good introduction to the matter, see Birocchi (2006).

10 The best example is David (1964).

11 For a review of the debate over Watson's ideas, see Cairns (2013: 637–696).

12 See the examples in Botero (2011), at 161–216.

References

Augustine. *A doutrina cristã* [The Christian doctrine]. 3a. ed. Translated by Nair de A. Oliveira. São Paulo: Paulus, 2011.

Ascarelli, Tullio. "Premesse allo studio del diritto comparato." In *Saggi Giuridici*, by Tullio Ascarelli, 3–40. Milano: Giuffrè, 1949.

Atienza, Manuel. "Estado de derecho, argumentación e interpretación." *Anuario de Filosofía del Derecho* 14 (1997): 465–484.

Audren, Frédéric. "Ouverture: dénationaliser l'histoire du droit?" *Clio@Thémis* 5 (2018).

Beck, Ulrich. *O que é globalização?* Translated by André Carone. Rio de Janeiro: Paz e Terra, 1999.

Birocchi, Italo, and Antonello Mattone. *Il diritto patrio - tra diritto comune e codificazione*. Roma: Viella, 2006.

Botero, Andrés. "Saberes y poderes: los grupos intelectuales en Colombia." In: *Revista Pensamiento Jurídico*, Universidad Nacional de Colombia, Bogotá, Facultad de Derecho, 30, (Jan.-April 2011): 161–216.

Cabral, Antonio Vanguerve. *Pratica judicial*. Coimbra: Antonio Simoens Ferreyra, 1730.

Caenegem, Raoul van. *Judges, legislators & professors*. Cambridge: Cambridge University Press, 1987.

Cairns, John W. "Watson, Walton and the history of legal transplants." *Georgia Journal of International and Comparative Law* 41 (2013): 637–696.

Cherfouh, Fatiha. "Les usages de l'hisoire et du droit romain dans les ouvrages d'introduction au droit." In *Histoire des manuels de droit*, by Anne-Sophie Chambost, 95–110. Paris: LGDJ Lextenso, 2014.

Conte, Emanuele. *Diritto comune*. Bologna: Il Mulino, 2009.

David, René. *Les grands systèmes de droit contemporains*. Paris: Dalloz, 1964.

Duve, Thomas. "European legal history: concepts, methods, challenges." In *Entanglements in legal history: conceptual approaches*, by Thomas Duve, 29–66. Frankfurt: Max-Planck Institute for European Legal History, 2014.

———. "História do direito europeu - perspectivas globais." *Revista da Faculdade de Direito – UFPR* 60 (2015): 383–412.

Escobar, Arturo. *Encountering development: the making and unmaking of the third world*. Princeton, NJ: Princeton University Press, 1995.

Ferguson, James. *The anti-politics machine*. Minneapolis, MN: University of Minnesota Press, 1994.

Freire, Pascoal José de Melo. *Institutiones juris civilis lusitani cum publici tum privati*. Coimbra: Typis Academicis (Tipografia da Universidade), 1789.

Grossi, Paolo. *Assolutismo giuridico e diritto privato*. Milano: Giuffrè, 1998.

———. *Mitologias jurídicas da modernidade*. Translated by Arno Dal Ri Júnior. Florianópolis: Fundação Boiteux, 2004.

Gruzinski, Serge. *La pensée métisse*. Paris: Fayard, 1999.

———. *L'aigle et le dragon*. Paris: Fayard, 2012.

Halpérin, Jean-Louis. "Histoire comparée du droit." In *L'Histoire du droit en France: nouvelles tendances, nouveaux territoires*, by Jacques Krynen and Bernard d'Alteroche, 183–201. Paris: Classiques Garner, 2014.

———. "Une histoire transnationale des idées juridiques?" *Clio@Thémis Revue Élétronique d,Histoire du Droit* 14 (2018).

Hespanha, A. M. "Porque é que existe e em que é que consiste um direito colonial brasileiro." *Quaderni Fiorentini per la storia del pensiero giuridico moderno* 35 (2006): 59–81.

Holston, James, and Appadurai, Arjun. "Preface." In *Cities and citizenship*, by James Holston, vii–viii. Durham, NC: Duke University Press, 1999.

Kelley, Donald. "Legal humanism and the sense of history." *Studies in the Renaissance* 13 (1966): 184–199.

MacCormick, Neil. "Contemporary legal philosophy: the rediscovery of practical reason." *Journal of Law & Society* 10 (1983): 1.

Mattei, Ugo. "Three patterns of law: taxonomy and change in the world's legal systems." *American Journal of Comparative law* 45 (1997): 5–44.

McCarty, Philip C. "Globalizing legal history." *Rechtsgeschite* (Max-Planck Institut für europäische Rechtsgeschichte) 22 (2015).

Oakeshott, Michael. *On human conduct*. Oxford: Oxford University Press, 1975.

Pegas, Manuel Alvarez. *Commentaria ad Ordinationes regni Portugalliae*. Lisboa: Typ. Michaelis Rodrigues, 1729.

Petit, Carlos. "Lambert en la Tour Eiffel, o el derecho comparado de la belle èpoque," en Padoa-Schioppa, Antonio (ed.), La comparazione giuridica tra Otto e Novecento. In ricordo di Mario Rotondi, Milano, Istituto Lombardo di Scienze e Lettere, 2001, 53–98.

Pocock, J. G. A. *The ancient constitution and the feudal law: English historical thought in the seventeenth century*. New York, NY: W. W. Norton, 1967.

Rabban, David. *Law's history: American legal thought and the transatlantic turn to history*. Cambridge: Cambridge University Press, 2013.

Raz, Joseph. *Practical reason and norms*. Princenton, NJ: Princeton University Press, 1990.

Renner, Karl. *The institutions of private law and their social function*. A cura di O. K. Freund. Traduzione di A. Schwarzchild. London: Routledge & Kegan Paul, 1949.

Sacco, Rodolfo. "Legal formants: a dynamic approach to comparative law." *The American Journal of Comparative Law* 39 (1991): 2–34.

Said, Edward W. *Culture and imperialism*. New York, NY: Vintage Books, 1994.

Sakrani, Raja. "The law of the other." *Rechtsgeschichte* (Max Planck Institute for European Legal History) 22 (2014): 90–118.

Tarello, Giovanni. *Storia della cultura giuridica moderna*. Bolgna: Il Mulino, 1976.

Von Wright, Georg Henrik. *Norma and action - a logical enquiry*. London: Routledge & Kegan Paul, 1963.

Watson, Alan. "Comparative law and legal change." *Cambridge Law Journal* 37 (1978): 313–336.

———. "Legal change: sources of law and legal culture." *University of Pennsylvania Law Review* 131 (1983): 1121–1157.

Part I

Legal history and legal culture across borders

1 Sincerity-based proper relationship

Socrates and Confucius

Chi-Shing Chen

This chapter will explore similarities between the thought of the Chinese philosopher Confucius (551 BCE–479 BCE) and the ancient Greek philosopher Socrates (c. 470 BCE–c. 399 BCE), as presented in the writings of his student Plato, with regard to the cultivation of one's virtues. These similarities are centered on a concept that may be described as a "sincerity-based proper relationship."

Sincerity is an indispensable element in Plato's explanation of Socratic elenchus.[1] In Plato's writings, Socrates claims to be the most knowledgeable person in Athens because he knows his own ignorance. One acknowledges one's ignorance in an elenctic endeavor after one holds two beliefs that are contradictory to each other. If either of these beliefs is not a true reflection of one's mind, the whole effort is futile. This is also the reason why Socrates always requires all interlocutors to say what they believe.

Confucius does not raise sincerity as a teaching in the *Analects*, but his frequent commendations of loyalty and trustworthiness foretell one of the most developed theories of sincerity for both political philosophy and metaphysics by later Confucians in the *Great Learning* and the *Centrality and Commonality*. One can also notice an omnipresence of sincerity in the Confucian teaching in the *Analects* if one realizes that all virtues have an internal dimension within oneself. No virtuous act can be rightly attributed to a person who is insincere.

Proper relationship is also emphasized by both Plato and Confucius. For Plato, self-knowledge refers to one's self-transformation, with an ordered soul as the final goal. In Plato's *Gorgias*, Socrates tells Callicles that the proper relationship within one's soul is called moderation, which is the basis for one's proper relationship with others, namely, justice. For Confucius, "Ren" means one's proper relationship with others in different contexts and under different roles, which is extensively discussed in the *Analects*.

Socratic virtue

This section seeks to point out that sincerity is not only emphasized by Plato in the early definitional dialogues; such emphasis is also necessary. Before I proceed to explore the Platonic idea of sincerity, I want to first survey Plato's exploration of the idea of soul for the purpose of illustrating the necessity and importance of sincerity in the Platonic idea of virtue in terms of accessing and improving one's soul.

In his discussion of the Socratic idea of virtue, especially the relationship between the specific parts of virtue such as piety, courage, moderation, justice, and virtue as a whole, Ferejohn argued we can better understand the idea by seeing virtue as "a single state-of-soul" (Ferejohn 1984). More recently, Ferejohn again made the argument that virtue in Plato's Socratic dialogues should be interpreted as a state-of-soul and that Socrates' search for definitions with his interlocutors really functions as a diagnosis of such a state in the early dialogues. Ferejohn believes our search effort will be in vain if we perceive Socrates as an intellectualist looking for a behavioral term in his definitional dialogues (Ferejohn 2011). Ferejohn hence believes Plato commits to a more radical idea than traditional wisdom admits. This chapter will argue that if one approaches Plato from the Confucian tradition, the Socratic view of virtue as the best state-of-soul is not radical in the least.[2]

Socratic exploration of the idea of the soul

In the *Apology of Socrates*, one of Plato's earliest writings, when Socrates defends himself in front of hundreds of judges in the Athenian court, Socrates did use the term "state of your soul." He explains what he is doing when he goes around and talks to people in his own particular way. "For I go around doing nothing but persuading both young and old among you not to care for your body or your wealth in preference to or as strongly as for the best possible state of your soul." Socrates believes that one's best possible state-of-soul, that is, one's excellence brings wealth and all other good things, and not vice versa.[3]

But before one can reach the best possible state of the soul, one first needs to be able to access or address one's soul. How could one do that? Words are one of the most widely discussed sensible means to address the soul in the Socratic definitional dialogues.

In the beginning of *Charmides*, Socrates is asked by Charmides to help treat his headache. Socrates suggests that before Charmides can treat his head, he needs to treat his whole body; and before doing that, based on what Socrates learnt from a Thracian doctor, Charmides needs to treat his soul. The soul is the source for both bodily health and disease[4]; the soul is cured by means of certain charms, which consist of beautiful words. It is these words that bring temperance to the soul, while a soul with temperance makes it easy to provide health for both the head and the rest of the body.[5]

The reason why Socrates goes around and talks to people is that words alone are qualitatively different from those in a dialogue, which Socrates once described as from soul to soul.[6] For Socrates, one should convey what one believes, that is, one should be sincere, in order to enable one's ideas to reach the soul of others. The content or words conveyed cannot be separated from one's manner. In *Euthydemus*, facing his interlocutors who are using an eristic approach by twisting the words to trap their discussants, Socrates asks whether things have sense because they have a soul. After Socrates receives an affirmative answer, he further raises the question "do you know any phrase that has soul?"[7]

In *Gorgias*, Socrates talks with Gorgias and two of his students, Polus and Callicles, about oratory which the three of them professionally practice. The idea of the soul is brought up frequently. It is with Polus that Socrates expresses clearly what he thinks of orators. He believes they are like pastry bakers, providing things people like but without a benefit that is equivalent to medicine for people's health. During the interchanges, Socrates brings up the issue of whether the soul governs the body, or the body governs itself. What Socrates wants to point out is that the soul, unlike the body, can choose between medicine and pastry baking. If one allows the body to make decisions based on the gratification it receives, one ends up living in a chaotic world where things are all mixed up.[8]

Socrates then argues with Polus regarding who is happier, those who are just or those who are unjust. Polus believes that unjust people, if not caught, are happier. In response to Polus, Socrates brings up the soul again. Socrates says that a soul that is disciplined is one that is admirable, just, and causes one to do good, which makes one better through getting rid of something bad in one's soul.[9] Yet the corruption of one's soul, that is, injustice, is the worst state of corruption, in comparison with the corruption of one's finances and body, which lead to poverty and disease.[10]

Callicles then replaces Polus. In the beginning of the dialogue between Socrates and Callicles, Socrates praises Callicles as a good partner for the adequate testing of one's soul. Socrates believes the knowledge of the interlocutor is important, for without that knowledge, the testing cannot go any deeper. Whether the interlocutor is concerned for his partner and the frankness of the interlocutor is also important. Lacking good will, the interlocutor will not speak the truth and the joint search will end up in vain. Socrates thinks both Gorgias and Polus are both wise and care for him, but they lack frankness since they are more ashamed than they need to be.[11]

In the previous discussion of the *Apology*, we considered Socrates' own confession that he goes around and talks to all walks of life. In Xenophon's *Memorabilia*, Socrates goes further and expresses his belief that he contributes to the public life of Athens best by talking to Athenians whenever he can about good citizenship.[12] In the debate between Socrates and Callicles, Socrates brings up the issue of what a good orator is, explaining that he should be the one that makes "the soul of people as good as possible" no matter "the audience will find it more pleasant or unpleasant." Socrates then challenges Callicles to say whether he has seen such a good orator.[13]

Toward the end of *Gorgias*, Socrates says something important about the soul, which I will further elaborate in the next section on Socratic proper relationship. Socrates says that "the name for the states of organization and order of the soul is 'lawful' and 'law,' which lead people to become law-abiding and orderly, and these are justice and self-control." This should guide a good orator: to enable justice, self-control, and excellence to exist in the soul of people.[14] Therefore, a self-controlled soul is a good one. A self-controlled man will do what's appropriate to both the gods and human beings, which are called piety and justice accordingly.[15]

In the definitional dialogues, Plato deals with human relationships mainly in terms of justice and friendship. Socrates discusses justice in *Republic I*, while friendship is dealt with in *Lysis*. In *Lysis*, searching with some young men for a definition for a friend, Socrates explores whether a person who is neither good nor bad in his soul, his body, or in both body and soul – because of this presence of evil becomes a friend of the good.[16] Friendship is a kind of belonging, in the soul or some characteristic, habit or aspect of the soul.[17] In *Republic I*, Socrates explores some exclusive functions of a soul: taking care of things, ruling, deliberating, and living. These are things that can be dealt with only by one's soul. A virtuous soul functions well with regard to these matters and enables one to live well.[18]

Socratic sincerity

Although Plato's interpretation of Socratic moral knowledge and the methodology to engage such knowledge, such as elenchus, have been extensively studied by the scholarly community, the Socratic requirement of sincerity has not been neglected: "Say what you believe" is a primary topic for such inquiry (Irwin 1993; Vlastos 1994). This subsection will explore this topic further.

One obvious example of the importance of sincerity, as discussed in the previous subsection, has to do with the Socratic observation that a quality test for self requires the partner to be knowledgeable, frank, and having good will. The requirement that the partner be knowledgeable has already been addressed. I focus here on the criteria of frankness and of being concerned for the interlocutor. Plato does not appear to have had a fully realized theory for these attitudinal requirements: rather, it seems that both of them are parts of the general requirement of sincerity, in a Socratic way of searching for truth.

I begin with an extended discussion of parts of *Alcibiades*, which was briefly touched upon in the previous subsection.[19] In the text, Socrates warns Alcibiades not to rush into politics before he is well educated, otherwise Alcibiades will be in the worst state of stupidity: he does not know that he does not know. Before Socrates reaches his judgment, he explains to Alcibiades how one knows that one does not know and illustrates the connection between knowing and the soul.

Socrates explains that if one gives conflicting answers about something that lacks meaning, it is a clear sign that one does not know. One's soul wavers when one does not know about something. However, a person's soul will not waver if he knows that he does not know. What we are meant to take from this is that our soul will not waver under two conditions: that we know or that we know we do not know. The third condition, in which we do not know that we do not know, is the worst condition one can be in: "the most disgraceful sort of stupidity."[20]

Socrates then encourages Alcibiades to think about how we can improve our condition to know and suggest that if we do not know what we are, it is hard for us to know what skills can make us better. "[I]f we know ourselves, then we might be able to know how to cultivate ourselves, but if we don't know ourselves, we'll never know how."[21] But what are we, our body, our soul, or our body and soul combined? Plato clarifies that we are our souls, and not our bodies, or our bodies and souls combined. Therefore, the dialogue between Socrates and Alcibiades can be described as being from soul to soul.

SOCRATES: So the right way of looking at it is that, when you and I talk to each other, one soul uses words to address another soul.

ALCIBIADES: Very true.

SOCRATES: That's just what we were saying a little while ago—that Socrates converses with Alcibiades not by saying words to his face, apparently, but by addressing his words to Alcibiades—in other words—to his soul.[22]

In my view, the process from soul to soul is key to understanding how sincerity is necessary and important. This process from soul to soul may be divided into three stages: from soul to what one expresses, from what one expresses to the senses of the interlocutor, and from what the interlocutor senses to his soul. In all three stages, frankness and good will are necessary and important to ensure the imparting of knowledge from soul to soul.

Frankness is key to the first stage, that is, from one's soul to what one expresses. If I do not mean what I say, then all three stages are flawed. What reaches the other soul will be indeterminate at least. The whole dialogue will be in vain and a waste of time, for improvement of one's soul and hence of the person cannot be expected.

Good will is critical to the other two stages. Since frankness focuses only on saying what I believe, that is, ensuring that my soul is truly reflected in my expression,[23] whether my expression has the needed force to reach the sense and soul of the interlocutor depends on another factor: whether the other party is sufficiently concerned about me. If I am truly concerned about the other party, I will not simply reflect my soul in my expression. Instead, I will attend to what the receiver is thinking and how my message can best be received and interpreted. In short, I will focus on whether what's in my soul can reside as it does in the soul of the receiver.

My interpretation is certainly influenced by the Confucian tradition. As I will discuss later in this chapter, although Confucius does not have a full theory of sincerity, he uses words that reflect many related ideas in the *Analects*. For example, Confucius further divides the idea of good will into the ideas of trust and respect. In terms of keeping one's promises, trust may have to do with the second stage, that is, abiding by what I express and what the other party receives. Respect has to do with the third stage, that is, caring how the other party may receive what I have chosen to impart. Failing in the early stage means that all the effort spent on the following stages would be in vain. Sincerity becomes one of the most extensively researched ideas by later Confucians and is first well developed in the book *Centrality and Commonality.*

One noteworthy development in the *Centrality and Commonality* related to the discussion here has to do with the soul and the divine. In this book, Confucius explains that if one practices sincerity well with one's soul, one can reach the law of nature[24] and be with it. By comparison, in *Alcibiades*, the relationship between joint search by the souls of the interlocutors and the gods is discussed toward the end of the book, though sincerity is not part of the discussion.

Considering the question of how both Socrates and Alcibiades can get the clearest knowledge of their souls, Socrates suggests looking at their interchanges as looking each other in the eyes. Such interchanges seem necessary because Socrates believes that "if an eye is to see itself, it must look at an eye, and at that region of it in which the good activity of an eye actually occurs, and this, I presume, is seeing." Likewise, "if the soul, Alcibiades, is to know itself, it must look at a soul, and especially at the region in which what makes a soul good, wisdom, occurs, and at anything else which is similar to it." Then, Socrates states that the best region of an eye and soul we need to look at is the one that resembles the divine.

> SOCRATES: Then that region in it resembles the divine, and someone who looked at that and grasped everything divine—vision and understanding—would have the best grasp of himself as well.[25]

Socratic proper relationship

To describe the Confucian idea of virtue as one's forming of proper relationships with others fits well with what Confucius says in the *Analects*, it is not as clear that the idea of proper relationship is relevant to understanding the Socratic idea of virtue. In this section, I want to present this reading as a plausible one. I also believe the reading provides a good contrast between the two important traditions.

The strongest textual support for my reading can be found toward the end of *Gorgias*. Plato clarifies that the proper relationship within one's soul makes one form a proper relationship with others and the gods. The virtues named after these three relationships are temperance, justice, and piety, respectively. In this section, I will provide the actual text and then trace how Plato arrives at such a conclusion in *Gorgias*. Then, I will discuss the three proper Socratic relationships. However, I can only touch on the virtues of justice and piety briefly since that reflects the reality in the early definitional Socratic dialogues. As will be shown in later sections, Confucius says little about political and cosmic order in the *Analects*. Yet both of them lay an important foundation and set the tone for later development.

Toward the end of *Gorgias*, Socrates concludes the following:

> SOCRATES: I say that if the self-controlled soul is a good one, then a soul that's been affected the opposite way of the self-controlled one is a bad one....

> And surely a self-controlled person would do what's appropriate with respect to both gods and human beings. For if he does what's inappropriate, he wouldn't be self-controlled.... And of course if he did what's appropriate with respect to human beings, he would be doing what's just, and with respect to gods he would be doing what's pious....[26]

It seems that, in Plato's telling, the Socratic concept of proper relationship means that one should form proper relationships with the gods, with others, and with oneself. Proper relationship with oneself seems to mean self-control, temperance, moderation, or proper relationship within one's soul. The text above suggests that self-control may be the basis for the other two proper relationships, but it is easy to exaggerate this point if one takes it out of context.[27] Plato's dialogue between Socrates and Callicles leading to this point starts with a dispute between the two regarding whether it is better for one to get as big a portion as possible verses to get an adequate portion. Tracing how Socrates develops his argument may shed light on how Plato sees one's proper relationship with one's own soul.

Callicles starts his argument[28] with Socrates by insisting that, although the stronger are not the majority, they should be granted the larger portion of material goods and, most importantly, should rule over the polis. But in reality, the stronger ones are limited by the law of the polis and are forced to share on an equal basis with their inferiors. Socrates responds by raising the issue of one's ruling of oneself.[29] At first, Callicles does not understand, so Socrates elaborates: "[j]ust what the many mean: being self-controlled and master of oneself, ruling the pleasure and appetites within oneself."[30]

Callicles continues his disagreement with Socrates on whether a self-controlled person is better. Socrates thinks that an uncontrolled person is like a leaking jar, which keeps filling up indefinitely and represents hard work without joy. Callicles counters this analogy with that of a stone for a disciplined person who always stays the same without joy. Socrates then changes gears and brings up the question of knowledge.[31]

The reason Socrates uses knowledge to refute and show Callicles is twofold. First of all, Socrates shows that knowledge is categorically different from pleasing senses; second, Plato has Socrates explain that a knowledgeable or craftsman-like person will not simply aim at getting more. A doctor may forbid his patient from getting any food if that could ruin the health of the patient. The Socratic effort is not well received by Callicles, but it helps us understand the Socratic idea of proper relationship.

To refute Callicles' claim that pleasant and good are the same, Socrates first gets Callicles to agree that it takes time to change from good to bad or vice versa. Then, Socrates secures Callicles' consent that when one is thirsty and drinks water, one feels pain and pleasure at the same time. The two, however, cannot be accepted together, but Callicles just does that. Socrates also refutes Callicles' claim that bravery and knowledge are different.[32] Since Callicles agrees that whether people are brave or not, they almost feel the same when enemies retreat (pleasure) or advance (pain), bravery cannot be categorically different from knowledge.

With regard to Callicles' claim that pleasure and good are the same in quality, Socrates presses further with the question of whether it is true that we should take actions, including pleasant ones, for the sake of good things and not the other way around. Socrates also posits that it takes a craftsman-like effort to achieve a purpose. Callicles agrees to both.[33] Socrates further elaborates that any craft needs a craftsman-like effort to put all the related pieces into an organized and ordered whole. What's required for an organized, ordered, and good body is health and strength.

> SOCRATES: And the name for the states of organization and order of the soul is "lawful" and "law," which lead people to become law-abiding and orderly, and these are justice and self-control....[34]

In addition to *Alicibiades* and *Gorgias, Charmides* contributes additional important insight to the achievement of the proper relationship within one's soul. First, in addition to knowledge, Socrates further brings in the idea of science. A doctor, having the craft knowledge of treating patients, may not have mastered the science of medicine, which may include why things need to be done that way. Second, true well-being means the integration of some craft knowledge, the science of science and absence of science, and the science of good and evil. Even the seer, one who knows all things in the past, present, and the future, is still one step short, since the seer[35] still needs to know all the good and evil for things in the past, present, and the future.[36]

The proper relationship with others has to do with the virtue of justice, which is not fully developed in the Socratic definitional dialogues. The same can be said regarding the *Analects* of Confucius. One reason may be that the internal proper relationship can actually be developed throughout one's life, bringing parts of one's soul and its whole constantly into a reflective mode. But proper relationship with others may not. Eric Brown's idea of complex unities may help to illustrate the difficulty. Brown suggests that "diverse elements constitute a complex unity, a whole, if and only if they are suitably organized in relation to each other and in relation to the whole that they constitute" (Brown 2012: 66). In other words, proper relationship with others consists of all relationships between one and all others in specific and in general, including the polis as a whole. The idea and practices of the whole of the polis is not something that one can critically experience; rather, one may approximately perceive it at best. This may be a reason why Plato starts using the methods of hypothesis, mathematics, and divided lines in the Republic to illustrate how to approach such tasks, and not simply relying on elenchus.

Sincerity in the *Analects*

If sincerity in Plato's conception of Socratic thought means frankness and concern for the interlocutors, as discussed in the previous two sections, then it primarily means trustworthiness, wholeheartedness, and reverence in the *Analects*.[37]

These three characteristics appear frequently in the *Analects*, and more often than not, they can be called manner-related. Using the communicative ideas developed previously, all three manner-related virtues have to do with the best attitudes to convey what one has in mind and how to make one's expression best received by others. This works both ways: one must care for others enough before one can formulate and express in the best possible manner to others.

There is another important meaning in calling these virtues manner-related: they are not substantive. Whether what is conveyed is good or right is independent of the manner in which the idea is conveyed. As shown in the article, Confucius greatly emphasizes learning, because if someone who is committed to being fully trustworthy, also commits wholeheartedly to everything he says without regard to learning, he may end up becoming a thief.[38] In addition to being attentive to the manner-related virtues, one who decides to become an exemplary person will also take care with respect to behaving well from a substantive perspective. Benevolence and justice are two primary virtues serving as evaluative criteria.

In this subsection, I will analyze how trustworthiness, wholeheartedness, and reverence[39] are used in the *Analects*, by classifying the contexts of their respective usages. First, I analyze the role of the moral agent associated with one of the virtues of manner. In the *Analects*, the subject of the manner virtues may be the exemplary person, ordinary people, the lord, the official, the father, or the son, I will then analyze the relationship between the moral agent and the object of the manner virtue in question. Most of the time, the manner virtue is a self-imposed ethical standard; it may also be used in the relationship between father and son, lord and official, among friends, etc.

In the *Analects*, the two words "trustworthiness" and "wholeheartedness" may be used together to denote a general principle: be sincere.[40] They also form part of the four teachings of Confucius: culture, moral conduct, doing one's best, and being trustworthy in what one says.[41] The word usually means being trustworthy in general or in a specific context[42]; but in at least two instances, it is used to denote faith.[43] Generally speaking, trustworthiness refers not to a permanent or long-term relationship, like between father and son or lord and official, but rather between friends. It serves as a basic virtue for anyone conducting himself in society. In fact, Confucius includes trustworthiness among friends as one of the three criteria for his ideal society.[44]

Wholeheartedness occurs less frequently. When one examines the *Analects* in detail, it is found to have more than one meaning. When asked how the common people should treat people with authority, Confucius uses trustworthiness to refer to loyalty in the sense of doing one's best with no reservation.[45] When asked about how one should speak or deal with friends or others, Confucius uses wholeheartedness more in relation to frankness and less to doing one's best.[46] In two occasions, wholeheartedness is used to denote concern or care for others, especially in how one should treat one's son or student.[47]

Reverence is used in various relationships in the *Analects*. It denotes how a subject or official should treat the ruler,[48] how common people should treat the ruler,[49] how sons or daughters should treat their parents,[50] the proper way one should treat others,[51] the proper way one should perform one's work,[52] the proper way one should conduct oneself generally,[53] the proper way one should perform ritual events,[54] and the proper way one should treat the deities.[55]

Proper relationship in the *Analects*

Confucius uses several terms relating to virtue that are highly interrelated. Together, they show what Confucius means in the *Analects* with regard to proper relationships. In this section, I use pairs of ideas to illustrate the Confucian virtues of proper relationships and the contexts in which they can be found in the *Analects*. Examining these pairs is the best way to visualize the whole picture. The four pairs of ideas are rites[56] and *ren*,[57] *ren* and exemplary person,[58] exemplary person and *yi*, and *yi* and *dao*.[59]

Confucius lived in the final years of the Spring and Autumn periods (722 BCE–481 BCE), which are believed to be the formative years for the ideas of rites and *ren*. Confucius further constructs these virtuous ideas and teaches those from all walks of life to live according to these virtues.[60] Specifically, the appropriateness of *li*, one's outward expression of one's proper relationship with others, depends upon *ren*, one's substantive inward intention and understanding of the appropriateness of that relationship.[61]

Confucius once praised one of his students for making an appropriate comparison between painting and rites. The student cited one of the poems in the *Book of Song* that points out the right way to paint is to apply the white color after the whole work is finished, in order to adequately express the beauty in the mind of the artist.[62] Likewise, rites express what is deemed proper, that is, *ren*, by the moral agent, but it is easily misunderstood to treat the ritual itself as determinative.[63] It is said that Confucius would quicken his step if he encountered people in mourning[64] and he would not sing if he cried that day.[65]

Rites are quite like customs. We usually see and deal with their end result, ignoring their interactive nature. Fuller points out that customs are actually the language of interaction. Wherever there are human interactions, there are customs. Treating customs as facts causes most people to lose the opportunity to make the needed change through interaction. Hence, the right way to evaluate a custom is to place it first in human interactive terms. Good customs to be kept are the ones that facilitate benign human interactions (Fuller 1969).

Whether one interacts with others or conducts oneself properly in a particular situation is inevitably controversial and requires critical thinking. One's outward expression and inward understanding of *ren* are also mutually influencing and enhancing. Without learning, one simply cannot take one's proper place in society. Here, Confucius is like Socrates, urging a craftsman-like effort once one sets his heart on the way of *ren*. To be benevolent is not a virtue, since "[t]o love benevolence without loving learning is liable to lead to foolishness."[66]

Similar to Plato not being able to achieve any definition in the early dialogues, Confucius does not provide a definition of *ren*; actually, he seldom alludes to *ren* by himself.[67] In response to the student he cherishes the most, Confucius said "[t]o return to the observance of the rites through overcoming the self constitutes benevolence."[68] In its negative facet, to be benevolent means not imposing on others what one does not desire[69]; in its positive aspect, benevolence means helping others to establish themselves in society as one would wish to establish oneself and helping others to accomplish the goal one would personally like to be able to achieve.[70]

Confucius admits that he himself has not accomplished what is needed for benevolence.[71] Benevolence aims at proper interpersonal relationships. As in Plato's Socratic dialogues, such proper relationships can only be reached when one arrives at the good, and by helping others to do well. If one commits oneself to the way of benevolence, one can be called an exemplary person. An exemplary person is also a person who achieves a proper relationship between his inner self and outward expression.[72] The right way, or *yi*, is what guides an exemplary person to reach this balance, in addition to benevolence.[73] The right way is always on the mind of the exemplary person. He follows the right way and guides his decision to what the rites demand.[74]

Unlike benevolence, which primarily involves proper interpersonal relationships, *yi* represents another proper relationship on a grander scale (Yu 2006). We need to understand the idea of way, or *dao*, before we can grasp the idea of *yi*. This is also a major difference between the ideas of virtue in Plato's Socratic dialogues and the writings of Confucius. In *Charmides*, Socrates did touch upon the idea of a seer, who knows the past, present, and future, but he did not further develop such a historical or evolutionary concept. The way, however, is a common concept frequently used in the *Analects*. As a matter of fact, it is so common that Confucius does not even explain its meaning because everyone knows it.

If we further analyze the meaning of the way, we can identify two types of usages in the *Analects*, one descriptive and one normative. Descriptively speaking, everyone follows his or her own way throughout his or her lifetime. We all live our lives and we can describe how we or others live their whole life. Normatively speaking, the way means the right way. For an exemplary person, to live a life of *ren*, benevolence, and *yi*, the right way, is what he is committed to do. It is not hard to realize that we need to learn and contemplate hard to get the ideas of *ren* and *yi*. Since we always live in communities, *ren* is relatively easier to comprehend. We are all quite experienced in dealing with others and we can learn from our successes and failures. *Yi* is understandably much harder to grasp, in the sense of the proper way according to the law of nature, or the right way for a state to develop.

Conclusion

As discussed in this chapter, Socrates (as presented in Plato's dialogues) and Confucius share many similarities in their thinking. Overall, they both approach life similarly. In short, both of them commit to truth. Socrates would rather die than to obey an unjust Athenian order of not to practice philosophy. Confucius also said that once one sees the right way in the morning, one can die with no regret in the evening.[75] If we think they are negative toward their life commitment, we are wrong. They both believe that to learn, ponder, and advance toward the truth is the best state one could possibly be in.

Socratic wisdom assures us that an examined life leads to one's well-being. Confucius is so full of joy in learning and thinking that it leaves no room for noticing the coming of his old age.[76] Borrowing the mirror metaphor in *Alcibiades*, we may as well try to let people see each other. If we try hard enough to get what they see, if we are lucky enough, we may be sure of heading the right way toward the good.

Neither Socrates nor Confucius was a legal philosopher, but both laid an important foundation for their students to develop legal philosophy.[77] Ideas of law as virtue are common to the two masters, though there is also great difference between the two masters and the schools of thought they founded. Shaped by their respective historical and social backgrounds, Socrates and his students focus more on the law of the city, whereas the Confucians emphasize more on the human interactive norms. I have previously written on the classical virtue ideas of law because I believe we need their help to think about the law in the contemporary globalized and interconnected world (Chen 2011). Sincerity and proper relationship are the starting place for the two masters in developing their respective schools of thought. They may also be what we should reflect on to address the legal issues we face today.

Notes

1 Since no original writings of Socrates survive, what we know of Socratic philosophy comes from the writings of Socrates' students, especially Plato (c. 427 BCE–347 BCE). This article uses "Socrates" and "Socratic" as shorthand for the idealized version of Socrates and Socratic thought that Plato presents in his writings. Vlastos classified early dialogs of Plato as elenctic or definitional; which included ***Apology, Charmides, Crito, Euthyphro, Gorgias, Hippias Minor, Ion, Laches, Protagoras,*** and ***Republic I.*** He believed these dialogs are Plato's early writings which reflect his understanding of Socrates' ideas. In the later writings of Plato, Socrates serves as the mouthpiece for Plato. Vlastos's view is accepted by the scholarly community in general. In this paper, I will focus mainly on the early dialogs in my discussion of Socrates.

2 See Ferejohn (1984: 383), contrasting the radical view of Socrates that Ferejohn believes Socrates actually holds, in comparison to what Vlastos holds.

3 Apology 30a6–b4. For translation, I used Cooper (1997).

4 156d1–157a3.

5 157a3–7.

6 In ***Alcibiades,*** Socrates discusses with Alcibiades how one can improve oneself. According to Plato, Socrates believes that one cannot know how to improve oneself without the knowledge of what one's self is. Moreover, the only possible way to know about oneself is through understanding itself. However, Socrates and Alcibiades then limit their discussion on what an individual self is. When Socrates reviews what both he and Alcibiades have done, he said "[s]o the right way of looking at it is that, when you and I talk to each other, one soul uses words to address another soul." 130d9–10.

7 287d9–13. In ***Ion,*** at one point, Ion also expresses that "[s]omehow you touch my soul you're your words, Socrates, …". 535a3–5.

8 465c9–d8.
9 476e5–477a24.
10 477b14–c5.
11 487a1–b2.
12 Memorabilia 1.6.15. Xenophon, "Memorabilia," ed. Bonnette (1994: 30).
13 503a5–b3.
14 504d1–e6.
15 507a5–c8.
16 218b6–c3.
17 222a1–4.
18 353d3–e11.
19 For insightful discussions of the same dialog, see Annas (1985) and Gill (2007).
20 117–118.
21 129a8–10.
22 130d8–e4.
23 In addition to truly reflecting what one has in mind, sincerity needs to be bi-directional, that is, truly reflect what is received from the other party to the soul. However, this dimension of sincerity is not as clear as the frankness Socrates insists in his elenchus, but he certainly recognizes that the reason he is considered the most knowledgeable person in Athens is because he knows his ignorance. Another related issue has to do with the strong erotic display of Socrates in his search for truth. This erotic character should not be considered a part of sincerity, but it frames the intensity of one's self-discipline of speaking one's belief and one's good will toward others.
24 I use the term "law of nature" since it can generally apply to both Socratic and Confucian traditions. However, such usage must be taken with caution since it is not widely used in Chinese philosophical community; instead, heaven or *dao* ("the way") is usually used.
25 132c6–133c7. Gill wisely suggests a triangular model to understand the joint search for truth, which takes place among the two interlocutors and the gods. Therefore, the search does not aim at truth in an intersubjective sense, but rather, an objective one. See Gill (2007: 109–111).
26 507a5–b4.
27 In *Memorabilia* 1.5., Socrates is also reported by Xenophon as stating that continence is the foundation of virtue and should be equipped first in the soul, Xenophon., 27. However, in light of the previous discussion of *Alcibiades*, the improvement of one's soul necessarily involves others. This is also further affirmed by the Socratic elenctic practice in the early dialogs where all walks of life may be his counterparts. Searching for proper relationship with others paralleling one's internal search for proper relationship is eminent in Plato's *Republic*. Socrates may also think that piety, justice, and moderation mutually improve one another.
28 Callicles enters the argument at 481b6.
29 491d8.
30 491d11–e2.
31 495c4.
32 495c7–12. I did not find exact textual support for such a claim of Callicles though he assents to what Socrates presents to him, 495c7–12. The best I can find is the several previous claims that by nature the intelligent and brave person is rare, and such persons should rule the many inferior people and should get more. See 491a7–b3, 491c6–d3, and 491e7–492c7. However, the instituted laws made by the inferior may require equal distribution; the latter, according to Socrates in the dialog, represents a self-controlled, knowledgeable, and craftsman-like way.
33 500a4–10.
34 504d1–3.
35 173e8–174a2.

36 As one of the cardinal virtues of Socrates, wisdom focuses on the right judgment regarding good and evil. In *Euthydemus*, Socrates says wisdom makes men fortunate because of doing right, 280a10–12; any good is not good by nature but due to it being controlled by wisdom and not by evil or ignorance, 281d4–e2; and love of wisdom or philosophy, is the acquisition of knowledge, knowledge of making and using knowledge, 288d9–289b6. Similarly, Socrates says in *Protagoras* that those with the right kind of knowledge are always more confident, and wisdom is courage, 350a9–c5; if someone were to know what is good and bad, then he would not be forced by anything to act otherwise than knowledge dictates, wisdom and knowledge are anything but the most powerful forces in human activity, 252a1–d2; and being overcome by pleasure is ignorance in its highest degree, to give in to oneself is nothing other than ignorance, and to control oneself is nothing other than wisdom, 357b6–358c5. In *Laches*, Socrates says courage is the knowledge of all goods and evils put together and therefore is not simply part of virtue, but virtue as a whole, 199c5–e6. However, Socrates does not mention wisdom there. In *Meno*, Socrates says that without wisdom, virtues or knowledge do not benefit us since a soul directed by wisdom makes things right and benefits us, 87e6–88e4.

37 For the index of *Analects*, I followed Lau (1992). I also used Lau's translation unless my translation differs.

38 *Analects* 17.8: "...To love trustworthiness in word without loving learning is liable to ultimately lead to harmful behavior." .... See also 13.20: ... "A man who insists in keeping his word and seeing his actions through to the end can, perhaps, qualify to come next, even though he shows a stubborn petty-mindedness."

39 Correspondingly, in Chinese, they mean: 信、忠、敬。

40 *Analects*: 1.8, 9.25, 12.10, 15.6. Lau's translation differs from mine.

41 *Ibid.*, 7.25.

42 *Ibid.*, 1.5, 1.6, 2.22, 5.10, 5.26, 8.16, 12.7, 13.4, 14.31, 15.18, 17.6, 17.8.

43 *Ibid.*, 7.1 which discussed previously; and in 8.13, the Master said, "[h]ave firm faith and be fond of learning, and abide to the death in the good way. ..." The variance of the words to denote sincerity reflects the fact that the idea of sincerity evolves over a very long period. For its early development, see Chen (2010); and Sato (2007).

44 *Ibid.*, 5.26, "... [t]o bring peace to the old, to have trust in my friends, and to cherish the young."

45 *Ibid.*, 2.20: Chi K'ang Tzu asked, "How can one get the common people to be reverent, to do their utmost and to be filled with enthusiasm?" The Master said, "Rule over them with dignity and they will be reverent; treat them with kindness and they will do their utmost; raise the good and instruct those who are backward and they will be filled with enthusiasm." 3.19: "...the ruler should employ the services of his subjects in accordance with the rites. A subject should serve his ruler by doing his utmost." See also 5.19 and 12.14 where Confucius uses wholeheartedness in a similar way to answer his student's question about governing.

46 *Ibid.*, 12.23: Tzu-kung asked about how friends should be treated. The Master said, "Advise them frankly and guide them properly, but stop when there is no hope of success. Do not ask to be snubbed." Lau translates "to the best of your ability" instead of "frankly" as I do here. 16:10: Confucius said, "There are nine things the gentleman turns his thought to: ... to being conscientious when he speaks ..."

47 *Ibid.*, 14.7: The Master said, "Can you love anyone without making him work hard? Can you be concerned for anyone without educating him?" Lau's translation differs. 13.19: Fan Ch'ih asked about benevolence. The Master said, "... care for others ..." Lau translates it differently.

48 *Ibid.*, 5.16, 15.38.

49 *Ibid.*, 2.20, 13.4, 15.33.

50 *Ibid.*, 2.7, 4.18.

51 *Ibid.*, 5.17.

52 *Ibid.*, 1.5, 13.19, 16.10.

53 *Ibid.*, 6.2, 14.42, 15.6.

54 *Ibid.*, 3.26.

55 *Ibid.*, 6.22.
56 In Chinese, 禮is also translated as li or "propriety."
57 In Chinese, 仁is also translated as Jen or "benevolence."
58 In Chinese, 君子, there are various ways to describe the ideal person of Confucius in the *Analects*; for example, superior man, better man, gentleman, or Xunzi.
59 In Chinese, 義 may be translated as "appropriateness" or "justice."
60 In Chinese, 道may be translated as "way."
61 Shi-an Yan believes that the transformation of rite from its ritual meaning to one that is spiritual is primarily the result of the union of the noble class from different clans to form a cultural circle, and their reaction to the threat of barbarian invasion, where the continuation of cultural China is in peril (Yan 2010; 2006). Yü-Sheng Lin (1974) points to two poems in the *Book of Song* he believes are written right before the beginning of the Spring and Autumn period. Ren is shown in both poems to describe someone with no one to compare.
62 *Analects* 3.3: The Master said, "What can a man who is not benevolent do with the rites? What can a man who is not benevolent do with music?"
63 *Ibid.*, 3.8. Lau's translation is different where the plain silk is there first, and the colors come afterwards.
64 See also *Ibid.*, 3.4: Lin Fang asked about the basis of the rites. The Master said,

> A noble question indeed! With the rites, it is better to err on the side of frugality than on the side of extravagance; in mourning, it is better to err on the side grief than on the side of indifference.

65 *Ibid.*, 9.10.
66 *Ibid.*, 17.8.
67 *Ibid.*, 9.1: The occasions on which the Master talked about profit, destiny and benevolence were rare.
68 *Ibid.*, 12.1.
69 *Ibid.*, 12.2.
70 *Ibid.*, 6.30.
71 *Ibid.*, 14.28: The Master said,

> There are three things constantly on the lips of the gentleman, none of which I have succeeded in following: 'A man of benevolence never worries, a man of wisdom is never in two minds, a man of courage is never afraid.'

72 *Ibid.*, 6.18: The Master said,

> When there is a preponderance of native substance over acquired refinement, the result will be churlishness. When there is a preponderance of acquired refinement over native substance, the result will be pedantry. Only a well-balanced admixture of the two will result in gentlemanliness.

73 *Ibid.*, 4.10: The Master said, "In his dealings with the world, the gentleman is not invariably for or against anything, He is on the side of the right way." Lau translates it differently.
74 *Ibid.*, 15.18: The Master said, "The exemplary person has yi as his basic stuff and by observing the rites puts it into practice, by being modest gives it expression, and by being trustworthy in word brings it to completion. Such is an exemplar indeed." I slightly modified Lau's translation.
75 *Ibid.*, 4.8.
76 *Ibid.*, 7.19.
77 I previously compared ideas of law between the students of Socrates and Confucius (Chen 2017). I am also working on a paper that compares the ideas of Aristotelian equity and the category of Xunzi. I believe that Confucius does not deal with a full idea of law until Xunzi. I also believe that Socrates has a virtue idea of law, but it requires great effort of interpretation and construction and is beyond the scope of this paper.

References

Annas, Julia. "Self-Knowledge in Early Plato." In *Platonic Investigation*, edited by Dominic O'Meara, 111–138. Washington, DC: Catholic University of America Press, 1985.

Brown, Eric. "The Unity of the Soul in Plato's Republic." In *Plato and the Divided Self*, edited by Tad Brennan, Rachel Barney and Charles Brittain, 53–73. Cambridge: Cambridge University Press, 2012.

Chen, Chi-Shing. "Greek Idea of Justice and the Contemporary Need to Expand the Internal Legal Point of View." In *Gerechtigkeit-Theorie Und Praxis. Justice-Theory and Practice*, edited by Shing-I Liu, Ulfrid Neumann, 41–60. Baden-Baden: Nomos, 2011.

———. "Justice and Law in the Republic and Mencius." *NTU Law Review* 12 (2017): 177.

Chen, Li-Kuei. "A Look at the Virtues of Loyalty and Honesty in the Pre-Chin Confucian Teachings from Confucian Documents and Records on Kuodian Bamboo Slips." *Bulletin of Chinese* 47 (2010): 1–36.

Cooper, John M., and Douglas S. Hutchinson. *Plato Complete Works*. Indianapolis, IN: Hackett Publishing Co., 1997.

Ferejohn, Michael. "The Diagnostic Function of Socratic Definitions." In *Socratic, Platonic and Aristotelian Studies: Essays in Honor of Gerasimos Santas*, edited by Georgios Anagnostopoulos, 1–17. Dordrecht: Springer, 2011.

———. "Socratic Virtue as the Parts of Itself." *Philosophy and Phenomenological Research* 44, no. 3 (1984): 377–388.

Fuller, Lon L. "Human Interaction and the Law." *Am. J. Juris.* 14 (1969): 1.

Gill, Christopher. "Self-Knowledge in Plato's Alcibiades." In *Reading Ancient Texts. Volume I: Presocratics and Plato*, edited by Suzanne Stern-Gillet and Kevin Corrigan, 95–112. Boston, MA: Brill, 2007.

Irwin, Terence Henry. "'Say What You Believe'." In *Virtue, Love and Form, Essays in Memory of Gregory Vlastos*, edited by Terence Irwin and Martha C. Nussbaum, 1–16. Alberta, Canada: Academic Printing, 1993.

Lau, Dim C. *Confucius: The Analects*. Hong Kong: Chinese University Press, 1992.

Lin, Yü-Sheng. "The Evolution of the Pre-Confucian Meaning of Jen 仁 and the Confucian Concept of Moral Autonomy." *Monumenta Serica* 31, no. 1 (1974): 172–204.

Sato, Masayuki. "A Study on the Concepts of Loyalty and Trustworthiness (Zhongxin) in Early Chinese Political Thought." *Genre* 37, no. 1 (2007): 1–34.

Vlastos, Gregory. "The Socratic Elenchus: Method Is All." In *Socratic Studies*, edited by Myles Burnyeat, 1–37. Cambridge: Cambridge University Press, 1994.

Xenophon. "Memorabilia." edited by Amy L. Bonnette. Ithaca, NY and London: Cornell University Press 1994.

Yan, Shi-an. "A Discussion of the Relationship between "Li" and "Ren" in the Analects." *Taiwan Journal of East Asian Studies* 7, no. 2 (2010): 345–359.

———. "Expansion of Public Kingdom Rites—Ways for the Formation of Ancient Huaxia Race." *The Journal of Jiangsu Administration Institute* 6 (2006): 127–132.

Yu, Jiyuan. "Yi: Practical Wisdom in Confucius's Analects." *Journal of Chinese Philosophy* 33, no. 3 (2006): 335–348.

2 Legal development from a comparative perspective

English contract law in the nineteenth century

Catharine MacMillan

The development of law within a nation-state is usually examined from a nationalist perspective through an examination of the internal forces that bring about change within a legal system. A comparative examination, however, brings a greater understanding to the development of law. When one examines how a legal system absorbs rules and principles from other legal systems and works to create a new set of rules or principles, one has a better understanding not only of the process but also of the end set of laws. In this sense, this is the study of a national legal system to explore the acceptance – and sometimes the rejection – of legal rules and concepts from other jurisdictions. Such a study combines elements of both comparative law and legal history.

Introduction

There are many explanations for legal change and development. These tend to take one of two forms: either a jurisprudential thesis advanced with little detailed historical or comparative study (Schauer 2003; Wilder 2012; Samaha 2014; Tokson 2015) or a detailed legal history with an explanation for the legal change within the particular study (Friedman 1973; Milsom 1976; Gordley 1991; Baker 2003). Alan Watson's work examining legal transplants fits between these two characterizations (Watson 1974, 1976, 1993, 1996). Watson's thesis is a complex one: legal transplants, "the moving of a rule or a system of law from one country to another, or from one people to another" (Watson 1974, 21) are not only common throughout history but are also the principal explanation behind legal change (Watson 1974, 95–101). Watson argues that the pattern of "continual massive borrowing and longevity of rules and institutions" means that "there was no simple relationship between a society and its law" (Watson 1974, 107). For Watson, this relationship of borrowing from one legal system to another is at the very heart of comparative law (Watson 1978, 316). This thesis has attracted criticism (Legrand 1997, 2003): two critics are significant to this essay. While Allison accepts that processes of transplantation have transferred legal ideas and theories from one legal system to another, he is concerned that "Watson's theoretical argument ... is flawed and his empirical work unconvincing" (Allison 1996, 14). Allison posits that legal transplants are rarely successful. A second critic, by implication, is Teubner who has introduced a competing construct, the "legal irritant" (Teubner 1998, 11). Teubner envisions legal institutions which are organic rather than mechanical and, thus, cannot be moved easily from one environment to another. To transplant implies that the borrowed law functions, if at all, as it did in the donor system. Teubner argues that "when a foreign rule is imposed on a domestic culture ... something else is happening ... it works as a fundamental irritation which triggers a whole series of new and unexpected events" (Teubner 1998, 12). The new rule, in short, irritates the recipient legal system such that there is a reconstruction of this legal system which produces something different both from the preexisting recipient legal system and also that of the donor legal system. A new dynamic is unleashed by this legal irritant.

This essay is concerned with how legal rules move from one jurisdiction to another by examining how certain legal "rules" moved from Louisiana and America to England. Essential to this movement is one nineteenth-century lawyer, Judah Philip Benjamin.[1] Lawyers have frequently been identified as agents of legal change. Most accounts of legal change indicate the primacy of lawmakers in particular and lawyers in general. Central to Watson's thesis of legal transplants is the argument that legal professionals control the internal mechanisms of legal change.[2] Baker observes that legal change in the common law arises in large part through the thoughts and actions of lawyers (Baker 2003, 12). Gordley emphasizes the central importance of the late scholastics in synthesizing Roman law with Greek philosophy, a synthesis later adopted by the natural lawyers, as central to the understanding of modern European private law (Gordley 1991, 2006).

It is in this context that the role of Benjamin as a lawyer effecting legal change in English contract law is examined. Watson's "Law-shaping Lawyers," act as forces of legal change because of "their knowledge of legal rules and of how law actually works means that they are particularly conscious of how the existing law or a change in the law affects their well-being" (Watson 1978, 328). Watson envisions law-shaping lawyers working as legislators or as judges or jurists. Their effect on the development of law is profound for "the law which emerges will therefore tend to be strongly influenced by the knowledge of this legal élite, by its imagination and training and by its experience of the world and of legal ideas" (Watson 1978, 328). In evaluating Benjamin as a member of this legal elite, we must also consider one final factor in legal change: accident or serendipity. Milsom considered that much of legal change occurred as a result of juristic accident as actors produced unintended results (Milsom 1976). This is an argument greatly strengthened by the work of Simpson, who presented legal change as arising from serendipitous combinations of circumstances. There was no overarching theory behind the change: "greater understanding of cases does not generate general theories; instead it brings out the complexity of affairs and the extreme difficulty of producing generalizations which have any empirical validity" (Simpson 1995, 12). As this essay demonstrates, the role of law-shaping lawyers is often one that arises in a serendipitous fashion as the lawyer pursues his own interests.

Judah Benjamin

Benjamin's role as an agent of legal change was itself an accident for fate brought him to London in 1865. He was probably a British subject by birth, born in the West Indies in 1811 to Sephardic Jewish parents who had recently arrived from London. Taken as a toddler to America, he spent his boyhood in South Carolina before attending Yale at fourteen. After three years, he left Yale in disgrace without taking his degree. Arriving as a penniless teenager to a booming New Orleans his intelligence, indefatigable efforts, enthusiasm, and personality ensured him a successful legal practice. By the 1840s, he was the preeminent commercial attorney of the city, married to the daughter of a prominent Creole businessman and a sugar plantation owner. Such success took him into politics and in 1842 he became a Whig Senator in Louisiana in 1842 and a US Senator a decade later.

It was his political activities which caused his arrival in England. When Louisiana seceded from the Union in 1861, Benjamin (a vocal proponent of states' rights) left his Senate seat and joined the Confederate cabinet at Jefferson Davis's invitation. Here, he occupied a number of key roles. Lee's surrender at Appomattox caused Benjamin and his fellow Confederate cabinet members to flee for their lives. Evading capture, Benjamin made his way to London. Describing himself as a "Political Exile,"[3] he was admitted to Lincoln's Inn in early 1866 and called to the Bar that summer. Rather surprisingly given his age, the repugnancy which attended his Confederate associations and the anti-Semitism of the day, Benjamin was to become London's leading barrister.

Benjamin's remarkable life equipped him with an impressive knowledge of the law and a unique set of legal skills and abilities. Because his early legal career had been in the mixed law jurisdiction of Louisiana, Benjamin had a detailed and profound understanding of civil law in both its French and Spanish forms. While this might have been thought to have been a barrier in common law England, it was to have become a source of his English success. This essay argues that a by-product of Benjamin's success was the transference of legal rules from Louisiana to England.

The English law of contract

In an early effort to alert London's legal world as to his abilities, Benjamin published A Treatise on the Law of Sale of Personal Property, with reference to the American Decisions and to the French Code and Civil Law (Benjamin 1868). He found the English law on the sale of goods "very different from the law of Louisiana" and "quite a difficult and troublesome branch of professional learning" in England.[4] In his treatise, Benjamin sought to organize, rationalize, and elucidate the principles of English law (ostensibly as established in English cases) by drawing upon the theoretical constructs of civilian jurists, notably Pothier. In undertaking this effort, Benjamin was both part of a larger process (Simpson 1975; Hamburger 1989; Swain 2007; Lobban 2010, 300–313) in which jurists were engaged in redefining English private law in the latter half of the nineteenth century (Leake 1867; Pollock 1876; Anson 1879) and, simultaneously, a stimulant to this process. What was particularly significant about Benjamin's efforts was that he had both an intellectual understanding of civil law and experience in its practice. That this was Louisiana mattered for it meant that Benjamin also had knowledge of American common law. While Benjamin modestly stated that he employed American decisions and the "authorities in the Civil law" to compensate for the "imperfections" of his attempts to develop the principles of the law of sale (Benjamin 1868, iii–iv), the real reasons were that he could not only draw upon the strengths of his experiences but also offer to English lawyers an analysis of their law with reference to the civilian systems which they admired. In doing this, Benjamin had a significant role in introducing civilian and American conceptions into English law. The treatise was greeted with immediate approval[5] and was to form an important source of legal information for both bench and bar. The majority of his civilian adoptions were not identified with specific references. It is argued in this essay that Benjamin in writing his treatise constructed it, at least in part, around elements of the Louisiana Civil Code and English judges, in accepting the positions he set out, acted to transfer elements of Louisiana law into English law.

The nature of consent

Scholars have already observed that nineteenth-century English jurists, in their attempts to construct principled contract treatises, borrowed a will theory of contract from civilian jurists (Simpson 1975; Hamburger 1989; Swain 2007; Lobban 2010, 300–313). A figure of particular importance for these authors was Pothier, the eighteenth-century French jurist, notably his 1761 *Traité des Obligations* (Pothier 1806). The attraction of Pothier's work to nineteenth-century English jurists was multifaceted. His writing was clear, elegant, and the legal structures he devised offered an intellectually attractive alternative to the common law system organized by forms of action or abridgements. Importantly, for common law jurists, his writings were full of examples for lawyers and judges who sought solutions to practical problems (Swain 2007, 166). Pothier defined contract as "a particular kind of agreement," and "an agreement is the consent of two or more persons to form some engagement, or to rescind or modify an engagement already made."[6] The consent, or will, of the parties to engage in a contract was at the center of Pothier's conception of contract.[7] Benjamin employed these principles and began from the premise that there were four requisite elements necessary to constitute a valid sale of which the mutual assent of the parties was one (Benjamin 1868, 1–2). While mutual assent was easily devised as a theoretical construct, the difficulty lay in the problems which could arising in ascertaining this mutual assent and those circumstances in which the assent was subject to disruption.

Benjamin recognized and dealt with these problems. A number of examples are considered. The first such instance lay in whether the required consent was objective or subjective. The second is the concordance of offer and acceptance in establishing a mutual assent through postal correspondence. The third is mistake. Benjamin's resolution of these problems left a lasting impact. An important part of the jurists' adoption of will theory into the common law of contract was the ability to both support the theory with English cases and also to explain the cases in light of the new theory. In this endeavor, some aspects of contract were easier to deal with than others[8] and some new doctrines of contract law were created.[9] It has been long recognized that jurists borrowed from Pothier in this process but what has not been recognized is that, through Benjamin, the borrowing came from Louisiana.

A major challenge for will theorist writers was resolving the discrepancy posed by the difference between the subjective intention posited by Pothier and the objective intention required by the common law. One manifestation of this discrepancy lay in the communication of an acceptance of an offer: what did an offeree need to do to accept an offer such that there was a meeting of the minds? English law at the beginning of the nineteenth century seemed to indicate that a subjective meeting of the minds was sufficient[10] but later cases cast doubt upon this and appeared to require an actual communication of the acceptance.[11] In *Smith* v *Hughes*, Blackburn J affirmed that the requisite standard was an objective one:

> If, whatever a man's real intention may be, he so conducts himself that a reasonable man would believe that he was assenting to the terms proposed by the other party, and that other party upon that belief enters into the contract with him, the man thus conducting himself would be equally bound as if he had intended to agree to the other party's terms.[12]

Blackburn's formulation was an unattributed borrowing from Benjamin's treatise, not only in the form of the words used but also the underlying rationale.[13] Benjamin provided Blackburn with a common law means of providing an objective requirement to support a subjective civilian requirement.

The impact of Benjamin as barrister in introducing Louisianan concepts into English law can be seen in *Parker* v *The South Eastern Railway Co.*[14] The issue in the case was whether or not Parker was bound by the railway's limitation of liability for the loss of Parker's bag, which the railway had taken into its cloakroom. The limitation was posted by notice and stated on the reverse of the ticket given to Parker. An earlier House of Lords case had decided that whether there was an assent to such terms was a question of fact: mere receipt of a ticket with conditions was not an assent to its terms.[15] The jury in the lower court found for Parker, largely upon the question of whether or not it was reasonable for him to read the conditions on the ticket.

The railway retained Benjamin to argue its case in the Court of Appeal. He began by arguing that there was no contract to keep the goods safely as the parties were not *ad idem*. He may have intended to rely upon the doctrine of mistake he had introduced into English law in his treatise or upon *Lewis* v *M'Kee*,[16] in which Willes J was of the view that where one party did not read the terms there was no contract. He was, in any event, stopped from further advancing this point by the interjection of Bramwell J.A. Benjamin then made a second argument that when Parker took the ticket this implied an assent to the terms on the ticket. This implied assent largely formed the basis for the judgment of Mellish L.J.[17] This concept of an implied assent was one not present in earlier, similar ticketing cases which had largely been concerned with the question of the reasonability or otherwise of the conduct of the parties. Although Benjamin relied upon English cases, his argument was framed with reference to the Louisiana Civil Code of 1825. The Code required the mutual assent of the parties and over twenty-one articles established rules concerned with the nature of the assent. Assent was necessary for a contract to be formed[18] and assent could be either express (by words, written or spoken) or implied.[19] An implied assent could arise through the inaction of a party, where it was "presumptive evidence of a contract, when they are done under circumstances that naturally imply a consent to such a contract."[20] These provision undoubtedly formed the basis for the reasoning in Benjamin's argument and it was to change the course of English contract law when adopted by the court.

Correspondence and consent

Benjamin's working knowledge of a civil law system enabled him to develop a more sophisticated analysis of the applicability of civilian conceptions to the common law.[21] A practical problem which bedeviled English law was the contract formed by correspondence. In an era of increasing commercial activity conducted at a distance between parties through the new medium of the penny post, questions arose as to how and when a contract was formed.[22] Two particular questions could arise. First, if an offeree posted their acceptance of an offer, when was the acceptance communicated to form a binding contract? Second, if an offeror posted their revocation of an offer, at what point was the revocation effective such that an offeree could no longer accept the offer? The existing case law was inconclusive and contradictory. In 1818, in *Adams* v *Lindsell*, it had been held that actual communication of an acceptance was not necessary to form a contract but that what was necessary was to locate a point at which the minds of the parties subjectively met.[23] In 1848, in a Scottish case, the House of Lords had held that when a letter of acceptance had been put in the post, the sender had done all that was necessary for him to do and was not responsible for late delivery occasioned by the fault of the Post Office.[24] In 1867, it was held that an acceptance was not binding until it was communicated to the proposer or his agent.[25] Benjamin set about to resolve the difficulty, for "the cases that arise in attempts to contract by correspondence present at times very singular complexity."[26]

His resolution of the difficulty was uniquely Louisianan as it drew upon both civil law and American law. He began with the proposition that a contract required the coexisting mutual assent of the parties. He drew this from the Louisiana Civil Code although without any attribution.[27] A binding contract, wrote Benjamin, required not only an offer but also an unconditional acceptance; this too was an unattributed borrowing from the Civil Code.[28] Because there was no contract until such an acceptance was given, a proposal could be withdrawn before acceptance, even where a time period was given for its acceptance.[29] To this general rule, the law admitted a "modification" where the parties lived at a distance and were compelled to treat by postal correspondence. The offeror could not withdraw his offer once the offeree had posted his acceptance, nor could the offeree retract his acceptance once posted and prior to the offeror's receipt of it.[30] Benjamin formulated this proposition on the basis of the British cases.[31] He rationalized these cases with a principle of mutual assent: "the acceptance of the offer was complete by the posting of the answer *before* the offer was retracted, in accordance with the principle which makes the bargain complete at the moment when *mutual* and *reciprocal* assent has been given."[32] *Adams* v *Lindsell* also precluded an effective revocation posted after the offer and even prior to acceptance.[33]

Benjamin then compared this result to those in America and civil law countries. Unsurprisingly, given his reliance upon Pothier, Benjamin found that the principles between these systems were not very different. A "striking exception," though, was that "the civil law permits what are termed quasi-contracts, and enforces obligations resulting from them."[34] In light of this distinction, Benjamin considered how problems raised by the common law requirement of recognizing a contract only once acceptance occurred. He began with the American criticism (Story 1853, § 127) of the English decision in *Cooke* v *Oxley*. Here, the defendants offered to sell the plaintiffs tobacco and gave them a set time to accept; before acceptance was made but within the time, they sold the tobacco to another. The court refused the plaintiffs' action as the promise to keep the offer open was not binding as a *nudum pactum*. Story thought the decision "unjust and inequitable" (Benjamin 1868, 46) but this, Benjamin explained, was based upon a misapprehension for there was no binding obligation to keep the acceptance time open. The case did not prevent the conclusion of contracts at a distance for *Adams* v *Lindsell* found that where the offer was withdrawn after acceptance a contract was formed. Benjamin then reconciled these cases on the basis of the relevant provision of the Louisiana Civil Code[35] and posited an underlying principle of mutual assent. Where there was mutual assent at the same moment in time, even where the acceptance was posted and unknown to the offeror, a contract was formed (Benjamin 1868, 50). In formulating this "English" principle, Benjamin made no mention of his reliance on the Louisiana Code.

With this principle as his basis, Benjamin employed two American decisions to elucidate principles applicable to the completion of contracts by correspondence.[36] The US Supreme Court's decision in *Tayloe* v *Merchants' Fire Insurance Company* was authority for the proposition that an offeror was bound to a posted acceptance even where the offeror had sought to withdraw the offer by post as yet unreceived by the acceptor. The decision was made on pragmatic grounds: it was illogical to require parties who had chosen to contract by post to have actual knowledge for this defeated the purpose of their mode of contracting. Benjamin contrasted this result with the civilian position in Pothier's *Contrat de Vente*. Pothier allowed the offeror to withdraw an offer sent by post even where the acceptance had already been made by post because any loss of the offeree could be made good by the offeror in quasi-contract. Benjamin had already stated that the common law refusal to acknowledge such a quasi-contractual liability was a major difference with the civil law (Benjamin 1868, 43) and Pothier's reasoning thus failed "to meet the difficulties of the case" (Benjamin 1868, 53). If Pothier's approach was to be rejected, what could be put in its place? Benjamin sought a principled rationale for the approach he proposed with *Tayloe* v *Merchants' Fire Insurance.* This was to be found in agency where the civil law and common law agreed and a strong analogy established with a contract of sale by correspondence (Benjamin 1868, 53). Where a principal sent an agent with a proposal, the agent's authority to make the proposal could not be revoked until the revocation actually reached the agent. The principal was bound once his agent received an acceptance regardless of the principal's awareness of the acceptance as long as the authority subsisted. Why should there be any difference when a proposer sent his proposal by public post:

> In reality, the true theory of the case seems to be that an offer sent by mail is an authority to the party to whom it is sent, to bind the sender by acceptance, and includes an implied promise that no revocation is to take effect till received by the agent.
>
> (Benjamin 1868, 55)

Benjamin's recommendation became English law a decade later in *The Household Fire and Carriage Accident Insurance Company (Limited)* v *Grant.*[37] The 1870s saw an increase in joint stock company failures and shareholders sought to deny their liability on the basis that they had no contract to purchase shares. Grant was one such litigant, arguing that to his posted offer to purchase shares he had never received an acceptance. Intriguingly, Thesiger LJ referred to Pollock's treatise (which rejected agency as a rationale for allowing contracts formed by post)[38] but made an unattributed borrowing from Benjamin's treatise. Thesiger LJ considered the English cases and concluded, following Benjamin, that the post office must be treated as the agent of the parties such that once the acceptance letter had been given to the post office, the contract was complete.[39] While Thesiger LJ might have been said to have acquired this basis from an earlier decision of Romilly MR[40] this seems unlikely for Romilly had later changed his mind on the point.[41] Instead, the borrowing from Benjamin is all the more apparent in Thesiger LJ's approval of Benjamin's central case – *Tayloe* v *Merchants Fire Insurance* – a decision not cited by either party. The adoption of Benjamin's agency analogy forms the basis for modern English contract law concerned with contractual formation at a distance.

Benjamin's determinative influence was completed in *Byrne & Co* v *Leon van Tienhoven & Co.*[42] A Cardiff defendant offered tinplate for sale to the New York plaintiff by post. The offer was revoked by post a week later, after the plaintiff had sent a letter of acceptance. Lindley J relied upon Benjamin's treatise[43] to resolve the issue of whether the posted revocation was effective upon posting or receipt. Pothier had posited that the revocation was immediately effective and prevented a contract's formation but, as Benjamin had noted, in a civilian legal system where the offeror was liable to the offeree in quasi-contract for any loss. Lindley J accepted Benjamin's reasoning for the rejection of Pothier in this instance and for the adoption of the US Supreme Court's decision in in *Tayloe* v *Merchants' Fire Insurance*. Revocations were, accordingly, effective in English law upon receipt and not posting.

Scholars have questioned how English law settled upon such a basis: the methods of comparative legal history demonstrate how the development of English law was critically influenced, through Benjamin, by American and Louisianan law. It was under Benjamin's aegis that English law both accepted elements of Pothier and rejected others and, in doing so, in favor of an American approach.

Mistake

Benjamin had a profound and decisive influence in shaping the doctrine of mistake in English contract law. While scholars have long recognized that the English doctrine was shaped with reference to Pothier what is less recognized is that this was Pothier à la Louisiane. Benjamin was the first treatise writer to write extensively about mistake in English contract law. In doing so, he drew directly upon Louisiana law as a conceptual framework around which to organize English cases and as an analytical device to rationalize these cases with a (new) principled bases. The centrality of consent in Pothier's theory of contract meant that he was particularly concerned with those elements which disrupted or prevented consent: error was the greatest defect to affect consent.[44] Error was "the greatest defect that can occur in a contract, for agreements can only be formed by the consent of the parties, and there can be no consent when the parties are in error."[45] The Louisiana Civil Code, in twenty-six articles, contained an even more detailed treatment of mistake based upon Pothier than the French Code Civil (Hoff 1978, 331). Benjamin's transposition of elements of the Louisiana Code on mistake was to shape English law.

Benjamin sought to give coherence to English law concerned with what he saw as mistake rather than to actively change English law. Thus, while the Louisiana Civil Code recognized that an error of law invalidated a contract;[46] Benjamin observed that in English law, a mistake of fact alone could prevent mutual assent and thus contractual formation.[47] The changes to English law brought about by employing Louisianan mistake were, however, new and profound albeit unintended.

Benjamin's reasoning lay behind the decision in *Smith* v *Hughes* which established circumstances in which a unilateral mistake avoided a contract. The case concerned a farmer who sold oats to a horse trainer by sample and without representation or warranty. The trainer thought these (new) oats were old. Both Blackburn J and Hannen J, in determining whether or not the sale was good, relied upon Benjamin's treatise. Benjamin conceived of mistake in an objective sense: the law gave effect to the intention manifested to the other party, not the actual intention of the party. Where a party had one intention, but manifested a different intention to another party to induce the latter to act upon it in contracting, the first party was "estopped from denying that the intention as manifested was his real intention" (Benjamin 1868, 39). For a mistake to form the grounds upon which a contract could be set aside, the mistake had to be a mutual one although, Benjamin allowed, in certain circumstances, the mistake could be of one party if the other party was aware of the mistake (Benjamin 1868, 306).[48] Again, Benjamin took a civilian proposition and supported it with the common law concept of estoppel:

> whatever a man's *real* intention may be, if he *manifests* an intention to another party, so as to induce that other party to act upon it, he will be estopped from denying that the intention as *manifested* was his *real* intention.
> (Benjamin 1868, 306)

Where the first party was aware that the second party had a different essential element in mind than the first party, there was no contract because the first party was in no position to show that he was induced to act by a manifestation of the second party's intention which was different from his real intention (Benjamin 1868, 306–307).

Benjamin's reasoning was largely derived from the Louisiana Civil Code. Following Pothier, it recognized error as a defect of consent which could invalidate a contract.[49] An error in motive or cause of the party in entering a contract would invalidate the contract where this was the principal cause and was the consideration without which the contract would not have been made.[50] No error in the motive invalidated a contract unless the other party was aware that it was the principal cause of the agreement or that the nature of the transaction was such that such awareness was to be presumed.[51] The contract was void where the motive was apparent and the error went to that motive.[52] The application of these provisions was not without difficulty in Louisiana but as Benjamin did not ascribe the origin of these principles he was not compelled to resolve these problems.[53]

Blackburn J, in another unattributed borrowing, employed Benjamin's proposition and relied upon the same estoppel case[54] and held that the where the parties were not *ad idem* as to terms there was no contract "unless the circumstances are such as to preclude one of the parties from denying that he has agreed to the terms of the other."[55] That Hannen J also echoed Benjamin's treatise further indicates the unattributed borrowing. Hannen J's requirement of mutual assent in relation to a unilateral mistake followed Benjamin's reasoning and made use of the same English cases[56] as support were both taken directly from Benjamin. In this manner, Benjamin was responsible for the introduction of a Louisianan approach to a unilateral mistake in English law. It is a curious anomaly that few if any cases will ever fit within this conception and that the Louisianans were to remove this from their Code.

Pothier has long been regarded as the source of the English doctrine of mistake as to identity.[57] Until the mid-nineteenth century, English jurists were uninterested in a mistake of identity despite its interest for civilian jurists. For Pothier, an error as to the person, where identity was a material consideration, destroyed consent and consequently annulled the agreement.[58] The Louisiana Civil Code, based upon this principle, dealt with error as to the person in seven articles,[59] and began from the rule that an "error as to the person with whom the contract is made, will invalidate it if the consideration of the person is the principal or only cause of the contract."[60] Benjamin, following the Louisiana Code, introduced the possibility of mistake of identity in English law. Before his arrival, English courts had struggled to deal with the consequences created by a rogue who, pretending to a credit-worthy individual, obtained goods on credit and then sold the goods to an innocent third party. The problems had not been easily resolved and was complicated by the procedures involved in the criminal acts perpetrated by the rogue. In contractual terms, the actions had been regarded as what they were: frauds.

It was from Benjamin's pen that these earlier cases[61] came to be regarded not as cases of fraud but of mistake and it was this characterization which was to permanently shape English law. Benjamin wrote that

> A mistake as to the person with whom the contract is made, may or may not avoid the sale, according to the circumstances ... where the identity of the person is an important element ... a mistake as to the person dealt with, prevents the contract from coming into existence for want of assent.
>
> (Benjamin 1868, 36)

This is a direct transposition of the civilian principle into English law and it required a precedential basis. This Benjamin found in re-explaining the earlier cases:

> the contracts in the cases[62] cited below were held void, on the ground of fraud, but they were equally void for mistake, or the absence of the assent necessary to bring them into existence.
>
> (Benjamin 1868, 36)

This brief passage marked the starting point for mistake of identity in English law because it was to form the basis of the decision in the leading case of *Cundy* v *Lindsay*.[63]

The case concerned the consequences of a long firm fraud. A habitual swindler set himself up to resemble a reputable London firm and in this guise obtained linen on credit from Lindsay, a Belfast merchant. The swindler sold the goods to a third party, Cundy. Upon discovering the swindler's deception, Lindsay sued Cundy on the basis that, relying on Benjamin's treatise, there was no contract between themselves and the swindler because there was "an entire mistake as to the person to whom they were selling."[64] And if the swindler had no contract with Lindsay, he could pass no property in the goods to Cundy. Lindsay advanced a second ground as to why they had property: the Larceny Act 1861[65] provided, as a matter of criminal law, that having prosecuted the swindler they had property. While this is likely the real reason why the court found in Lindsay's favor, the decision was based on Benjamin's treatise: Lindsay had no intent to deal with the swindler. It was on this case that English treatise writers based their doctrine of mistake as to identity and it became English law (MacMillan 2005, 711).

Benjamin's final influence upon mistake was to take a case concerned with an innocent misrepresentation, *Kennedy* v *The Panama, New Zealand and Australian Royal Mail Company*,[66] and explain it as an example of a mistake (Benjamin 1868, 328–329). He wrote approvingly of the Roman analogies used in the adjudication of the case. This was unsurprising for it accorded with the provisions of the Louisiana Civil Code concerned with an error of substance.[67] Later, authors of his treatise were to develop this further and explain the case as an example of an error in substantia[68] and in the twentieth century this case came to be used as a part of the basis for the House of Lords' recognition of mistake.[69]

Conclusion

The above examination of English contract law demonstrates how a comparative legal history approach informs the understanding of a national legal system. Elements of Louisiana civil law and American common law entered into English contract law. This transference occurred as a result of Benjamin. While he was a member of a Watsonian "legal elite," English law changed not as a result of an intentional form of law-shaping driven by political, economic, or social considerations but through a series of fortuitous events. The explanation is rather simple, if un-theoretical, in many ways. Benjamin's arrival at the English Bar, at a time in which English lawyers sought to recast their law, was serendipitous. As an outsider, his need to establish himself was considerable and he did this through the construction of a treatise. The rapid rate at which this was written required the reliance on an existing structure. In Benjamin's case, this existing structure was the Louisiana Civil Code of 1825. It is only through an examination of this Code and the comparison with the position in English law – and the role of Benjamin's treatise in the construction of this law – that it becomes apparent how and why the transference occurred. Benjamin's reliance upon the Louisiana Code was largely unattributed. This is not surprising for what English barrister, jurist, or judge would rely upon a work on the civilian law of an American state as authority to resolve the problems bedeviling their own law?

What Benjamin did with his unattributed borrowings was to construct a treatise devised, seemingly, upon rational and scientific juristic concepts supported by English cases. His unattributed borrowings from the Louisiana Code were, in turn, the subject of largely unattributed borrowings of English judges as the bases for their own decisions. These legal decisions then became the basis not only for other contract treatises but also the basis of later English cases. And so a cycle of transference began.

Notes

1 The three major biographies of Benjamin are: Pierce Butler, *Judah P. Benjamin* (Philadelphia: George W. Jacobs & Co., 1907), Robert Douthat Meade, *Judah P. Benjamin, Confederate Statesman* (New York: Oxford University Press, 1943; Baton Rouge: Louisiana State University Press, 2001) and Eli N. Evans, *Judah P. Benjamin, The Jewish Confederate* (New York: Free Press, 1989). Aspects of their work

are challenged in Catharine MacMillan, "Judah Benjamin: marginalised outsider or admitted insider?" *Journal of Law and Society* 42, no. 1 (2015), 150.

2 Alan Watson, *Failures of the Legal Imagination* (Edinburgh: Scottish Academic Press, 1988) chs 1 and 2. Thus, for Watson, the lawmakers of one society share more in common with the lawmakers of another society than the law does with the particular political, economic, or societal demands of the society from which it is said to emanate: ibid., 105. See, also, Roger Cotterrell, "Is There a Logic of Legal Transplants?" in D Nelken and J Feest (eds) *Adapting Legal Cultures* (Oxford/Portland OR, Hart Publishing, 2001).

3 *The Black Books of Lincoln's Inn* (1866) Book XXXI, 133.

4 Letter to Penina Kruttschnitt, 22 February 1868, quoted in Butler, *Judah P. Benjamin*, 392.

5 See, for examples, the anonymous review in 13 *Solicitors' Journal and Reporter*, 14 November 1868, 28 and the observations of Willes J in *Seymour* v *The London and Provincial Marine Ins Co* (1872) 41 LJNS CP 198.

6 Pothier, *Law of Obligations*, pt I, ch I, s I, Art I, §1, p 3.

7 *Ibid.*, §2.

8 Consideration proved largely impervious to change: Swain "The Will Theory", 370–372.

9 Mistake is one such area: Catharine MacMillan, *Mistakes in Contract Law* (Oxford: Hart, 2010).

10 *Adams* v *Lindsell* (1818) 1 B & Ald. 681 at 683.

11 *Dunlop* v *Higgins* (1848) 1 H.L.C. 381 and *Felthouse* v *Bindley* (1862) 11 C.B. N.S. 869.

12 LR 6QB 597, 607.

13 Benjamin, *A Treatise on the Law of Sale*, 39. He reaffirmed the point in his second edition, after *Smith* v *Hughes*: J.P. Benjamin, *A Treatise on the Law of Sale of Personal Property*, 2nd ed (London: Sweet and Maxwell, 1873) 45, 388–389.

14 (1877) 2 C.P.D. 416.

15 *Henderson* v *Stevenson* (1875) Law Rep. 2 H.L., Sc 470, 481.

16 (1868–1869) L.R. 4 Ex 58 at 62.

17 *Parker* v *South Eastern Railway*, 421.

18 Article 1794.

19 Article 1805.

20 Article 1810. A specific example in the article was the terms upon which a deposit was made.

21 An example can be seen in his discussion of the civilian recognition of quasi-contracts: *A Treatise on the Law of Sale*, 43.

22 "[T]his class is one of great and increasing importance – namely, where a contract is entered into by correspondence between persons at a distance": Pollock, *Principles of Contract*, 11. The impact of changing technological development upon the law is considered in Simon Gardner, "Trashing with Trollope: A Deconstruction of the Postal Acceptance Rules in Contract", *Oxford Journal of Legal Studies* 12, no. 2 (1992), 170.

23 1 B & Ald 681, 683; 106 ER 250, 251.

24 *Dunlop* v *Higgins*.

25 *In re National Savings Bank Association* v *Hebb's case* (1867) LR 4 Eq 9.

26 Benjamin, *A Treatise on the Law of Sale*, 55.

27 Article 1759, Civil Code of the State of Louisiana (1825). The requirement was derived from Pothier *Law of Obligations*: Wheelock S. Upton and Needler R. Jennings, *Civil Code of the State of Louisiana; with Annotations* (New Orleans: E Johns and Company, 1838).

28 Articles 1792 and 1794.

29 Benjamin, *A treatise on the Law of Sale*, 30 relying upon *Cooke* v *Oxley* (1790) 3 T.R. 653. On the significance of the case, see Lobban, *Oxford History of English Law*, 333–335.

30 Benjamin, *A Treatise on the Law of Sale*, 33.

31 *Adams* v *Lindsell*; *Dunlop* v *Higgins*; *Potter* v *Saunders* (1847) 6 Hare 1, 67 ER 1057; and *Duncan* v *Topham* (1849) 8 CB 225, 137 ER 495. Surprisingly, Benjamin, *A Treatise on the Law of Sale*, 12 did not consider Romilly MR's observation *In re National Savings Bank Association* v *Hebb's Case* (1867) LR 4 Eq 9 that *Dunlop* v *Higgins* arose because the "the Post Office is the common agent of both parties."
32 Benjamin, *A Treatise on the Law of Sale*, 34.
33 *Ibid.*, 34–35.
34 *Ibid.*, 43.
35 Article 1795 presumed that a proposer continued in the intention which his proposal received if he did not signify a changed intention before receiving acceptance and that the proposer was bound by his proposal if the proposal had been made in terms which evinced an intention to allow the acceptor the right of contracting by his assent.
36 *Ibid*, 50. The cases were *Mactier's Admr's* v *Frith* (1830), 6 Wendell (New York) 104 and *Tayloe* v *Merchants' Fire Insurance Co* (1850) 9 How. 390.
37 (1878–1879) LR 4 Ex D 216. Benjamin, *A Treatise on the Law of Sale*, 2nd ed, 56–61.
38 Pollock, *Principles of Contract*, 10–11. Pollock thought it is better to allow the contract on the basis that the post was a reasonable mode of communication.
39 *Household Fire Insurance* v *Grant*, 221.
40 *In re National Savings Bank Association* v *Hebb's case*.
41 *In re Constantinople and Alexandria Hotel Company* v *Reidpath's Case* (1870–1871) LR 11 Eq 86.
42 (1880) 5 CPD 344.
43 He relied also upon a volume dedicated to him, Pollock's "excellent work" (*Principles of Contract*), which was itself based upon Benjamin's treatise and Leake's *Elementary Digest of the Law of Contracts*.
44 These elements he described as "defects which may occur in contracts" and considered "error, force, fraud, inequality, want of consideration, and want of obligation": Pothier, *Law of Obligations*, pt I, ch. I, s I, Art III, p 12.
45 *Ibid.*
46 Article 1840.
47 Benjamin, *A Treatise on the Law of Sale* 36, 307–308 but by a curious slip to Louisiana law, he began by noting that a mistake alleged as a reason for avoiding a contract could be "a mistake of law or of fact": 303.
48 Benjamin, *A Treatise on the Law of Sale*, 306.
49 Article 1813.
50 Article 1819.
51 Article 1820.
52 Article 1821.
53 S Litvinoff, "Vices of Consent, Error, Fraud, Duress and an Epilogue on Lesion" *La. L. Rev.* 50 (1989): 1, 47. A particular problem in Louisiana was whether one party had to know of the motive *and* the mistake of the other or only one of these elements.
54 *Freeman* v *Cooke* (1848) 2 Ex 654; 154 ER 652.
55 LR 6 QB 597, 607.
56 *Raffles* v *Wichelhaus* (1864) 2 H & C 906; 159 ER 375 and *Scott* v *Littledale* (1858) 8 E & Bl 815; 120 ER 304.
57 *Lewis* v *Avery* [1972] 1 QB 198, 206.
58 Pothier, *Law of Obligations*, pt I, ch I, s I, Art III § 1, p 13.
59 Articles 1828–1834.
60 Article 1828.
61 *Hardman* v *Booth* (1863) 1 H & C 803; 158 ER 1107 and *Higgons* v *Burton* (1857) 26 LJ Ex 342.
62 *Hardman* v *Booth* and *Higgons* v *Burton*.
63 (1877–1878) LR 3 App Cas 459.

64 *Cundy* v *Lindsay* (1875–1876) LR 1 QBD 348, 350.
65 24 & 25 Vict, c 96, s. 100.
66 (1867) LR 2 QB 580.
67 Articles 1835–1839.
68 The case stood for the proposition that only a mistake as to an essential matter such that "there must be a difference in substance between the thing contracted for and that actually existing, so as to constitute a failure of consideration": JP Benjamin, *A Treatise on the Law of Sale of Personal Property*, 6th edn, W.A.C. Ker (ed) (London: Sweet and Maxwell, 1920), 113.
69 *Bell* v *Lever Bros* (1932) AC 161, per Lord Atkin, 219.

References

Allison, John W.F., *A Continental Distinction in the Common Law: A Historical and Comparative Perspective on English Public Law* (Oxford: Clarendon Press, 1996).

Anson, Sir William Reynell, *Principles of the English Law of Contract* (Oxford: Clarendon Press, 1879).

Baker, John Hamilton, *Oxford History of the Laws of England 1483–1558*, vol 6 (Oxford: Oxford University Press, 2003).

Benjamin, Judah P., *A Treatise on the Law of Sale of Personal Property; with Reference to the American Decisions and to the French Code and Civil Law* (London: Sweet and Maxwell, 1868).

———, *A Treatise on the Law of Sale of Personal Property*, 2nd ed (London: Sweet and Maxwell, 1873).

———, *A Treatise on the Law of Sale of Personal Property*, 6th ed, WAC Ker (ed) (London: Sweet and Maxwell, 1920).

Butler, Pierce, *Judah P. Benjamin* (Philadelphia, PA: George W. Jacobs & Co., 1907).

Cotterrell, Roger, 'Is There a Logic of Legal Transplants?' in D Nelken and J Feest (eds) *Adapting Legal Cultures* (Oxford/Portland, OR: Hart Publishing, 2001).

Evans, Eli N., *Judah P. Benjamin, the Jewish Confederate* (New York, NY: Free Press, 1989).

Friedman, Lawrence, *A History of American Law*, 3rd ed (New York, NY: Simon and Schuster, 1973).

Gardner, Simon, "Trashing with Trollope: A Deconstruction of the Postal Acceptance Rules in Contract", *Oxford Journal of Legal Studies* 12, no. 2 (1992), 170.

Gordley, James, *The Philosophical Origins of Modern Contract Doctrine* (Oxford: Clarendon Press, 1991).

———, *Foundations of Private Law: Property, Tort, Contract, Unjust Enrichment* (Oxford: Oxford University Press, 2006).

Hamburger, Philip A., "The Development of the Nineteenth-Century Consensus Theory of Contract", *Law and History Review* 7, no. 2 (1989), 241–329.

Hoff, Timothy, "Error in the Formation of Contracts in Louisiana: A Comparative Analysis", *Tulane Lane Review* 53 (1978), 329.

Leake, Stephen Martin, *The Elements of the Law of Contract* (London: Stevens and Sons, 1867).

Legrand, Pierre, "The Impossibility of 'Legal Transplants'", *Maastricht Journal of European and Comparative Law* 4, no. 2 (1997), 111–124.

——— 'The Same and the Different' in P Legrand and R Munday (eds) *Comparative Legal Studies: Traditions and Transitions* (Cambridge: Cambridge University Press, 2003).

Litvinoff, Saul, "Vices of Consent, Error, Fraud, Duress and an Epilogue on Lesion", *Louisiana Law Review* 50 (1989), 1.

Lobban, Michael, *The Oxford History of the Laws of England*, vol XII (Oxford: Oxford University Press, 2010).
MacMillan, Catharine, "Judah Benjamin: Marginalised Outsider or Admitted Insider?" *Journal of Law and Society* 42, no. 1 (2015), 150.
——— *Mistakes in Contract Law* (Oxford: Hart, 2010).
——— "Rogues, Swindlers and Cheats: The Development of Mistake of Identity in English Contract Law", *The Cambridge Law Journal* 64, no. 3 (2005), 711–744.
Meade, Robert Douthat, *Judah P. Benjamin, Confederate Statesman* (New York: Oxford University Press, 1943; Baton Rouge: Louisiana State University Press, 2001).
Milsom, Stroud Francis Charles, *The Legal Framework of English Feudalism* (Cambridge: Cambridge University Press, 1976).
Pollock, Frederick, *Principles of Contract at Law and in Equity* (London: Stevens and Sons, 1876).
Pothier, Robert Joseph, *A Treatise on the Law of Obligations or Contracts*, trans W.D. Evans (London 1806; reprinted Clark, NJ, 2003).
Samaha, Adam M., "On the Problem of Legal Change", *Georgetown Law Journal* 103, no. 1 (November 2014), 97–155.
Schauer, Frederick, "Legal Development and the Problem of Systemic Transition", *Journal of Contemporary Legal Issues* 13, no. 1 (2003), 261–278.
Simpson, Alfred William Brian, *Leading Cases in the Common Law* (Oxford: Clarendon Press, 1995).
——— "Innovation in Nineteenth Century Contract Law", *Law Quarterly Review* 91, no. 362 (1975), 247.
Story, William W., *A Treatise on the Law of Sales of Personal Property*, 2nd ed (Boston, MA: Little, Brown and Co, 1853).
Swain, Warren, 'The Will Theory of Contract in the Nineteenth Century: Its Influence and Its Limitations' in A Lewis, P Brand, and P Mitchell (eds) *Law in the City* (Dublin: Four Courts Press, 2007), 162–180.
Teubner, Gunther, "Legal Irritants: Good Faith in British Law or How Unifying Law Ends up in New Divergences", *The Modern Law Review* 61, no. 1 (1998), 11–32.
The records of the Honorable Society of Lincoln's Inn. The Black books (Abingdon, Oxfordshire: Published for the Honourable Society of Lincoln's Inn by Professional Book Supplies, 1991–2001), Book XXXI.
Tokson, Matthew, "Judicial Resistance and Legal Change", *University of Chicago Law Review* 82, no. 2 (Spring 2015), 901–973.
Upton, Wheelock S., and Needler R. Jennings, *Civil Code of the State of Louisiana; with Annotations* (New Orleans, LA: E Johns and Company, 1838).
Watson, Alan, *Legal Transplants: An Approach to Comparative Law* (Edinburgh: Scottish Academic Press, 1974); republished as *Legal Transplants: An Approach to Comparative Law*, 2nd ed (Athens, GA: University of Georgia Press, 1993).
——— "Legal Transplants and Law Reform", *Law Quarterly Review* 92, no. Jan (1976), 79.
——— "Aspects of Reception of Law", *American Journal of Comparative Law* 44 (1996), 335.
——— "Comparative law and legal change", *The Cambridge Law Journal* 37, no. 2 (1978), 313.
———, *Failures of the Legal Imagination* (Edinburgh: Scottish Academic Press, 1988).
Wilder, Colin F., "Teaching Old Dogs New Tricks: Four Motifs of Legal Change from Early Modern Europe", *History and Theory* 51, no. 1 (2012), 18–41.

3 Legal history and comparative perspective

A study of the Cuban experience

Fabricio Mulet Martínez

Introduction

Legal history, considered as the academic discipline we know today, has a close relationship with comparative law. It could even be said that both fields of knowledge come from the same epistemological roots, given that their scientific origins may be found in very similar contexts. This relationship is maintained not only for that reason but also because it is useful. Paolo Grossi, in an interesting paper about the Italian professor Filippo Vassalli, asserted that only history and comparison would give jurists the awareness of relativity and restore the complexity of a normative fact that takes the risk of being simplified and misunderstood (Grossi 1997: 390–391).

Despite the thin line that separates both fields of knowledge, the dynamic between them has not been reciprocal. Although historicism has been present in almost every comparative legal exercise, comparative perspective has not always accompanied the development of legal historiography. In recent times, comparative legal history has become prominent in some important academic centers, mainly in the United States and Europe, where societies have even been created to promote this approach. However, comparative legal history has not yet reached sufficient force in Latin America, where historical-legal research has maintained a predominantly nationalist scope, although recently there have been some exceptions (Uribe and Ortiz 2000, Aguirre and Salvatore 2017; Marquardt and Llinás 2018).

At present, it is imperative to cultivate in Latin America a legal history capable of going far beyond the limits of national borders and the comparative method will be critical to this effort. The aim is not only the improvement of traditional methodological tools but also discovering new approaches that, instead of comprehending Latin American legal evolution as a unitary and uniform progression, take into account all the differences and particularities among the region's historical experiences. In addition, there are processes that cannot be understood by the interpretation of an isolated national case, and their development must be studied in various countries and epochs.

The comparative method of the present day is not rigid. Apart from the traditional systematic comparative analysis, there are other perspectives defended by authors like Professor Heikki Pihlajamäki (2015: 69–70), who advocates for a type of historical-legal comparison that requires assuming a wider framework. This means locating a research object in an international context, regardless of whether this research object is a national or regional institution. The present chapter will consider how the history of comparative law in Cuba offers a helpful case study contributing to the development of an eventual comparative legal history of Latin America.

Comparative method in Cuban legal science during the nineteenth century

The Royal and Pontifical University of Saint Jerome of Havana, the first university built on the island of Cuba, was officially founded on January 5, 1728. It was created through a Royal Decree dictated by Philip V, King of Spain, and a Papal Bull issued by Innocent XIII. The university was initially under the auspices of the Dominicans of San Juan de Letrán's convent, and it included a College of Civil and Canon Law. Like the great majority of peninsular or American universities of the time, one of its missions was to provide the Catholic Church with clerical experts in the different branches of knowledge offered in its classrooms so that these graduates could assume different ecclesiastic positions and other functions (Hernández 1992: 77).

Although not all the students were priests, the fact that university studies were in the hands of a religious order meant, among other things, that it was generally permeated by the most ancient scholastic ideas and by dogmatic rigidity in terms of the knowledge transmitted and the authors read. This was clearly detrimental to the quality of the education imparted, which turned its back on rational thought and recent advances in the scientific field. This level of general backwardness university suffered had a direct impact on the study of jurisprudence. However, in 1842, a Spanish reform that would be extended to Cuba would entail the secularization and modernization of the university, which would cease to be called Royal and Pontifical and would be renamed as the Royal and Literary University of Havana. With this reform, the university would be subject to government control.

It is essential to remember that, while most countries in the New World reached their independence during the first decades of the nineteenth century, the island of Cuba would remain under Spanish colonial domination until the end of the nineteenth century. There are several factors behind Cuba's belated independence, but one important reason is vested mostly on causes of economic nature because the Cuban oligarchy avoided entering a war that would damage their commercial interests. This topic, which has been discussed by historians like José Antonio Piqueras Arenas (2002: 465–483) and Antonio Santamaría García (2011: 149–150), does not represent our work's main purpose, but the truth is that this condition implied that the destinies of both colony and metropolis would be inextricably linked, and that would be evidenced in different aspects. In the area of law, especially in the academic context, this phenomenon meant that during those years, the same programs of study that were followed in the metropolis constituted the principal reference for Cuban jurists, as well as the texts and authors read in Spain, *La Madre Patria*.

In addition to these academic issues, other points are worth noting. During these years, profound political, social, and cultural changes had been brewing on the island. A Creole oligarchy was gaining more and more strength, becoming what would be known as *sacrocracia or plantocracia*. This powerful social class was imbued with the principles of liberalism and adhered to a conception of progress strongly linked to scientific knowledge. As a result, this elite group, with its plantationist mentality, would enhance the idea of acquiring knowledge so as to increase agricultural production, especially of sugar, which had become the Cuban economy's main export line (Moreno 1996: 150). These conditions would stimulate the flowering of scientific and rational thought within Cuban intellectual circles.

During the second half of the nineteenth century and the beginning of the twentieth century, Spain would receive the thrust of comparative legal studies that gained popularity throughout the European continent. In the field of jurisprudence, the use of the comparative method in the sense in which it is known today goes back to the nineteenth century, a century that is marked by the triumph of the codifying project in the western hemisphere. The promulgation of the French Civil Code, in 1804, unleashed a trend that would rapidly spread throughout Europe and would also deeply penetrate the new national states that emerged in Latin America. A genuine product of rationalism and enlightened thought, the Code represented a legal body whose precepts were perfectly systematized and followed a coherent and unitary order. This would bring deep transformations not only in the sphere of the production of law but also in its conception and understanding, as well as upending the established system of legal sources since the production of legal norms had come to be practically monopolized by the State. Codification would also greatly influence legal science, promoting the movement known as exegesis. More than doctrine, exegesis constituted a hermeneutic method that reduced the legal analysis to the textual interpretation of written legal norms. This stream of thought would have a great impact on judicial practice and legal education.

The codification paradigm expanded all over the European continent during the nineteenth century, with the French Civil Code being followed by countless texts, including the Austrian ABGB in 1811, the Netherlands Civil Code in 1838, the first Italian Unitary Code in 1865, and the Portuguese Civil Code in 1867 (Grossi 2010: 90–93). There were separate examples like Spain and Germany, where civil codification did not crystallize until the end of the century. In the case of Germany, authors like Anton Friedrich Justus Thibaut proclaimed the necessity of reworking all the German Civil Laws and condensing them into a clear, unequivocal, and exhaustive code, which would govern all Germany and evade the arbitrariness of particular governments (Thibaut 2015: 13). However, this movement also had detractors.

One of the most famous opponents of codification was Friedrich Carl von Savigny, emblematic figure of the German Historical School, who in response to

Thibaut espoused the idea that Law was a historical product rooted in life itself, housed in the spirit of the people. For this reason, it was in constant organic interaction with all the constituent elements of the identity of a nation, such as its character, its traditions, and even its language. In addition, its process of formation and development was determined by the incidence of purely internal forces, without the need for legislative intervention (Savigny 2015: 20–21). With these postulates, Savigny not only reaffirmed the legal phenomenon's historicity but also refuted the rationalist notion that the law could be separated from the fabric of social life or confined in an abstract order. Law was not a universal truth, but an eminently national reality. Hence, Savigny insisted that any precept or legal concept ought to be approached from a historical perspective, something that would establish the premises for the construction of a rich and effective national law, based on a solid scientific education (Savigny 2015: 20–21).

Years later, positivism would gain remarkable relevance, which led to the penetration of the study of social phenomena by methods implemented in the natural sciences. As a consequence, historical and comparative observation became the basis of true scientific research within the spectrum of the so-called social sciences, which obviously included legal science. To this, we must add a peculiar interest towards foreign legal norms, which took hold in Europe during the second half of the twentieth century. At first, this interest manifested through the narrow prism of the so-called comparative legislation. In 1869, Henry Sumner Maine was appointed as lecturer in Historical and Comparative Jurisprudence at Oxford University. That same year, the Society for Comparative Legislation was created in France, a country where that academic discipline expanded its boundaries and gained autonomy as a legal branch during the subsequent decades. The first international conference on comparative law, celebrated in Paris in 1900, was a significant achievement (Grossi 2010: 125–126). This is how comparative law was born: a comparative law that, as the Spanish professor Carlos Petit affirms, was set apart from the traditional comparative legislation and provided a study method that should be accessible to every jurist (Petit 1995: 130). At this moment, jurists like Francois Gény, Raymond Saleilles, and Édouard Lambert excelled, defying exegetic method and pondering other legal sources such as custom and jurisprudence.

This influence of the comparative method would eventually reach Spain, where chairs would be inaugurated in Comparative Legislation. In this sense, one of the most outstanding figures was that of Professor Gumersindo de Azcárate, whose work combined philosophical-historical science with legal science. This should encompass the historical law, in each of its manifestations, and the comparison of laws, without their study being restricted to a particular sphere of legislation or to a specific period of legal history (Azcárate 1874: 6). However, Azcárate was conscious that Comparative Legislation and legal history, even if they shared some common ground, were two different disciplines that needed to be separated. He recognized legal history's scientific nature, and although he admitted that the study of Comparative Legislation required the knowledge of universal legal history, he affirmed that history's mission was to expose the facts in a systematic form and adjust to the reality of the way in which they were produced. Comparative legislation, on the other hand, on the contrary, was meant to judge those facts exposed by history (Azcárate 1874: 11–12).

This acritical function of history was developed in other legal-comparative incursions during the nineteenth century. Rafael María de Labra, a Spanish politician born in Havana and an active abolitionist, affirmed in his 1876 book about Black Codes that

> there is no place for certain disquisitions here. I want only to expose the slave legislation of some countries; I try a mere historical work, of pure reference. The comments, the deductions, the applications, will be done by the readers (...) In purity, now I intend to do with the Black Codes what I would do with the Spanish *Fuero Real* or the Portuguese *Ordenanzas Alfonsinas.* Neither the moralist nor the politician speaks. It is the historian.
>
> (6)

This lack of criticism, in addition to the limited compass of the discipline, would be attacked during the first years of twentieth centuries by authors like Adolfo Posada (1906: 222–223) and the historian Rafael Altamira (1903: 49–59).

In Cuba, the comparative method would be embraced as "one of the most characteristic and fertile products of modern culture in all its manifestations" (Montoro 1889: 39). Following the example of the Spanish metropolis, a chair of Comparative Legislation was created, filled by eminent professors such as José Manuel Mestre Domínguez and José María Céspedes y Orellano. José Manuel Mestre Domínguez was one of the figures of greatest intellectual importance during the nineteenth century in Cuba, mainly known due to his contributions in the philosophical field, including his well-known work *About Philosophy in Havana.* (Mestre 1862). One of the most influential authors in nineteenth-century Cuba was undoubtedly the German philosopher Karl Christian Friedrich Krause. Regarding his impact on Cuban science, we have as one of the most authentic examples the relevant book by Antonio Bachiller y Morales, *Natural Law Course* (Bachiller 1857), which is full of references to Heinrich Ahrens, one of Krause's followers, who managed to transpose many of his philosophical ideas into the area of jurisprudence. José Manuel Mestre was one of many scholars to further this trend. In fact, when he occupied the legal philosophy chair at Havana University, he replaced Bachiller y Morales' text with Ahrens' (Sappez 2016: 553).

At present, we have limited information about the work developed by Mestre while he held the comparative legislation chair. There are a few references to the program he elaborated and published, in which he divided the academic course into sixty lessons, paying special attention to issues of private international law (Céspedes 1895: 3). Unfortunately, we do not have any access to that program's text. Scrutinizing Cuban legal historiography related to the colonial period, as well as any aspect of legal teaching or legal science within that time, can become a very complex task, mainly due to the scarcity of bibliographic and documentary resources. Much valuable information has been lost over time. Numerous works by notable jurists have come to be impossible to find in libraries or private collections throughout the country because they simply do not exist. Similar obstacles exist with regard to the study of some of the most outstanding figures of the Cuban legal past, particularly from the nineteenth century, which is the moment when certain signs of its flowering first emerged. This fact becomes much more evident if one attempts to explore the life and work of the former professors of Havana University, whose academic and administrative files are either missing, mutilated, or have a severe level of physical deterioration. This not only makes the extraction of vital data very difficult but also obstructs the total reconstruction of the disciplinary itinerary followed by legal history throughout the development of the Cuban cultural universe. Despite the challenges presented in any attempt to undertake an exhaustive survey of published doctrinal works, we may nonetheless mark the principal milestones and analyze the documents that have survived to the present day.

As noted, the other comparative legislation professor was José María Céspedes Orellano, who was born in Bayamo on April 10, 1829. He obtained his degree in Jurisprudence from Havana University in 1852 and achieved his doctor's degree in 1856. Years later, he would occupy the chair of Criminal Law and Civil and Criminal Procedures, replacing Antonio Zambrana (Calcagno 1878: 190–191) and would write a manual on procedural matters (Céspedes 1862). After the outbreak of the Cuban War of Independence, he would settle for a few years in Costa Rica, a country that received a large number of Cuban families fleeing from the conflict. In that Central American country, Céspedes Orellano had the opportunity to join Saint Thomas University, where he held the chairs of International Law, Public Law, Roman Law, and Rational Philosophy. So significant was his work in Costa Rica, and so great was its impact, that he is recognized as the scholar who introduced positivist philosophy to that country (Vargas 2006: 37–38). Indeed, he always showed great admiration for the figure of Auguste Comte and the philosophical system he created, which he considered superior to other existing currents. About positivism, Céspedes (1895) affirmed that this was

> a philosophy based on real and proven facts and will always be more respectable and more credible for the generality of men, than the one which relies only on metaphysical hypotheses, even if they are created by the most exalted geniuses from Germany.
>
> (282)

Once the war ended, José María Céspedes y Orellano returned to Cuba and was able to rejoin Havana University. Having previously held the comparative legislation chair, he became the first professor to occupy the chair of General Spanish Legal History, created in 1883 under the Gamazo Plan. Céspedes was aware that historicity was a feature inherent to the legal phenomenon, and the latter could not be understood in isolation from the society that gave it life. Law was inseparable from the successive and constant transformations of the community in which it germinated (*Disertación* 1886: 113). Hence, law could not develop in the same way in all periods or in all social groups, but its modulations obeyed internal and external conditions of each specific historical moment (Céspedes 1885: 13).

José María Céspedes y Orellano would apparently implement these criteria when dictating his comparative legislation lessons. The only surviving evidence of his work with regard to the subject is the opening speech of the 1880–1881 academic year. In this speech, he proposed to expand the subject matter's limits toward the confines of the critical history of the social state and the norms that had ruled the ancient peoples of the East, of Greece, and Rome. All of these aspects should necessarily be redirected to the study of the critical history of the social state and the norms that governed modern societies. In order to satisfactorily fulfill the itinerary outlined, he emphasized the point that it was indispensable to resort to legal philosophy since all this wealth of knowledge had to be based on solid and accurate principles (Céspedes 1895: 2).

After examining the scope that Céspedes intended to give the comparative legislation chair, it is possible to glimpse the role he assigned to historical analysis. A fundamental position in his thought was that every glance at the legal past had to be justified and could not serve banal and unsuccessful purposes. History could not come out by the mere display of erudition. No one should evoke it with the vague desire of filling pages because its indiscriminate use did nothing but denote an inability to generate one's own ideas (Céspedes 1895: 435–436). Céspedes understood that all knowledge was profitable, but it was impossible to cover it entirely. Therefore, it was prudent to focus on those studies that, regardless of their nature or object, were the most useful and indispensable for the optimal performance of the legal profession (*Disertación* 1886: 4). However, his opinions did not imply the rejection of the historical-legal perspective. On the contrary, he never stopped stressing that law had to be observed through history's prism, "ascending to its concrete origins and descending to its always infinite and relative ethnic evolutions" (*Disertación* 1886: 5). Paradoxically, although the comparative legislation chair assigned an important role to the historical perspective, the chair of General History of Spanish Law did not seem to make space for the comparative method. It focused on a purely nationalist approach, as evidenced by the program drafted by Juan Francisco O'Farrill, successor of Céspedes y Orellano in the latter chair. This program enclosed a series of methods to study legal history. The methods considered were the geographical, the ethnographical, the chronological, and the synchronous, with no mention of a comparative approach (O'Farrill 1892: 5–6). Other works published by the same author also lack references to the comparative approach (1895).

Comparative perspective and legal-historical analysis in the first half of the twentieth century

Spanish colonial domination on the Cuban island would cease in 1898. After a period of American military intervention, Cuba would arise as an independent national state in 1902. The new Republic demanded a new university, one capable of consolidating a national culture that was barely emerging while fostering the most innovative scientific contributions achieved in the various fields of human knowledge. Positivist currents gained universal popularity within the scientific work of the country. Although positivism had been present in the work of some Cuban jurists since the second half of the nineteenth century, a generation of teachers would now bridge the gap between nineteenth-century legal science and twentieth-century legal science. That is why both the comparative and historical visions would be conceived as the basis of any scientific examination of legal institutions. There, we have the cases of José Antonio González Lanuza (1893: 9–15), professor of Criminal Law, and Ricardo Dolz y Arango (1895: 3), professor of Procedural Law, who reserved a space for historical explanation as a prelude to the theoretical and doctrinal assumptions of their respective subjects. In addition, Antonio Sánchez de Bustamante y Sirvén (1896: 173–174), perhaps the most famous Cuban jurist worldwide, pondered the historical method in the first volume of his *Treatise of International Private Law*, as an alternative to the unearthing of "scientific curiosities" that would "theoretically build organisms that achieve the greatest possible perfection." Among this generation were other teachers who also included history as a predominant part of the contents imparted by them. For example, this can be seen in the *Program of Political and Administrative Law* redacted by Domingo Guerrero (n.d.) and in Bernardo del Riesgo's *Elements of Commercial Law* (del Riesgo 1881: 15–28) whose second chapter was completely dedicated to that discipline's historical evolution. This was a common practice during the time in question, generally restricted to the acritical exposition of the chronological legal sources. Even so, it represented an advance in the context of scientific teaching and research.

At the beginning of the twentieth century, praiseworthy efforts were undertaken by José Antonio González Lanuza and Enrique José Varona, who successively occupied the Secretariat of Public Instruction during the first intervening government and would develop at the time two programs with a positivist orientation. In this sense, González Lanuza, who would also become the Law Faculty's Dean, during the inaugural speech of the 1902–1903 academic year recalled the importance of considering law historically as a *sine qua non* requirement of any truly scientific approach (1902: 16). He understood that the appropriate method for legal positivist research required observing the social phenomena regulated by law, as well as engaging in a historical, philosophical, and comparative analysis. He viewed history as the laboratory in which society could be analyzed in its constant dynamic of transformation and restructuring. These cognitive procedures were, according to José Antonio González Lanuza, "the only ones capable of providing positive results" (1902: 16), but it was necessary to harmonize historical knowledge with current law and legal technique, so as not to be mere scholars but jurists with sufficient skills to operate in the domains of theory and practice.

During the first half of the twentieth century, there were attempts in the field of legal history to go beyond the purely nationalist approach and to undertake global or at least regional approaches. Such were the efforts of the Argentine professor Ricardo Levene with the Spanish colonial law (Derecho Indiano) and the German Franz Wieacker with his book *History of Private Law in Europe* (Wieacker 1995). By contrast, in Cuba, this period was characterized by a quest for a national legal historiography. One of the consequences of this phenomenon was the suppression of legal history from the university curriculum. While at first such a measure may seem paradoxical, it can be justified by considering that according to the paradigms of that time, the legal-historical analysis reduced its spectrum to categories such as legal norms and political institutions. Therefore, it was logical to eliminate a discipline that focused narrowly on an immediate past in which only metropolitan norms and colonial institutions could be glimpsed. Here is one of the possible obstacles when explaining the absence of a national legal history in the university classrooms: from the normative and institutional point of view, a previous Cuban law did not property exist. Some decades would pass before Cuban legal history was taught at Havana University—more specifically, Cuban constitutional history, imparted by Professors Ramón Infiesta (1942) and Enrique Hernández Corujo (1960). However, as we already pointed out, throughout the indicated period a series of historical-legal subjects made their presence felt in academic programs.

As early as 1906, a chair of Municipal Government and History of Local Institutions was created at the University of Havana, on the initiative of the prestigious professor Francisco Carrera Jústiz, who is acknowledged as the father of Cuban municipal science and as one of the precursors of legal positivism on the island. Carrera Jústiz proposed an institutional history that deviated from the one cultivated during the preceding century. In this case, the methodology he opted to implement was based on a sociological perspective. His methodology aimed to unravel the actions of the political and social forces that marked the origins of local institutions and the trends that shaped their evolution through the different periods, as well as the phenomena that revealed the ways of life of the communities in each determined historical moment (Carrera 1905: XI–XII).

Francisco Carrera Jústiz believed that Cuba's institutional life blossomed from its municipalities, which he viewed as critical to the genesis of the recently founded Cuban state. His work embarks on a sociological journey through the history of the Cuban municipalities, going back to Roman Spain, with the intention of highlighting their Latin roots, and engaging in a comparative analysis with the European, Hispanic American, and North American municipalities. In Professor Carrera Jústiz's (1905) own words, the comparative approach was the only way to undertake a truly scientific exam of any institution:

> The scientific study of Cuban local institutions consists not only in their historical description, referring data and dates; but in exposing these institutions in relation to their analogues of other countries, to interlock them with their institutional genealogical precedents, to unravel whatever the old strain, which as an active political principle has traditionally been animating

> the current collective life of Cuban local society, and finally, to set their rightful place in the great universal family of political institutions worldwide. (9)

That is the reason why, although this study delved into the municipal legislation that governed in Cuba during the colonial regime, the analysis of the corresponding legal norms did not stagnate in simple exegetical interpretation but ventured to evaluate vital issues such as their effective validity and their social impact.

Within Cuban legal historiography, Francisco Carrera Jústiz was possibly the only scholar to develop a comparative analysis during the second half of the twentieth century. However, there were other historians who, despite not assuming a comparative approach, tried to use wider frameworks. According to the 1940–1941 program, a legal history chair was inaugurated and the professor in charge was Domingo Herrera Barruete. This subject's content did not encompass Cuban Law or even any particular national Law, but it instead pretended to focus on a universal legal history, capable of evaluating the legal phenomenon in its entirety and not in an isolated or fragmented way:

> We understand that true legal history must be considered as a whole, and the phenomenon of its evolution in time must be treated and studied as a whole as well. Scientific legal history ... is not reached by the gathering of isolated news and pieces without connection of legal institutions; the mission of legal history ... is to recognize the set of institutions and acquire a total image of the interior of Law's development ... Legal history is not the isolated sum of its institutions.
>
> (Herrera n.d.: 4)

In that sense, the proposed itinerary encompassed the historical phase that went from Justinian's *Corpus Iuris Civilis* to nineteenth-century codification. Outside the scope of university education, it was possible during this era to find books with a similar approach, like *Historical Fundaments of Merchant Law*, written by the already mentioned Ramón Infiesta (1939). These works, as we said, stand out because of the attempt to embrace wider frameworks beyond national boundaries. However, none of them involved a comparative exercise in the strictest sense. This situation would not change during the revolutionary period, that is, after 1959.

The revolutionary period

On January 1, 1959, Cuba would witness one of the most crucial twentieth-century events in Latin America and the world. That date famously witnessed the triumph of a revolutionary movement that empowered a government that would establish a socialist regime in the country. The implantation of the socialist system would not be limited only to the substitution of the political order.

The revolution would project a set of deep transformations in the economic, social, and cultural sphered. In the coming years, the university played a very active role in the construction of a society governed by principles totally opposed to the model that was intended to be left behind. It also had to contribute to the formation of the so-called "new man," promoting new cultural tendencies and offering the ideological foundations deemed suitable in order to reach the established goals.

According to the new political conceptions, the law school would undergo considerable changes. As a result, legal-historical studies would be expanded in such a way that legal history would be divided into two different subjects: History of the State and Law in Cuba and General History of the State and Law. Soviet models of legal education then began to serve as a reference, and at the same time, the use of Marxist analytical categories was inserted into the historical reading. History of the State and Law in Cuba initially had Orestes Hernández Más as the principal professor. Orestes Hernández Más had many academic merits throughout his life. One of them was to introduce a subject that would try to show a general panorama of Cuban legal history in the halls of Havana University for the first time. However, due to his sudden and premature death, his course was left incomplete, and his lessons barely reached the dawn of the nineteenth century (Hernández: 2). After he died, the matter would continue to be imparted successively by Julio Carreras (1981) and then Julio Fernández Bulté (2005), who would write respective manuals and increase the content developed by his predecessor.

With regard to the matter General History of the State and Law, Julio Fernández Bulté was in charge since the course's creation and until very recent times. Two voluminous tomes entitled *History of State and Law in Ancient Times* (Fernández 1971) sprung from his pen, serving as the basic text. This new subject pretended to gather a series of historical milestones on the genesis and evolution of the State and Law, from ancient times to modernity, but tempered with the dialectical-materialist approach imposed by the new historical conditions. Meanwhile, General History of the State and Law tried to comprehend a vision as universal as possible of legal history while also giving considerable space to contents of Roman Law. Nevertheless, as occurred with the legal history course taught during the prerevolutionary republican period, the new course could not embrace a comparative perspective.

Conclusion

Although the Cuban case has been taken as the central point of our analysis, the comparative legal history of Latin America more generally is in its early stages, with most scholarship taking a narrow national focus. To develop a truly Latin American legal history would require much more work than is possible here. However, it is evident that the use of a comparative perspective could contribute to the reencounter with our common past. This is true whether we follow a traditional comparative method, of a systematic nature, or a more flexible one.

Any of these variants would be valid as long as a serious and solid comparative exercise is carried out: a comparative exercise that not only pursues a glimpse of our common past and demonstrates everything that unites our countries but also brings out the particularities of each pertinent case in our different formation processes. A comparative history of Latin American law should highlight our contrasts and our differences, as well as situate the different experiences of our countries in each historical moment. This should do nothing but contribute to the rescue and the vindication of Latin American legal culture.

References

Aguirre, Carlos and Salvatore, Ricardo D. (2017) "Escribir la Historia del Derecho, el Delito y el Castigo en América Latina". *Historia y Justicia* 8: 224–252.

Altamira, Rafael (1903) *Historia del Derecho Español*. Madrid: Librería General de Victoriano Suárez.

Azcárate, Gumersindo (1874) *Ensayo de una Introducción al Estudio de la Legislación Comparada y Programa de Esta Asignatura*. Madrid: Imprenta de la Revista de Legislación.

Bachiller y Morales, Antonio (1857) *Elementos de la Filosofía del Derecho o Curso de Derecho Natural*. La Habana: Imprenta del Tiempo.

Calcagno, Francisco (1878) *Diccionario bibliográfico cubano*. New York: Imprenta y Librería N. Ponce de León.

Carrera Jústiz, Francisco (1905) *Introducción a la Historia de las instituciones locales de Cuba. Tomo Primero*. La Habana: Lib. e Imp. "La Moderna Poesía".

Carreras, Julio (1981) *Historia del Estado y el Derecho en Cuba*. La Habana: Ministerio de Educación Superior.

Céspedes y Orellano, José María (1895) "Abuso de la Historia". Céspedes y Orellano, José María, *Discursos, escritos y artículos*. La Habana: Establecimiento Tipográfico, Teniente Rey 23: 435–437.

——— (1885) "Antropología y Derecho Penal". *Revista Cubana. Periódico Mensual de Ciencias, Filosofía, Literatura y Bellas Artes* 1: 107–122.

——— (1895) "Discurso de Apertura de la Cátedra de Legislación Comparada en la Universidad de La Habana en el Año Académico de 1880 a 1881". Céspedes y Orellano, José María, *Discursos, escritos y artículos*. La Habana: Establecimiento Tipográfico, Teniente Rey 23: 5–20.

——— (1895) "El Comtismo". Céspedes y Orellano, Céspedes y Orellano, José María, *Discursos, escritos y artículos*. La Habana: Establecimiento Tipográfico, Teniente Rey 23: 281–297.

——— (1862) *Elementos teórico-prácticos de procedimientos civiles con aplicación a la isla de Cuba*. La Habana: Imprenta "La Antilla."

Discurso inaugural de las Academias de Derecho (Curso 1902–1903) leído por el Dr. José Antonio González Lanuza (Profesor de Derecho Penal). Domingo 2 de noviembre de 1902 (1902) La Habana: Imprenta de Rambla y Bouza.

Discurso para el doctorado en Derecho, sección del Civil y el Canónico, leído y sostenido el 18 de junio de 1884 por el Ldo. Juan Francisco O'Farrill y Chappotín. (1844) La Habana: Establecimiento Tipográfico de Soler, Álvarez y Compañía.

Disertación leída en la sesión de apertura de la Academia de Derecho en la Real Universidad de La Habana por el Doctor Don José María Céspedes y Orellano, Catedrático Numerario de la Facultad de Derecho, celebrada el día 7 de noviembre de 1886, sobre la siguiente tesis: El Derecho, su clasificación y sus relaciones con las otras ciencias (1886) La Habana: Imprenta del gobierno y Capitanía General por S. M.

Dolz y Arango, Ricardo (1895) "Ventajas del plan y del método de enseñanza desarrollados en el programa de Derecho Procesal Civil, Penal, Canónico y Administrativo, y Teoría y Práctica de redacción de instrumentos públicos". *Revista del Foro* III: 70–120.

Fernández Bulté, Julio (2005) *Historia del Estado y el Derecho en Cuba*. La Habana: Editorial Félix Varela.

——— (1971) *Historia del Estado y el Derecho en la Antigüedad*. La Habana: Instituto cubano del libro.

González Lanuza, José Antonio (1893) *Programa de Derecho Penal. Curso 1893–1894*. La Habana: Imp. "La Moderna".

Grossi, Paolo (1997) "Il Disagio di un Legislatore (Filippo Vassalli e le Apporìe dell'Assolutismo Giuridico)". *Quaderni Fiorentini per la Storia del Pensiero Giuridico Moderno* 26: 377–405.

——— (2010) *A History of European Law*. UK: Wiley-Blackwell.

Hernández Corujo, Enrique (1960) *Historia Constitucional de Cuba*. La Habana: Compañía Editorial de Libros y Folletos.

Hernández Más, Orestes (n.d) *Historia del Estado y el Derecho en Cuba*. La Habana: Universidad de La Habana. Facultad de Derecho.

Hernández Sandoica, Elena (1992) "La Universidad de La Habana, 1728–1898 (Implantación cultural, estatus científico y nacionalismo bajo el dominio español)". *Historia de la educación: Revista universitaria* 11: 73–89.

Herrera, Domingo (n.d.) *Historia del Derecho (Copias de Clases)*. La Habana: Departamento de publicaciones de la Universidad de La Habana).

Infiesta, Ramón (1939) *Fundamentos históricos del Derecho Mercantil*. La Habana: Jesús Montero, Editor.

——— (1942) *Historia Constitucional de Cuba*. La Habana: Editorial Selecta.

Labra, Rafal M. de (1879) *Los Códigos Negros. Estudio de Legislación Comparada*. Madrid: Imprenta de Aurelio J. Alaria.

Marquardt, Bernd and Llinás, David (eds.) (2018) *Historia comparada del derecho público latinoamericano del siglo XIX. Anuario VII de constitucionalismo comparado*. Bogotá: Grupo Editorial Ibáñez.

Mestre, José Manuel (1862) *De la Filosofía en La Habana*. La Habana: Imprenta "La Antilla".

Montoro, Rafael (1889) "Estudios Comparativos sobre el Bandolerismo y su Represión". *Revista General de Derecho* 6: 39–49; 319–328.

Moreno Fraginals, Manuel (1996) *Cuba/España. España/Cuba. Historia Común*. Barcelona: Crítica.

O'Farrill, Juan Francisco (1895) *La España romana. Discurso leído en la Apertura del 10º curso de la Academia de Derecho*. La Habana: Imprenta y Papelería "La Universal," de Ruiz y Hermano.

——— (1892) *Programa de Historia General del Derecho Español*. (La Habana: Imprenta y Papelería "La Universal" de Ruiz y Hermano.

Petit, Carlos (1995) "Absolutismo jurídico y derecho comparado: método comparativo y sistema de fuentes en la obra de Edouard Lambert". *De la Ilustración al Liberalismo: Symposium en honor al profesor Paolo Grossi*. Madrid: CEC, 1995.

Pihlajamäki, Heikki (2015) "Comparative Contexts in Legal History: are we all comparatists now?" *Sequência* 70: 57–75.

Piqueras Arenas, José A. (2002) "La Política de los Intereses en Cuba y la Revolución (1810–1914)". Terán, Marta and Serrano Ortega, José Antonio (eds.), *Las*

Guerras de Independencia en la América Española. México, El Colegio de Michoacán: 465–484.

Posada, Adolfo (1906) *Derecho Político Comparado*. Madrid: Librería General de Victoriano Suárez.

Programa de las materias correspondientes a las asignaturas de Derecho Político y Administrativo Español, a cargo del Dr. José Domingo Guerrero (n.d.) La Habana: Universidad de La Habana.

Riesgo, Bernardo del (1881) *Elementos de Derecho Mercantil*. La Habana: La Propaganda Literaria.

Sánchez de Bustamante y Sirvén, Antonio (1896) *Tratado de Derecho Internacional Privado. Tomo I. Nociones Preliminares. Historia del Derecho Positivo. Historia del Derecho Científico*. La Habana: Imprenta y Papelería "La Universal" de Ruiz y Hermano.

Santamaría García, Antonio (2011) "Las Islas Españolas del Azúcar (1760–1898). Grandes Debates en Perspectiva Comparada y Caribeña". *América Latina en la Historia Económica* 35: 149–176.

Sappez, Delphine (2016) "El Krausismo en la Formación del Movimiento Reformista y Liberal en Cuba (Siglo XIX)". *Revista de Indias* 267: 543–572.

Savigny, Friedrich Carl von (2015) *De la vocación de nuestra época para la legislación y la ciencia del Derecho*. Madrid: Universidad Carlos III de Madrid.

Thibaut, Anton Friedrich Justus (2015) Sobre *la necesidad de un Derecho Civil General para Alemania*. (Madrid: Universidad Carlos III de Madrid.

Uribe Urán, Víctor Manuel and Ortiz Mesa, Luis Javier (eds.) (2000) *Naciones, gentes y territorios. Ensayos de historia e historiografía comparada de América Latina y el Caribe*. Medellín: Colección Clío, Editorial y Facultad de Ciencias Humanas y Económicas de la Universidad Nacional de Colombia, Sede Medellín.

Vargas Araya, Armando (2006) *El Doctor Zambrana*. San José, Costa Rica: Editorial Universidad Estatal a Distancia.

Wieacker, Franz (1995) *A history of private law in Europe with particular reference to Germany*. Oxford: Clarendon Press.

4 Bar associations and the circulation of legal knowledge

Argentina and Brazil, 1917–1943

Mariana de Moraes Silveira

Introduction[1]

Even though legal historians have shown a growing interest in comparative, transnational, and global approaches in the past few years (Pihlajamäki 2015, 57–75; Duve 2016), not many studies pay attention to the circulation of ideas within Latin American countries. The existing analyses tend to emphasize dialogues lawyers from that region established with their colleagues in Europe or the United States.[2] During the first half of the twentieth century, however, several initiatives aimed at enhancing contacts between Ibero-American lawyers took place alongside debates regarding Pan-Americanism, the impact of the World Wars and subsequent assessment of foreign ideas and theories, and pressing concerns about the nation and the ideal path of its progress.

This chapter analyzes the role legal organizations played in promoting exchanges between Brazil and Argentina, both who were profoundly engaged in those debates. More precisely, this chapter reconstitutes the activities sponsored by the Institute of Brazilian Lawyers (IAB) and the Buenos Aires Bar Association (CABA), the primary associations of their kind in their respective countries.[3] In doing so, I argue the often-overlooked dialogues between Argentinian and Brazilian lawyers were crucial for articulating public actions domestically and for creating transnational forums for debate.

I place legal and intellectual histories into a productive dialogue by attending to concrete mechanisms through which the legal knowledge transcended national borders between 1917 and 1943.[4] In 1917, CABA invited the Brazilian jurist, politician, and diplomat Afrânio de Melo Franco to speak in a solemn session held in its headquarters, and in 1943, the Inter-American Bar Association (IABA) (founded during The Eighth American Scientific Congress in 1940) held its second meeting in Rio de Janeiro. The texts produced from these conventions include meeting minutes, conference proceedings, legal journals, and daily newspapers. Attention from the press demonstrates that lawyers held prestigious social and political positions in Argentina and Brazil, and that the activities they promoted concerned a public far broader than the legal profession.

I start by providing background information on the IAB and CABA, retracing the contexts of their development and emphasizing how both institutions acted in the public arena. The next section contains brief chronological descriptions of three key moments in which those organizations engaged in cross-border dialogues: early initiatives in the late 1910s, often connected to the actions of diplomats and politicians; the development of more articulate efforts for improving exchanges throughout the 1920s and 1930s; and the founding of IABA under the watchful eye of the United States in a world immersed in World War II. The closing section discusses the intriguing questions of *why* and *how* official discourses and historiography ignored reciprocal gazes in spite of their vitality and the anticipation surrounding them.

Neighboring countries, distinctive professional organizations: the entangled histories of the IAB and the CABA

Although IAB and CABA developed closely knit ties throughout the first decades of the twentieth century and became key actors in the transmission of legal knowledge across the borders of Argentina and Brazil, their trajectories differ considerably. They were established seven decades apart, and it is not unreasonable to assume that at least part of the Argentinian lawyers' interest in strengthening bonds with Brazilian colleagues stemmed from their search for legitimization within a similar and more established institution. The Brazilian organization was more successful in securing positions of relevance for its members and gathering support from the state for its projects.[5] Nonetheless, one striking resemblance connects both institutions: their activities were never limited to professional matters, but often sought to intervene or even take the lead in public debates and political controversies.

In the case of the Institute of Brazilian Lawyers, this trait dates to their founding in 1843 as a sort of semi-official institution by a group of prominent lawyers.[6] Throughout the nineteenth century, the Institute managed to build the public image of a selfless, abnegated society of learned men whose chief commitment was to the consolidation of a legal order for the newly independent nation while counting several politicians among its members and developing its activities under the auspices of Emperor Dom Pedro II. More importantly, the IAB created a niche for their congregation of experts who needed to be heard in governmental decision-making, especially during the drafting of new legislation.

Following the Proclamation of the Republic in November 1889, the group could no longer take its privileged access to the state for granted. The IAB's activities were all but suspended in the wake of the political disruption and did not regain their regularity until April 1892. Little by little, however, the Institute sought to rebuild its position in the public scene. One crucial mechanism it employed was the promotion of academic gatherings, strategically designed to coincide with larger festivities. Beginning in London in 1851, conferences blossomed alongside World's Fairs, helping consolidate an international arena for science and scholarly debate (Rasmussen 2017, 599–604). Law was no exception. During the 1900 Universal Exhibition in Paris, a large international gathering on comparative law witnessed increasing interest in legal knowledge transcending borders (Petit 2001, 53–98). That May, amid celebrations of the fourth centennial of the first Portuguese fleet's arrival on what would become Brazilian territory, the IAB held the American Juridical Congress. Eight years later, it would host the First Brazilian Juridical Conference during the hundredth anniversary of the opening of Brazilian harbors for trade with nations other than its metropolis. Similarly, a Juridical Congress Celebrating Independence took place in September 1922 alongside the international exhibition that marked hundred years of Brazilian political emancipation (Galvão 2017, 377–401).

While the Institute regained its position as a group of expert consultants for the writing of novel legislation, it also created clearer definitions of its public ambitions by rewriting its bylaws. In 1893, the rules that governed IAB's actions started to emphasize the organization's role in promoting "the study of law in its widest development, in its practical applications, and in comparison with several branches of foreign legislation." Additionally, they established that the Institute should "send memoranda to public powers about bills, projects and regulations" (Guimarães, Bessone and Motta 2003, 26–27). In 1928, the goal of acting in favor of the "diffusion of legal culture in the country" was added. Initially conceived as a means to promote the betterment of legal education, this new goal provided the basis for a series of interventions in public life (122–127). One central aspiration of the Institute, however, remained unaccomplished for almost a century. Claims for professional regulation constituted part of the reason why IAB was first established, but they would only be enacted in the early 1930s as an attribution of a different institution, the Order of Attorneys of Brazil (OAB).[7]

The Buenos Aires Bar Association, in turn, was established in 1913.[8] Passed the following year, its first bylaws defined "the promotion and the sustainment of righteousness and illustration when exerting attorneyship and in lawyers' decorum" as its central goals. Shortly after, the document clearly articulated that the new professional society's cultural and political ambitions were vast: it would seek to guarantee the passing of bills regulating the legal professions, create a library, promote "conferences, assemblies or scientific congresses on juridical matters," and produce opinions "about matters of public interest" whenever required (Colegio 1914, 3). The institutional aims became more poignant in 1926 with the addition of the intent "to favor the improvement of justice administration and the progress of legislation" (Colegio 1926, 3).

Half a decade earlier, Argentinian jurists had already shown signs of their investment in institutional development. Created in 1921, the Argentinian Federation of Bar Associations (FACA) aimed to congregate organizations representing lawyers throughout the country, and to stimulate the creation of similar institutions where they did not yet exist (Federación 1923, 9–14). Working in close connection with CABA, the Federation started holding National Conferences of Lawyers in 1924. At first, the debates were limited to matters of judicial organization and procedural law, but they would quickly expand to virtually all domains of legal expertise (Federación 1925, 7–8). Those meetings soon encompassed foreign colleagues: Brazilian and Chilean lawyers took part in its fourth edition, held in Tucumán in 1936 (Federación 1937, 14). In the following conference (Santa Fé in 1940), these delegates were again present, as well as Paraguayan, Peruvian, and Uruguayan colleagues (Federación 1941, 25).

Furthermore, these national jurist gatherings were at the origin of the Argentinian Institute for Legislative Studies. Subordinate to FACA and established in 1935, the organization was designed as a permanent body of experts able to advise government on the drafting of new bills and other matters of public interest (Federación [193–]). Although a similar institution never formed on the opposite bank of the Plata River, the desire to advise and affect the legislative process was something the Brazilian and Argentinian bar associations undeniably shared. Uncoincidentally, projects for legal reforms constituted one of the main topics of their dialogues.

The IAB, CABA, FACA, and the OAB all engaged in publishing policies that sought to spread their messages, as well as to perpetuate events such as public talks and conferences. Despite the irregularity of its *Boletim*, the Institute of Brazilian Lawyers could rely on the *Jornal do Comércio*, then Rio de Janeiro's main newspaper, to publicize accounts of its activities. The Buenos Aires Bar Association launched its more routinely published *Revista* in 1921, but articles on the association frequently appeared in *La Prensa*, the Argentinian capital's leading daily at the start of the twentieth century. CABA managed one of the biggest legal libraries of Buenos Aires, whose social prestige was raised by its housing in the Supreme Court of Justice's building. Starting in the late 1920s, the IAB and CABA also made intelligent use of novel communication technologies. The IAB sponsored a series of radio lectures fostering the "popularization of legal knowledge" (Carneiro 1930, 144–145). Meanwhile, other radio stations made offers to promote CABA's activities (Colegio 1934–1938, 187–188; 1938–1944, 240).

Argentinian and Brazilian jurists had longed shared connections, reciprocal gazes, and mutual projects when lawyers of the entire continent established the IABA in 1940. J. Honorio Silgueira, FACA's President and leader of Argentina's delegation to the IABA's second conference, took a keen interest in retracing the steps of this rapprochement. In his farewell speech after the meeting held in Rio de Janeiro in August 1943, Silgueira developed a thorough chronicle of activities that demonstrated the strength of such exchanges: sustained contacts between bar associations, international conferences, book donations, and special delegations' travel. The Argentinian lawyer believed these actions had built "a new luminous arch of Argentinian-Brazilian comprehension between Guanabara [Bay] and the Plata [River], between the two countries' jurists," opening "a large road of promising confraternity" (Silgueira 1943, 209–211). The Department of Press and Propaganda (DIP), the organization in charge of censorship and official advertising during the Estado Novo or "New State," the authoritarian Brazilian regime under President Getúlio Vargas (1937–1945), broadcast Silgueira's speech on Brazilian and Argentinian radio, suggesting that the activities bar associations promoted resonated in the political world. Paying close attention to those ties to power, the next section provides a critical account of central steps between CABA's first official invitation to a Brazilian colleague and Silgueira's exultant speech.

Setting legal knowledge in motion: itineraries of the first half of the twentieth century

In the footsteps of diplomats and politicians: early attempts at enhancing the contacts between Argentina and Brazil

When Afrânio de Melo Franco (1917) spoke about the "correlation between Brazilian and Argentinian law," he had not come to Buenos Aires as only a guest of the city's bar association. He was on his way back from an official mission to represent his country in the new Bolivian president's inauguration ceremony. His itinerary to Rio de Janeiro also included stops in Santiago and Montevideo. In each of these cities, he met with local authorities and took part in public events. Franco's presence at CABA constitutes a typical example of how contacts between South American bar associations unraveled during the late 1910s. These contacts blossomed primarily through the actions of law graduates who were polygraphs *par excellence*, traveling between different domains of expertise and serving in political or diplomatic posts. Therefore, exchanges often stemmed from circumstances that had little to do with law in principle such as travel for official or even personal purposes, activities sponsored by literary societies and the press, and Rio de Janeiro's position as a stop on naval routes between Argentina and Europe.

However, a more attentive reading of the peculiarities surrounding Franco's speech shows it was strategically conceived to facilitate general exchanges between Argentinian and Brazilian lawyers, as well as particular contacts between those countries' bar associations. Shortly after this public session, CABA arranged for the talk to be published. An explanatory note from Oscar Rodríguez Saráchaga, the director of CABA's library, accompanied the transcription. Amid a eulogizing account of the session held at the Palace of Justice, Rodríguez Saráchaga emphasized how the speaker was not only a diplomat and politician but also "a distinguished professional, member of Rio de Janeiro's Institute of Lawyers" (Franco 1917, 4).

The note also highlighted the role Franco played in the parliamentary commission that examined Clovis Bevilaqua's draft for his country's first civil code. Passed in 1916 and enacted a few months before Franco visited Buenos Aires, the codification was quickly received with high praise in Argentina where it was often seen as a modern body of laws, providing useful insights into the renewal of the country's nearly fifty-year-old civil code (Abásolo 2017, 425–442). The new legislation constituted the subject of roughly half of the diplomat's remarks, and Franco implied that such choice of emphasis was not his own, but a request from CABA (Franco 1917, 22).

Franco portrayed Brazil's passing of a civil code more than nine decades after its declaration of independence as a sign of pride and distinction for his country and the American continent. He took a particular interest in describing how Dalmacio Vélez Sarsfield, while drafting the text that would be approved as the Argentinian Civil Code in 1869 and enacted in 1871, had drawn inspiration from Augusto Teixeira de Freitas's 1864 "sketch" for a Brazilian equivalent – a plea several of his compatriots and neighbors would echo while attempting to prove the bonds between Brazil and Argentina had deep historical roots. Franco underscored the quality of those exchanges, by claiming that, when making use of each other's legal writings and institutions, Argentinian and Brazilian lawyers remained attentive to the "peculiar features of both nationalities" and managed to undertake "an intelligent work that honors both nations, and not an unconscious and servile adaptation" (Franco 1917, 8).

The praise for the connection between Freitas and Vélez Sarsfield also appeared amid commemorations of the centennial of Brazil's independence in 1922. CABA adhered to public festivities held in Argentina to mark the occasion while the University of Buenos Aires's law school promoted a solemn session in honor of the neighboring country and sent a special delegation to Rio de Janeiro (Colegio 1922, 13; Facultad 1923). The group that traveled to the Brazilian capital took a bronze plaque honoring the memory of Freitas, and the nineteenth-century jurist was a ubiquitous presence in speeches pronounced by lawyers from both countries. Originally meant as a gift to Rio's law school, the plaque was installed instead at IAB, following a suggestion from Sá Vianna, one of its long-standing members who was responsible for greeting the Argentinian delegation. However much symbolic investment went into those actions, an articulate project to strengthen bonds between the two countries' bar associations would not be created for another half decade.

The "Plan for cultural and juridical exchange" and the delegations of lawyers

J. Honorio Silgueira's initial motivations for his 1926 trip to Brazil were quite mundane, although he started weaving connections with local lawyers. He traveled to Rio de Janeiro as one of the representatives of the Buenos Aires Jockey Club, and inaugurated the new facilities of its homologue. If we believe Silgueira's account of the facts, a casual conversation with a journalist (who happened to be a correspondent of Buenos Aires's *La Nación*) was the starting point of his contact with Brazilian jurists. In a move that's telling of the sociability of law graduates, the IAB promoted a lunch party in Silgueira's honor, also at the Jockey Club. Subsequently, they named him an honorary member of the Institute in a ceremony attended by the Brazilian Minister of Foreign Affairs, the Argentinian ambassador in Rio, and other representatives of American countries (Silgueira 1943, 209–210).

Before those solemnities, Silgueira gave an interview to the *Jornal do Comércio* describing the activities and aims of the FACA, an organization over which he then presided. The reporter praised his presence in Brazil as a sign of a cordial climate between the two countries. The newspaper article also mentioned the previous president of the Federation, Manuel B. Gonnet, and his status as a correspondent member of the IAB. The interview concluded with what Silgueira described as a "plan for juridical and cultural rapprochement." After praising the Institute of Brazilian Lawyers as the "doyen of the Americas," he expressed his certainty that

> It may be, it must be useful to the strengthening of the ties between friends, neighbors and efficient factors of the juridical progress of America, to bring the lawyers of Brazil in contact with those of Argentina in a frequent exchange, so that, knowing each other, they can propagate their culture, examine or study together the problems regarding legislation in general, political organization and issues of private and public international law which are of most interest to both peoples.
>
> (*Jornal do Comércio*, July 15, 1926)

Silgueira argued a useful means towards that end would be to establish regular, yearly visits of Brazilian lawyers to Buenos Aires, and of their Argentinian colleagues to Rio de Janeiro. In his view, these expeditions would generate reciprocal knowledge to the benefit of both countries, as they would allow jurists to develop "a safe study of comparative law" and to better understand each nation's "legislation, its march and orientation from the social, political, economic and labor points of view" (*Jornal do Comércio*, July 15, 1926). Silgueira's proposal would soon find resonance within the IAB. In his inaugural speech as President of the Institute for the 1926–1928 term, Rodrigo Octavio referred to the Argentinian colleague's recent reception as honorary member to encourage the IAB's engaging in "crossing country borders" of "democratic and sister America," in order to achieve the ideals the institution shared with foreign bar associations (1927, 8).

A few months later, Octavio, who was a seasoned diplomat, a recognized expert of international law, and founding member of the Brazilian Academy of Letters, led the first concrete effort stemming from Silgueira's proposal. Between March 10 and 20, 1927, a group including Octavio, Eduardo Theiler (the IAB's treasurer) and Haroldo Valladão (a young professor of private international law who later engaged in projects to promote "continental solidarity" in the Americas) traveled not only to Buenos Aires but also to Rosario and Cordoba. A group of prominent Argentinian lawyers accompanied the delegation in each city, and scholars and professionals from both nations gave speeches on topics ranging from general praise of "Argentinian-Brazilian friendship" to procedural law, and from professional ethics to the 1926 reform of the Brazilian constitution. Octavio was appointed honorary member of CABA, whereas Theiler and Valladão received the title of correspondent members (Valladão 1940, 221–230).

The Argentinian bar associations insisted on reciprocating the visit. The choice of date came from the IAB, suggesting the colleagues should travel to Brazil in August 1927 so they could take part in the centennial celebrations of the founding of law faculties in Brazil (Instituto 1927). When the Argentinian delegation was about to leave for Rio de Janeiro, *La Prensa* published an editorial about "legal and juridical exchange" in which it praised the "practical measure" of taking a number of law books as a donation to the IAB's library

(August 3, 1927). The newspaper argued that constituted "an evidently useful procedure" for "establishing a true exchange" between the two nations. Reciprocal book donations featured consistently in the contact between Brazilian and Argentinian bar associations. However, none of them would be the object of as much attention as the exchange made in August 1927, revealing its significance and relevance.

J. Honorio Silgueira presided over the delegation, which included Carlos A. Berghmans Doncel, FACA's secretary, Víctor N. Romero del Prado, Domingo A. Derisi, and Ricardo A. Lagos representing the bar associations of Cordoba, San Nicolás, and Rosario, respectively (Federación 1927, 309–313). The choice of members suggests an intention of representing different parts of the country in events that would take place across the border. Like the Brazilians in Argentina a few months earlier, the foreign lawyers took part in several public ceremonies in Rio de Janeiro and in São Paulo and gave a series of talks, only this time with a resonance heightened by the commemorative date. The hundredth anniversary of the Brazilian law schools was marked by a conference about higher education in which the Argentinian lawyers participated as guests of honor (Faculdade 1928–1929).

Despite this promising start, Silgueira's desire to make these delegation exchanges a yearly program would not thrive. It was not until the mid-1930s that organized groups of lawyers crossed the Plata basin again, and they often did so as part of larger efforts for cultural exchange. In July 1934, a delegation of the Buenos Aires-based Argentinian-Brazilian Institute of Culture visited Rio de Janeiro. Rodolfo Rivarola, a prominent lawyer and politician who had already visited Brazil in the early 1920s, led the group as they took part in receptions and gave talks at the IAB (Intercambio 1934, 301). In November 1935, a "Brazilian Intellectual Embassy" visited the Argentinian capital. Led once again by Rodrigo Octavio, the delegation was often referred to by the press as "the group of Brazilian lawyers," but its activities were not limited to the legal realm (Embajada 1935, 501–507).

One possible explanation for the disruptions in international travel is the economic depression following 1929. Furthermore, Argentina and Brazil underwent coups d'état in 1930, leading General José Félix Uriburu and Getúlio Vargas to power. However, these institutional ruptures fostered new connections, as intentions to lead the continent in times of political turmoil made Argentina and Brazil more eager to strengthen their bonds, especially with concerns of the Chaco War.[9] In 1933, the Argentinian president Agustín P. Justo visited Brazil; Vargas reciprocated in 1935. During the Brazilian president's stay in Argentina, the University of Cordoba held a special session in his honor where Professor Enrique Martínez Paz (1935) gave a talk about Brazilian legal ideas and the country's main jurists. Vargas's visit was also celebrated with a luxurious book containing speeches and notes about the events that took place during his stay in Argentina. Among them was a comment about the initiative of CABA library director Oscar Rodríguez Saráchaga to give Vargas a bust of nineteenth-century Argentinian state builder and intellectual Domingo Faustino Sarmiento, asking that the President give a portrait of himself, a copy of his doctoral thesis, and a Brazilian flag to the library in return (Comisión 1935, 241). The strong presence of lawyers in the public acts surrounding Vargas's trip is an important example of how bar associations were able to find alternative paths to enhance their cross-border exchanges. Even though the delegations Silgueira dreamed of failed to travel regularly, Argentinian law never ceased to draw attention from Brazilian jurists and vice versa.

The founding of the IABA and its first two conferences

The engagement of bar associations in the diffusion of legal knowledge took a decisive turn as a deadly conflict was becoming more global. During the Eighth American Scientific Congress, held in Washington, DC in May 1940, the IABA was created. Its constitution, made available throughout the event to all those who were interested in signing up, stated the following purposes:

> To establish and maintain relations between associations and organizations of lawyers, national and local, in the various countries of the Americas, to *provide a forum for exchanges of views.*
>
> To *advance the science of jurisprudence* in all its phases and particularly the *study of comparative law*; to *promote uniformity of commercial legislation*; to *further the diffusion of knowledge of the laws of the various countries* throughout the Americas.
>
> To *uphold the honor of the profession of the law*; and to encourage cordial intercourse among the lawyers of the Western Hemisphere.
>
> To *meet in Conference from time to time* for discussion and for the purposes of the Association.
>
> (Federación 1941, 8, emphasis added)

The list suggests that learned exchange was the nodal point of the program, and that periodic conferences would be the mechanism of choice to execute this goal. More significantly, the strengthening of bonds between legal experts of the Americas was thought to serve the practical purpose of making trade among those nations smoother. The IABA also intended to enhance lawyers' presence in the public scene.

The constitution stated that membership was open to national, state, and local bar associations, as well as to professional associations devoted to specialized branches of law. Nonetheless, representation in the IABA's council was only granted to the most relevant institution of the respective national territory (Federación 1941, 8–9). The association was to have a rotating presidency, as well as one vice-president representing each country. In practical terms, the position of president seems to have been more honorific than effective. For several years after the IABA's inception, the leading figure appears to have been William Roy Vallance, a member of the American Bar Association who served as secretary general at the IABA's Washington headquarters. Elsewhere, the United States was overwhelmingly overrepresented among the founding members, as several of its state and specialized institutions, including women's bar associations, joined the IABA, whereas most countries appeared on the list with a single institution.[10] Both Brazil and Argentina were early adherents: the IAB joined the Federation via the signatures of Edmundo Miranda Jordão and Filadelfo Azevedo, who presided over the institute at different times, and FACA was represented by Enrique Gil, a lawyer who had studied in the United States, had strong bonds with the country, and served as director of CABA's *Revista*.

The 1940 edition of the *Bulletin of the Pan-American Union* published a note about the creation of the IABA, praising the new organization as the result of old aspirations of "internationally-minded" jurists of the continent (Inter-American 1940, 597). Evidence of previous mobilizations can be found in the speech pronounced by Carlos A. Berghmans Doncel at the IAB's session held in August 1927 to honor the Argentinian lawyers and to commemorate a hundred years of legal education in Brazil. He described the Brazilian delegation's previous visit to Argentina as "one of the main chapters" in FACA's history because it served as "the starting point to the masterpiece that the Federation is set out to accomplish and that could be called: International Federation of Lawyers." A draft on the establishment of the organization, written by a special commission of the Argentinian Federation, was read aloud by Berghmans Doncel with the purpose of gaining support from his Brazilian colleagues (1927, 324–328). The Cuban lawyer who served as the IABA's first president, Manuel Fernández Supervielle, later evoked the Brazilian Edmundo de Miranda Jordão and Argentinians J. Honorio Silgueira and Enrique Gil among the men whose efforts in the preceding two decades had been crucial to the emergence of an organization aimed at bringing the lawyers of the continent together (Federación 1941, 64).

The IABA's inaugural conference was originally planned in the highly symbolic Panamá City, where the canal linking the Atlantic and the Pacific oceans provided a fitting metaphorical background to the desires of American union. For reasons that remain unclear (perhaps due to the choice of Fernández Superveille as provisional first president), the conference ended up taking place in Havana. Between March 24 and 28, 1941, lawyers from different parts of the continent gathered in the Cuban capital, where they were greeted with warmth by local authorities. The Caribbean island's House of Representatives provided the setting for the meeting, while the nation's vice-president acted as the chair of the opening session.

Then, Cuba's Minister of Foreign affairs, José Manuel Cortina, gave an incisive speech in one of the plenary sessions, referring to the context of war to justify a prominent public position for lawyers and a renewed role for the Americas in the global scenario. "Jurists," he claimed, "acting as statesmen are the persons who, through their technical skill, assume the difficult role of uniting people through treaties of peace, of friendship or of commerce." Since the lawyer was "the technician who studies and interprets the laws," he should be in charge of making international unity legally possible. Cortina's final remarks were a firm defense of Pan-Americanism; he claimed America should function as "a laboratory of human improvement" (Federación 1941, 53–58).

Enrique Gil's "An opinion on American solidarity," the first proper paper presented at the conference, followed a similar path except it defended the leadership of the United States on the continent. The resolutions he proposed concerned teaching and enforcing professional ethics, including the adoption of the American Bar Association's code in other countries, a proposal that did not appear in the final resolutions. His first suggestion concerned the founding of libraries by bar associations or by judicial authorities to serve as professional tools for those involved in the administration of justice and was fully endorsed by the members of the conference. Gil finished by asking delegates to avoid using the word "foreign" when referring to their colleagues or their origins, and also that the term be erased from the proceedings (Federación 1941, 80–81, 168).

If Argentina was featured prominently at the beginning of the conference, Brazil would take the center stage at its end, as Edmundo Miranda Jordão was responsible for the closing speech (Federación 1941, 142–145). Praised as the pioneer of an association uniting lawyers of the Americas at several occasions, J. Honorio Silgueira was chosen as the next IABA President. The association's second conference should have taken place in Buenos Aires in mid-1942, but it would only happen a year later and in a different setting: Rio de Janeiro. Some accounts hold the meeting was postponed due to travel difficulties caused by the war, but it is not unreasonable to assume Argentina's ambiguous posture towards the world conflict may have played a role in that change of plans.

Such possibility adds further significance to Brazil's choice; the country had recently entered World War II on the Allies' side and had become a crucial partner to the United States. The conference also carried a symbolic weight, coinciding with the celebration of the IAB's hundredth anniversary. Even if relations between President Getúlio Vargas and Brazilian lawyers had grown strained by August 1943, official propaganda was strongly invested in the meeting (Silveira 2016, 454–455). Other than the aforementioned initiative to broadcast Silgueira's farewell speech, the event had a notable repercussion in the censored daily press, and Vargas appeared as President of Honor of the gathering. A panoply of social and cultural activities in honor of the delegates took place, including an official reception in the presidential palace. Even in such a troubled context, belief in the diffusion of legal knowledge as a means to secure progress and peace persisted. Among the twenty commissions around which the work of the conference organized, "Post-war problems" coexisted with the search to establish "National centers of legal documentation and bibliographical indexes of law," thought to be crucial to ensuring better communication and understanding between lawyers of different nationalities (Federação 1948–1950).

Closing remarks: on the limits of Argentinian-Brazilian exchange and the lingering narrative of mutual ignorance

A few years before Afrânio de Melo Franco spoke of the "correlation between Brazilian and Argentinian law," another polymath diplomat and politician who had studied law, the Argentinian Martín García Mérou published an extensive account of intellectual life in Brazil (1900, 1). At the opening of his book, he claimed, "Out of all the South American literatures, none is so little known among us as that of Brazil." Driven by his intentions to build stronger bonds between the neighboring countries, the Argentinian seems to have remained oblivious to how the very fact that he was writing such a book denied, to a certain extent, his claim or perhaps he deliberately chose the hook as a rhetorical tool. Either way, the examples and key moments of exchange between the aforementioned bar associations stand in clear contrast to García Mérou's diagnosis. One could argue that nearly two decades came between the publishing of *El Brasil Intelectual* and Franco's speech at CABA, but those dialogues were by no means an early twentieth-century invention, as the constant references to the bonds between Vélez Sarsfield and Teixeira de Freitas suggest.

The examples evoked show exchanges between Brazilian and Argentinian lawyers were by no means negligible even if they were discontinuous and often relied on events that had little to do with law in principle. Then why is "mutual ignorance" still the dominant narrative about the cultural relations between these countries? Paying attention to asymmetries in power could be a crucial step towards understanding the perpetuation of this narrative. Although the IABA was dreamt of and talked about in the southernmost part of the American continent since at least the late 1920s, it could only become concrete under considerable North-American influence, and as part of the Pan-American project.

The "Mérou formula," what Gustavo Sorá (2003) has called the lingering interpretation according to which Argentinians and Brazilians take little interest in each other's intellectual life, is so powerful because it corresponds to certain (pre)conceptions and aspirations of these countries' learned men. By studying translations of Brazilian authors in Argentina, Sorá was able to show that a relevant corpus of publications formed and was met with interest by the Argentinian public. This is usually erased from memory as Argentinians and Brazilians are keen to favor their connections with nations deemed more "civilized" or "developed" over the exchanges they established among themselves. A similar line of reasoning applies to jurists, who never ceased to take European (or, increasingly throughout the 1900s, North-American) authors as ideal points of reference while seeking recognition from across the Atlantic as the ultimate form of distinction.

In certain circumstances, perceived geographic and cultural proximity would challenge the "Mérou formula." Kátia Baggio has drawn attention to how men sought to make knowledge about neighboring countries a useful means for developing solutions to their own nation's problems in her studies about travel narratives of Brazilian intellectuals who visited Hispanic American countries and those in the former Spanish colonies who took the opposite route (2013, 167–171). She has also shown the reciprocal gazes these intellectuals exchanged conveyed a mix of proximity and distance, identity and difference, familiarity and estrangement.

Brazilians who went to Argentina often interpreted the trip as a *Bildungsreise*, a formative journey comparable to those they took to Europe or the United

States. Buenos Aires appeared as a symbol of modernity and progress, a South American Paris of sorts, and Brazilian intellectuals were often fascinated by its elevated levels of literacy and the development of the Argentinian editorial market. A paradigmatic example is Oliveira Lima, who, as a retired diplomat, lived in Argentina between mid-1918 and early 1919. During that time, the Brazilian visited several of the country's cities, becoming acquainted with the political, economic, and social life in the Plata basin. Most importantly, he established a lively exchange with some of the most prominent local intellectuals such as Estanislao Zeballos and Ernesto Quesada. Upon returning to his homeland, Lima published a book with a profoundly positive panorama of the neighboring country. The implicit message was that Argentina could and should provide reference points for the development of Brazil (Lima 1920; Baggio 2010, 96–138).

The actions of Argentinian and Brazilian bar associations should serve as invitations to look for alternative paths of knowledge circulation when read in the context of transformations in legal thought spreading internationally at the start of the twentieth century, such as the consolidation of studies in comparative law and concerns with "rethinking law as a purposive activity, as a regulatory mechanism that could and should facilitate the evolution of social life in accordance with ever greater perceived social interdependence" (Kennedy 2006, 22). Doing so could illuminate complex interactions between national and transnational dynamics and challenge "diffusion" models of intellectual history, according to which ideas always originate in "central" countries and can only exist in the "periphery" under distorted, incomplete, or inadequate forms (Zimmermann 2009, 547).

Notes

1 This paper is part of an ongoing PhD project developed at the University of São Paulo under the supervision of Professor Gabriela Pellegrino Soares and funded by the Brazilian National Council for Scientific and Technological Development (CNPq). I would like to thank Professors José Reinaldo de Lima Lopes, Andrés Botero Bernal, Joshua Tate, Laura Beck Varela, Matthew Dyson, and Rafael Mafei Rabelo Queiroz for their feedback on drafts of this text. I am also grateful to the Centro de Investigación y Docencia Económicas (CIDE, Mexico City), which provided a travel grant that allowed me to attend the 2017 International Meeting on Law and Society, where I presented an initial draft of this paper.

2 See Ezequiel Abásolo (2014); Thomas Duve (2014); Herrera (2014, 97–119); Massimo Meccarelli and Paolo Palchetti (2015); Massimo Meccarelli and María Julia Solla Sastre (2016); Lucia Barbosa del Picchia (2012); María Rosario Polotto, Thorsten Keiser and Thomas Duve (2015); Juan Pablo Scarfi (2017); and Eduardo Zimmermann (2015, 421–438). Ezequiel Abásolo (2011, 415–427; 2016, 332–341; 2017, 425–442) is one of the few legal historians to have addressed the exchanges between Argentina and Brazil.

3 I primarily refer to the institutions by their acronyms in their native language: Instituto dos Advogados Brasileiros (IAB), Colegio de Abogados de Buenos Aires (CABA), the Order of Attorneys of Brazil [Ordem dos Advogados Brasileiros] (OAB), and the Argentinian Federation of Bar Associations [Federación Argentina de Colegios de Abogados] (FACA).

4 See Frédéric Audren (2015) regarding the possibility of merging legal and intellectual histories.

5 One likely reason for this contrast is the existence of a more complex and diversified intellectual life in Argentina with higher literacy rates, a vibrant publishing market, longer standing universities, and an earlier establishment of degrees in subjects such as Sociology and Economics, which provided the state with alternative experts (Soares 2007, 31–50; Jackson and Blanco 2014).

6 Studies about the IAB's history are fairly abundant (Bonelli 2002, 29–81); (Guimarães, Bessone and Motta 2003); (Pena 2001).

7 Both the IAB and the OAB still exist, but the latter's public prominence has far surpassed the former since the 1960s, possibly due to the OAB's status of mandatory bar. During the timeframe of this research, their attributions were not clearly differentiated, but the OAB tended to concentrate on professional regulation, whereas the IAB was more likely to engage in public and academic activities.

8 I have only been able to locate one work about the Buenos Aires Bar Association, which is more of an institutional memoir than it is a piece of scholarship (Leiva 2005).

9 The Chaco War between Bolivia and Paraguay lasted from 1932 to 1935.

10 Out of the sixty-eight members listed on the proceedings of the Havana conference, forty-five were based in the United States. The only other countries represented by more than one association were Cuba (five) and Canada (two) (Federación 1941, 27–28).

References

Abásolo, Ezequiel. "Interés argentino en la cultura jurídica brasileña a mediados del siglo XX: el caso de la revista *La Ley* durante el quinquenio 1941–1945." *Revista do Instituto Histórico e Geográfico Brasileiro*, vol. 452, no. 172 (2011): 415–427.

———, ed. *La cultura jurídica latinoamericana y la circulación de ideas durante la primera mitad del siglo XX*. Buenos Aires: Instituto de Investigaciones de Historia del Derecho, 2014.

———. "La Argentina y lo argentino en los primeros debates constituyentes del Brasil republicano (1891–1946)." *Em tempo*, vol. 14 (March 2016): 332–341.

———."El pensamiento de Clóvis Beviláqua y su impacto en los debates jurídicos argentinos de la primera mitad del siglo XX." *Revista do Instituto Histórico e Geográfico Brasileiro*, vol. 473, no. 178 (2017): 425–442.

Audren, Frédéric. "Introduction: l'histoire intellectuelle du droit ou la fin du 'Grand Partage'." *Clio@Thémis* IX (December 2015). http://www.cliothemis.com/Introduction-l-histoire,112.

Baggio, Kátia Gerab. "La Argentina según Oliveira Lima. Impresiones de viaje, vida política y sociabilidad intelectual (1918–1919)." In *Pensar al otro / pensar la nación. Intelectuales y cultura popular en Argentina y América Latina*, edited by Alejandra Mailhe, 96–138. La Plata: Al Margen, 2010.

———. "Brasil e Hispano-América: representações e trocas intelectuais." In *O Brasil em dois tempos*, edited by Eliana de Freitas Dutra, 167–183. Belo Horizonte: Autêntica, 2013.

Berghmans Doncel, Carlos. "La Federación de Colegios de Abogados de La República y la Federación Internacional de Abogados." *Revista del Colegio de Abogados de Buenos Aires*, vol. 3–4 (1927): 324–328.

Bonelli, Maria da Gloria. *Profissionalismo e política no mundo do direito*. São Carlos: EdUFSCar: Sumaré, 2002.

Carneiro, Levi. "Características atuais do direito positivo brasileiro." *Boletim do IAB*, vols. 3–4, no. VII (1930): 144–145.

Colegio de Abogados de Buenos Aires. *Estatutos del Colegio de Abogados de la Ciudad de Buenos Aires*. Buenos Aires: Imp. Busnelli, Caldelas y Cia, 1914.

———. *Memoria, balance y cuentas e informe del director de la Biblioteca*. Buenos Aires: J. Bodner, 1922.

———. *Estatuto del Colegio de Abogados de la Ciudad de Buenos Aires*. Buenos Aires: Editorial Argentina de Ciencias Políticas, 1926.

———. Board Minutes. Colegio de Abogados de Buenos Aires Library, Buenos Aires, vols. 2–3, 1934–1938; 1938–1944.

Comisión de recepción. *Visita a la Argentina del Excmo. Sr. Presidente de los EE. UU. Del Brasil Dr. Getulio D. Vargas*. Buenos Aires: Talleres Graficos de Araujo Hnos, 1935.

Duve, Thomas, ed. *Entanglements in Legal History*. Frankfurt: Max-Planck-Institut für Europäische Rechtsgeschichte, 2014.

———. "Global Legal History – A Methodological Approach." *Max Planck Institute for European Legal History Research Paper Series*, no. 04 (2016). http://dx.doi.org/10.2139/ssrn.2781104.

"Embajada intelectual brasileña." *Revista del Colegio de Abogados de Buenos Aires*, vol. 6, no. XIII (1935): 501–507.

Faculdade de Direito da Universidade do Rio de Janeiro. *Livro do Centenário dos Cursos Jurídicos (1827–1927)*. Rio de Janeiro: Imprensa Nacional, 1928 (volume 1); 1929 (volume 2).

Facultad de Derecho y Ciencias Sociales de la Universidad de Buenos Aires. *Homenaje al Brasil con motivo del centenario de su emancipación (1822–1922)*. Buenos Aires: Talleres Gráficos Caracciolo y Plantié, 1923.

Federação Inter-Americana de Advogados. *Anais da segunda conferência*. Rio de Janeiro: Imprensa Nacional, 1948–1950 (6 volumes).

Federación Argentina de Colegios de Abogados. *Memoria Correspondiente al Primer Ejercicio*. Buenos Aires, 1923.

———. *Conferencia Nacional de Abogados*. Buenos Aires: Talleres Gráficos de la Penitenciaría Nacional, 1925.

———. "Intercambio jurídico-cultural argentino-brasileño." *Revista del Colegio de Abogados de Buenos Aires*, vol. V, no. 3–4 (1927): 309–313.

———. *Instituto de Estudios Legislativos*. N. p., [193–].

———. *Cuarta Conferencia Nacional de Abogados* Buenos Aires: Imprenta del Congreso Nacional, 1937.

———. *Quinta Conferencia Nacional de Abogados*. Buenos Aires: Compañia Impresora Argentina, 1941.

Federación Interamericana de Abogados. *Organización de la asociación y memoria de la Primera Conferencia*. Baltimore: The Lord Baltimore Press, 1941.

Franco, Afrânio de Melo. *Correlação do direito brasileiro e argentino*. Buenos Aires: Imprenta de José Tragant, 1917.

Galvão, Laila Maia. "Espaços de construção da interpretação constitucional: análise dos congressos jurídicos da Primeira República." *Revista Jurídica da Presidência*, vol. 19, no. 118 (2017): 377–401.

García Mérou, Martín. *El Brasil intelectual*. Buenos Aires: Félix Lajouane, 1900.

Guimarães, Lúcia Maria Paschoal, Tânia Maria Tavares Bessone, and Marly Silva Motta. *História da Ordem dos Advogados do Brasil*. Brasília: OAB, 2003 (volume 3).

Herrera, Carlos Miguel. "Jean Jaurès y Léon Duguit en Buenos Aires: el político, el científico, lo social." In *Visitas culturales en la Argentina (1898–1936)*, edited by Paula Bruno, 97–119. Buenos Aires: Biblos, 2014.

Instituto dos Advogados Brasileiros. Minutes of the meeting held on May 12. Institute of Brazilian Lawyers Library, Rio de Janeiro, 1927.

"Inter-American Bar Association." *Bulletin of the Pan-American Union*, vol. LXXIV (1940): 597–598.

"Intercambio jurídico-cultural con el Brasil." *Revista del Colegio de Abogados de Buenos Aires*, vol. XII, no. 4 (1934): 301.

Jackson, Luiz Carlos, and Alejandro Blanco. *Sociologia no Espelho.* São Paulo: Editora 34 34, 2014.

Kennedy, Duncan. "Three Globalizations of Law and Legal Thought: 1850–2000." In *The New Law and Economic Development*, edited by David Trubek and Álvaro Santos, 19–73. New York: Cambridge University Press, 2006.

Leiva, Alberto David. *Historia del Colegio de Abogados de la Ciudad de Buenos Aires.* Buenos Aires: Ad-Hoc, 2005.

Lima, Oliveira. *Na Argentina (Impressões 1918–19).* São Paulo: Rio de Janeiro: Weisflog Irmãos, 1920.

Martínez Paz, Enrique. *El proceso de las ideas jurídicas del Brasil a través de sus jurisconsultos.* Córdoba: Universidad Nacional de Córdoba, 1935.

Meccarelli, Massimo, and Paolo Palchetti, eds. *Derecho en movimiento.* Madrid: Dykinson, 2015.

Meccarelli, Massimo, and María Julia Solla Sastre, eds. *Spatial and Temporal Dimensions for Legal History.* Frankfurt: Max-Planck-Institut für Europäische Rechtsgeschichte, 2016.

Octavio, Rodrigo. "Discurso de posse." *Boletim do IAB*, vol. III, no. 5 (1927): 3–9.

Pena, Eduardo Spiller. *Pajens da casa imperial.* Campinas: Unicamp, 2001.

Petit, Carlos. "Lambert en la Tour Eiffel, o el derecho comparado de la Belle Époque." In *La comparazione giuridica tra Otto e Novecento*, edited by Antonio Padoa-Schioppa, 53–98. Milan: Instituto Lombardo di Scienze e Lettere, 2001.

Picchia, Lucia Barbosa del. "Estado, democracia e direitos na crise do constitucionalismo liberal: uma comparação entre o pensamento jurídico francês e o brasileiro." PhD dissertation, University of São Paulo, 2012.

Pihlajamäki, Heikki. "Comparative contexts in legal history. Are we all comparatists now?" *Seqüência*, vol. 70 (January–June 2015): 57–75.

Polotto, María Rosario, Keiser, Thorsten and Duve, Thomas, eds. *Derecho privado y modernización.* Frankfurt: Max-Planck-Institut für Europäische Rechtsgeschichte, 2015.

Rasmussen, Anne. "L'arène internationale de la science (1860–1914)." In *La vie intellectuelle en France*, edited by Christophe Charle and Laurent Jeanpierre, 599–604. Paris: Seuil, 2017 (volume 1).

Scarfi, Juan Pablo. *The hidden history of international law in the Americas.* New York: Oxford University Press, 2017.

Silgueira, J. Honorio. "Conferência, em 17 de Agosto de 1943, no IAB." *Boletim do IAB*, vol. 2 (July–August–September 1943): 209–216.

Silveira, Mariana de Moraes. "Direito, ciência do social: o lugar dos juristas nos debates do Brasil dos anos 1930 e 1940." *Estudos Históricos*, vol. 29, no. 58 (2016): 441–460.

Soares, Gabriela Pellegrino. *Semear Horizontes.* Belo Horizonte: UFMG, 2007.

Sorá, Gustavo. *Traducir el Brasil.* Buenos Aires: Libros del Zorzal, 2003.

Valladão, Haroldo. *O ensino e o estudo do Direito especialmente do Direito Internacional Privado no Velho e no Novo Mundo*. São Paulo: Revista dos Tribunais, 1940.

Zimmermann, Eduardo. "Intellectual elites." In *The Palgrave Dictionary of Transnational History*, edited by Akira Iriye and Pierre-Ives Saunier, 547–551. London: Palgrave/Macmillan, 2009.

———. "Circulation des savoirs juridiques: le droit administratif et l'État en Argentina." In *Les Savoirs-Mondes*, edited by Pilar González Bernaldo and Liliana Hilaire-Pérez, 421–438. Rennes: Presses Universitaires de Rennes, 2015.

Part II

Constitutional experiences in global perspective

5 Lessons from the history of courts on the review of constitutional amendments in Colombia

Mario Alberto Cajas-Sarria

Introduction: Why does Colombia matter for comparative legal history: "Unconstitutional" constitutional amendments in a complex political context?

The role of the courts

The year 2017 will be remembered for the high intensity of legal and political debates on the implementation of peace agreements signed between the Colombian government and the rebels of the leftist Revolutionary Armed Forces of Colombia (Farc) (OACP 2018). These peace agreements were achieved after four years of negotiations and three decades of failed attempts to end an armed conflict that lasted fifty-two years and killed more than 200,000 people (*The Guardian* 2016). The Final Agreement (FA) has polarized political elites and public opinion, to the point that the 2018 presidential election is divided between those who support the peace agreements and those who reject them outright[1]. Most of the discussion regarding the peace agreements places the Constitutional Court at the center of the legal and political debate because it will have the last word on the constitutional amendments, laws, and decrees needed to make real the agreements; for instance, the reforms that established a system of transnational justice (Special Jurisdiction for Peace); the responsibility for crimes; and the rights of the former guerrillas in political participation (Bernal 2018).

But this kind of role of the Court is not a novelty. A historical approach allows us to appreciate that constitutional judges have had a leading role in the review of constitutional amendments in different junctures of the political regime during the twentieth and twenty-first centuries. Thus, the Colombian case is interesting for a Comparative Legal History due to several factors: (1) the recurrent constitutional reforms, many of them passed outside the formal rules of amendment established by the constitutions; (2) the early creation of the Public Action of Unconstitutionality (PAU) in 1910;[2] in this way, in a context of constitutional reformism and an easily accessible judicial mechanism, it is possible to trace the rich trajectory of judicial interventions in the political and legal disputes over constitutional amendments; (3) the history of constitutional amendments, and their judicial review, is also the history of a country that has a long and complex political regime, one that has dealt with different kinds of political violence over more than sixty years and also had a short military rule in the mid-twentieth century and then a return to a "restricted democracy," as well as guerrilla and drug trafficking violence, two constitutions, and also two constitutional judges: first the Supreme Court and now the Constitutional Court.

But the complexity of the political regime is not the only area of interest when analyzing this history of the courts on the review of constitutional amendments. Indeed, constitutional judges have refrained from deciding in moments of serious political tensions, but they also acted at critical junctures against all the predictions. In addition, they interpreted the Constitutions of 1886 and 1991, both to limit and to extend their jurisdiction to review constitutional amendments.

Filling the "gap" in the field of unconstitutional constitutional amendments

An overview of the theoretical literature on the role of the courts over "unconstitutional constitutional amendments" as well on "judicial review of constitutional amendments" allows us to appreciate that the accent of the legal scholars has been placed on the theoretical debates on the political legitimacy of this type of review, or on the limits to the interpretation of the amendments clauses, or on whether the institutional designs or decisions of courts contribute or not to limit the excesses of authoritarianism and populism in the amendments to the Constitution. This last one comes with greater emphasis in Latin America, when in the last decade the amendments and attempts at amendments were increased to allow presidential reelection in several countries, some of them making use of populism and drawing on mechanisms of popular participation (Colon 2014; Landau 2018; Cárdenas & Corredor 2018). Similarly, other types of studies have focused more on the global expansion of the judicial review of amendments, or on the successful "migration" of doctrines such as the "Basic Structure Doctrine" of India (Yaniv 2013; Landau 2017; Albert 2018).

The history of the role of the courts on the review of constitutional amendments in Colombia, in a complex political context, is a place that is little frequented, either by Comparative Legal History or by Comparative Constitutional Law.[3] This chapter examines this history with a critical perspective, from the time the PAU was established in 1910 until the present time.

This approach is necessary, given the limitations offered by those perspectives that only deal with legal doctrines such as the "unconstitutional constitutional amendments" or which legitimize the judicial review of amendments as restrictions to power. In effect, those tend to reduce the complexity of particular political factors and institutional trajectories of each country, which affects the review of the amendments. As such, it is considered that this rich legal history is of interest to those who undertake a comparative analysis of the judicial review of constitutional amendments, which intends to go beyond the current Colombian doctrine of the "substitution of the Constitution," which, as it is known, is one of the most studied by comparatists worldwide (Yaniv 2017).

First, this chapter briefly describes the path to the creation of the PAU, which entrusted the Supreme Court with the responsibility of deciding the petitions of citizens for unconstitutionality of the laws and decrees of the executive. Second, it deals with the review of constitutional amendments by the same Court between 1955 and 1990. This section evolves in four stages: It takes as a starting point the military rule in the mid-twentieth century, when citizens began to challenge constitutional amendments. Second, it discusses when the Court allowed the call for a plebiscite to amend the Constitution for the return to civil rule in 1957. Third, it shows the path to decisions that declared unconstitutional two amendments in 1978 and 1981. And fourth, it reviews the time when the Court in 1990 allowed the enactment of a new Constitution by a constitutional assembly. Then finally, it deals with decisions of the Constitutional Court under the Constitution of 1991 regarding the political regime between 1992 and the current time.

The Constitution of 1886 and the judicial review of its amendments

From the constitution of 1886 to the public action of unconstitutionality in 1910

The Constitution of 1886 materialized the political projects that converged in the so-called "Regeneration" led by President Rafael Nuñez. Thus, it embodied the conservative, centralist, confessional, and authoritarian reaction against the liberal and federal regime that dominated much of the second half of the nineteenth century. It also established the Supreme Court as the head of the judiciary, and then a legal reform decided that the same institution would be a "Court de Cassation." One of the measures that sought to ensure the dominance of the executive over the Court ensured that the justices would be appointed by the first and confirmed by the Senate. Indeed, the "first Court" was composed of a majority of justices of a conservative origin, faithful to the "regenerative" ideal (Cajas 2013).

But the authoritarian "regenerators" and the exclusion of the Liberal Party paved the way for the bloody *Thousand Days War*, a civil armed conflict that pitted the Liberals against the Conservative government between 1899 and 1902, and from which the latter emerged victorious. Then, in 1904, the conservative Rafael Reyes reached the presidency and tried to govern without the politicians and rebuild the country after the civil war. With the opposition of Congress to his ambitious reforms, Reyes decided to close it in 1905. The same year he confronted the Court and persuaded a constitutional assembly, which replaced the Congress, to approve a constitutional amendment that set terms of five years for the justices. He also forced the "retirement" of the full court and quickly replaced it with a new one (Cajas 2015: 106).

An alliance between Conservative and Liberal factions created opposition with the "Republican Union" movement, which forced the elections to Congress in 1909, and then the convocation of a new constituent assembly in 1910, in which the opposition won a majority of seats. With the end of the "soft" dictatorship of Reyes, path-breaking constitutional amendments were enacted by the assembly in 1910, all aimed at guaranteeing a true system of checks and balances, limiting presidential power, and maintaining political peace. For instance, the amendments established that the justices of the Supreme Court would be elected by Congress from a short list of three candidates whom the executive would nominate.

It is important to say that, although it is little known in the literature on Comparative Legal History, Colombia had rich experiences of judicial defense of the Constitution throughout the nineteenth century, which cannot necessarily be associated with the traditional "American model."[4] But, undoubtedly, one of the most important milestones of this trajectory was the creation of the PAU in the Legislative Act (LA) 03 of 1910, which for the first time allowed any citizen to challenge the constitutionality of laws and decrees before the Supreme Court (Grant 1954). Indeed, Colombia was among the first countries to establish in its Constitution a public action of judicial review of legislation.[5]

To sum up, under the institutional design of 1910 and the PAU, the Court was modeled as a kind of "arbitrator" between the legislative and the executive, in a political regime with a history of great "presidentialism" and extreme civil armed conflicts between political parties. Indeed, its defense of the Constitution as a "neutral power" would be a way to prevent political war in a context of frequent political polarization.[6]

As we will see next, a few decades later, the Court would not only have to decide on the constitutionality of the laws but on the amendments to the Constitution.

"Unconstitutional" constitutional amendments during the military rule

Colombia reached the middle of the twentieth century with a new conflict between Liberals and Conservatives. In 1950, at the highest peaks of bipartisan political violence ("La Violencia"), Laureano Gómez won the presidency in an election in which the Liberal Party withdrew its candidate claiming lack of conditions. Gómez was a Conservative and recognized anti-communist, who had been ambassador in Spain and showed great sympathy for the General Franco regime. Due to President Gomez's health breaks, his position was replaced by the Presidential Designated, Roberto Urdaneta, since November 1951.

In 1952, a Conservative Congress approved an LA that created a National Constituent Assembly (ANAC) that would amend the Constitution to establish an ultraconservative Constitution inspired by Spanish Francoism. A Commission prepared the bill of amendment, but it never saw the light of day because, when President Gómez tried to regain power from Acting President Urdaneta on June 13, 1953, General Gustavo Rojas Pinilla, commander of the Armed Forces, assumed the presidency.

The Colombian military rule lasted five years and is not comparable with any other experiences of bloody armed coup in South America. Rojas, a prestigious military leader, took power with the support of the Liberals, a Conservative faction opposed to Gomez, and also a broad sector of public opinion (Valencia 2011). The *coup d'état* was pacific, and Rojas initially embodied the messiah who would end the sharp political violence that had intensified under the government of Gomez. This explains to a large extent why the ANAC, right after the general assumed power, approved the LA 01 of June 18, 1953, stating that on June 13, "The presidency of the Republic had become vacant" so that "the title of the current president of the Republic, Lieutenant General Gustavo Rojas Pinilla, was legitimate." He would hold this position for the rest of the presidential term; that is, until 1954 (Cajas 2015).

The same amendment established that if by 1954 there were no conditions for free elections, the date of the presidential elections may be extended, or the ANAC could be convened to elect the president of the Republic, in which case General Rojas would stay in government until the possession of his successor. Then, the LA 01 of 1954 determined that on August 3, the ANAC itself would choose the president for the constitutional period from 1954 to 1958.

Perhaps because of opposition to the military rule, which began to become authoritarian around 1955, for the first time in Colombian history the citizens began to challenge the unconstitutionality of LA. The Court that decided the petitions was appointed in 1954, after the full court resigned due to a confrontation with Rojas.[7]

A citizen challenged the constitutionality of the two mentioned LA. In its decision of October 28, 1955, the Court stated that the petition was related to an "act of constituent power" approved by "the National Assembly created by LA 01 of 1952," whose purpose was to "amend the Constitution" in accordance with the procedure established by the same Charter. That is, it considered the ANAC as the competent body for such reform, even though the same LA of 1952 enacted by Congress had expressly stated that the ANAC would only make the "next constitutional reform," not that it would be the "constituent power" from now on (Supreme Court of Colombia 1955: 362). Then, the Court rejected the petition on the grounds that it lacked jurisdiction to review constitutional amendments. The argument for this was the textual interpretation of the Constitution, which, according to the Court, excluded it from judging LA. It also asserted it was not logical that a "constituted power" such as the Court would exercise the judicial review of a *constituent power*, as it was the Congress (Cajas 2017).

On January 30, 1956, the Court also rejected a challenge of unconstitutionality to LA 02 of August 24, 1954, under which, from July 20, 1955, the ANAC would not be a constituent power, but a legislative one, and this also extended the period of the ANAC until August 7, 1958. According to the petitioner, the amendment violated the Constitution, and especially the LA 01 of 1952, which exclusively convened the ANAC to amend the Constitution (Supreme Court 1956). The Court reiterated its precedent of the lack of jurisdiction to review constitutional amendments.

As we can see, the first two citizen actions of unconstitutionality against LA that are known in Colombian history were rejected by the Court. Both petitions dealt with key constitutional amendments that served as legal framework to the military rule, but in a formalist approach, the Court avoided an almost certain confrontation with the executive branch.

Finally, it is important to say that during the military rule, a leading legal scholar proposed a full judicial review of constitutional amendments in Colombia. In fact, Leopoldo Uprimny, a declared naturalist Thomist and refugee from the European War, wrote a paper defending the idea that the Supreme Court had full jurisdiction to review amendments on procedural grounds but also by its content (Uprimny 1957: 31). He argued that a constitutional amendment becomes unconstitutional not only when it had been approved with procedural defects in its procedure but also when this amendment manifestly contradicted "fundamental principles of justice or Natural Law" (Uprimny 1957).

Uprimny also analyzed the two aforementioned decisions of the Court, and he stated that it had made a mistake by declaring its lack of jurisdiction to review the LA approved by the ANAC. In his opinion, it was clear that constitutional amendments only could be approved by Congress, so he considered that it was incompatible with the *Rule of Law* that the Court argued that the constituent power had no limits, since even the Colombian Constitution itself defined rules for reviewing the laws, within which the amendments to the Constitution should be understood as "constitutional laws."

The plebiscitary amendment of 1957: the road to the "National Front"

General Rojas resigned from the presidency and left power to a military junta amid the collapse of his regime in May 1957. The return to civil government was agreed upon by the Liberal and Conservative elites, and had the approval of the junta. The alliance would guarantee the exercise of power by the two parties, and the exclusion of other possible political forces for an initial term of twelve years (the so-called National Front [NF]). For this, both parties agreed on a constitutional amendment.

As Congress had been closed since 1952 and the ANAC was discredited for serving the Rojas government, the political parties proposed a plebiscite to amend the Constitution. Then, the military junta, in the framework of the *state of siege*, enacted the Legislative Decrees No. 0247 and 0251 of October 4 and 9, 1957, which called the people to a plebiscite.

A citizen opposed to the NF challenged the constitutionality of the decrees because the Constitution of 1886 established that the only party authorized to amend the Constitution was Congress. On November 28, 1957, a Supreme Court, appointed by General Rojas in 1956 after he established a "Constitutional Affairs Chamber" within the Court itself, refused to judge the constitutionality of the decrees. The Court considered that the military junta had its origin in the resignation of General Rojas, who legitimately exercised the presidency, and the source of power of that body was a "revolutionary movement" that had broad-based support. Similarly, it argued that democracy should be conceived as a system that hinged on political parties, which in this case had reached an agreement surrounded by the broader "popular outcry." Likewise, the Court reiterated that it lacked jurisdiction to review "amendment acts of the Constitution." In its opinion, even though the legislative decrees calling for a plebiscite had been enacted in the context of the *state of siege*, their content was "constitutional" and, therefore, not under the jurisdiction of the Court (Supreme Court of Colombia 1957).

Seven of 19 justices dissented. They pointed out that the Court had been subject to political pressure, as even party leaders had indicated their intention to dissolve the Court. According to them, the junta was not a partially revolutionary and de facto government, and therefore, its acts could not be on the fringes of the judicial review. In addition, they considered that the Court had full jurisdiction to review the decrees issued by the junta, even if they sought a constitutional amendment. Other evidence of that political environment denounced by dissenting justices would soon appear: the day after the decision was issued, six of the justices resigned their positions (Cajas 2015-I).

As we can see, the Court allowed the transition to the civil government, although the plebiscite reform contradicted the formal rules of constitutional amendment. Three days after the decision, the plebiscite was approved on an election day in which female voters participated for the first time in Colombian history.

Finally, it is important to say that the amendment of 1957 established that both parties would integrate the Supreme Court on an equal basis, that the justices would have a lifetime appointment, and that the vacancies would be filled by the Court itself (a co-optation system).

From the "lack of jurisdiction" to the "unconstitutional constitutional amendments": 1968–1981

The debate on the constitutional amendment of 1968: procedural vices?

One of the most important amendments of the NF was the LA 01 of 1968, which largely modified the structure of the state and public branches to increase the power of the executive, and made the public administration more technical.[8]

The LA 01 of 1968 did not alter the judiciary nor the Supreme Court. Indeed, the amendment project had initially contemplated the creation of a Constitutional Court that would replace the Supreme Court as guardian of the Constitution. The proposal would establish a specialized and concentrated constitutional tribunal inspired by the European model or "Austrian Kelsenian model." Although the initiative achieved its approval in several debates in Congress, it was finally rejected, in part by opposition from legal scholars and by the Supreme Court itself (Cajas 2015-II). However, the amendment established a constitutional chamber within the Court, which would be composed of justices who were public law experts, and whose function would be to draft the decisions for the rulings of the full chamber of the Court (Congress of Colombia 1968).

The LA 01/1968 was repeatedly challenged for unconstitutionality by citizens who stated that Congress had violated several rules of procedure when processing it. While in all these challenges, the Court upheld the doctrine of its lack of jurisdiction to review LA, in the decision of April 16, 1971, six of twenty-four justices signed dissenting votes requiring the Court to take jurisdiction over the constitutional amendments. The dissenting opinion held that Congress had limited amending powers and stated, "In the current circumstances that the country is in, the prime of its legal evolution (…), the Court cannot refuse to decide about an unconstitutionality challenge of an amending act of the Constitution…" They also recalled that the 1957 plebiscite had entrusted to Congress the power of the constitutional amendment, so the Court was responsible for enforcing the amendment rules established by the Constitution (Supreme Court 1971).

The Court declined to judge the controversial amendment, which ultimately was the product of the consensus among the political forces and factions in power so that it maintained the *status quo* of the two traditional parties in the NF. At the same time, the dissident votes show that the favorable trend in the Court had already begun to expand to exercise jurisdiction over LA on procedural grounds.

The unconstitutional constitutional amendments of 1977 and 1979

During the *NF*, the judiciary began to take shape as a centralized management of the national order in a unitary state, in which the Court was the highest nominator of the judges as it appointed the magistrates of the Superior District Courts (*Tribunales Superiores de Distrito*), and these, in turn, appointed the Judges of Appeal (*Jueces de Circuito*) and the first instance judges (*Jueces Municipales*), who were appointed for terms and might be reappointed. That is to say, the "chain of command" placed the Court in the vortex of the pyramid.

For all of this, it is likely that the NF helped to form a kind of "*esprit de corps*" in the judicial branch that might even have to do with the failure of a number of constitutional amendments to the Court, and to the judiciary during the second half of the twentieth century (Cajas 2015-II). In fact, in the late 1970s, Congress approved two constitutional amendments that affected the judiciary and, at that moment, the Court decided to declare them unconstitutional, radically altering its legal doctrine of the lack of jurisdiction to review LA.

First, the LA 02 of 1977 determined that the citizens would elect representatives to a *Constituent Assembly* who would be in charge of reforming the current Constitution. The amendment was challenged by several petitioners before the Court. On May 5, 1978, with 10 of 24 justices expressing their dissenting opinions, the Court declared the amendment unconstitutional. According to the Court, Congress could not delegate its power to amend the Constitution because it was a constituted power. This means that the amendments to the Constitution should be made under the rules it provided for processing the LA. Similarly, the Court stated that when exercising its powers of constitutional judgment, it had to do it on the laws as LA since the Constitution was a "systematic whole." Thus, it estimated that, when the Constitution provided that the amendments could only be made by Congress, it clearly fixed an exclusive competence represented by that branch, which in no way could be supplanted. The Court also stated that, if people are the primary constituent, and the Congress is a constituted power, the latter could not give the ability to amend the Constitution, or to cede its powers to a constituent assembly (Supreme Court 1978).

One of the proposals that the *Little Constituent* would consider was a profound amendment to the head of the judiciary, and especially to the Supreme Court, which would only retain its role as a Court of Cassation since it was planned to create a Constitutional Court. Due to all this, its abrupt change in precedent was perceived as a ruling that protected the Court itself.

Then, the LA 01 of 1979 mostly tried for a deep transformation of the judiciary. For example, it abolished the life tenure of justices in the Court and Council of State, so they would be in their posts for eight-year periods, with no possibility of reelection. It also attributed new functions to the Constitutional Chamber and took them off of the full Supreme Court. On November 3, 1981, the Court, with 11 dissenting opinions, struck down the amendment (Supreme Court 1981).

In its decision, the Court established that Congress had committed serious errors on procedural grounds in the issuance of the amendment parties (Supreme Court 1981). For instance, Congress ignored the rights of parliamentary minorities because the election of the Committees of the Congress had taken place without paying attention to the electoral quotient system, which allowed the proportional representation of those same committees to approve the constitutional amendment. Also, it was noted that there was an "undue accumulation of bills of amendments" (Arboleda 1981).

The Supreme Court and the "change" of the constitution of 1886 by the constitution of 1991

Since the mid-1980s, Colombia seemed to be heading towards a failed state: the increase in guerrilla violence was remarkable,[9] along with the terrorist attacks and murders attributed to the drug trafficker Pablo Escobar, who had challenged the state to oppose his extradition to the United States of America. Among the most disturbing cases, there were the murder of the Minister of Justice in 1984; a terrorist attack that brought down a commercial plane; a bomb that destroyed the DAS headquarters (state intelligence agency); and the murder of the Attorney General of the Nation, a Supreme Court Justice; as well as the murder of the most eligible candidate to reach the presidency in 1990, Luis Carlos Galan.

Thus, as the presidential elections approached in 1989, three candidates had been killed. In addition, between 1988 and 1990, the attempts at constitutional amendments to open the political system had also failed in Congress. Added to this was the climate of violence that the country breathed, and the "legal obstacles" to amend the Constitution that had imposed the aforementioned decisions of the Supreme Court. In this scenario emerged the initiative called "The Student Movement of the Seventh Ballot," mainly composed of university students who proposed a large citizen mobilization to renew institutions as a countermeasure to the collapse of them.

The "Seventh Ballot" proposal consisted of convoking a constituent assembly to amend the Constitution. After a great citizen mobilization, which brought together the most diverse sectors of the country and which had the support of the main political parties, the government accepted the proposal and, within the framework of the state of siege, it issued Decree 927 of May 3, 1990, to summon citizens to express themselves in favor of the constituent. The Court would take great prominence, as it should review the constitutionality of the aforementioned decree. By then, peace agreements had just been signed with the M-19 guerrilla group, and three other groups announced that they were demobilizing and laying down their arms, attracted by the possibilities of political change.

On May 23, 1990, in Decision 59, the Court declared Decree 927 as constitutional. In its ruling, it reconstructed the context of violence that the country was facing. In general terms, the Court determined that convening the people to express their opinion in pursuit of the institutional change to face the crisis was within the authority that the government had, understanding that such action did not imply the amendment of the Constitution (Corte Suprema de Justicia 1993).

Citizens approved the convocation to the Constituent with an overwhelming majority of 88.89% of the votes cast. Shortly after, the newly elected president César Gaviria issued a state of siege Decree No. 1926 of August 24, 1990, which called for the election of a Constituent Assembly (CA) that would reform the Constitution on some specific topics. Again, the final decision on the origin of the CA would depend on the Court.

The Supreme Court declared Decree 1926 as constitutional in its decision from October 9, 1990 (Supreme Court 1990). For the Court, the goals sought by the decree should be considered; namely, the achievement of peace as the central value of the political community. Likewise, it resorted to the notion of "primary constituent power" to assert that the people were the holders of the political power and that, therefore, it did not give up to this power, due to the fact that Congress had the constitutional power to amend the Constitution. But the Court went beyond what was ordered by the decree of the state of siege, and determined that the CA would have full powers to modify all the contents of the current Constitution; that is, it was "sovereign."

Eleven of the twenty-four justices dissented. They considered that the Court had exceeded its jurisdiction by ruling on the advisability of the call to the CA. The dissenters also denounced that the Court allowed the extension of the executive powers of the state of siege to the point of accepting an amendment to the Constitution, as this was exclusive to Congress (Cajas 2015-II).

Thus, thanks to the two rulings, the CA was elected on December 9, 1990, which approved the Constitution of 1991 and repealed the Constitution of 1886.

With its decisions, the Court seemed to recognize the complex context where it operated, but what it could not predict was that the same CA would radically transform the structure of the judiciary, and would create a Constitutional Court.

The Constitutional Court and the "unconstitutional constitutional amendments"

From the "literal interpretation" to the "substitution" doctrine

The Constitution of 1991 expressly empowered the Constitutional Court to review the constitutional amendments in its Article 241 # 1–3, but just "for procedural vices."

The Constitution has been amended 45 times up to the year 2017.[10] Between the years 1992 and 2003, the Court literally interpreted Article 241 of the Constitution and judged several of these LA on the grounds that Congress violated procedure (Cajas 2008). However, the doctrine would change when, in its decision C-551 from July 9, 2003, the Court found that it also had jurisdiction to review the constitutional amendments for "competence vices" when the Congress "was replacing the Constitution."

The ruling arose in a complex political environment. President Álvaro Uribe Vélez, a politician from the right wing, was elected in 2002 and promoted a referendum that first sought to deeply amend the Constitution (Cepeda 2005: 78). The law calling for a constitutional referendum was passed by Congress, and then it was reviewed by the Constitutional Court before asking the people if they agreed with this amendment.

Thus, with the decision C-551/2003, the Court began building its *constitutional replacement doctrine* that was initially called "*competence vices.*" According to the Court, the Congress cannot replace the Constitution, but only amend it. In this way, when the Congress exceeds its power of amendment, it violates the current Constitution because the only entity enabled by the Constitution to replace it is the primary constituent (the people), although the Constitution does not expressly determine this. When such replacement occurs, stated the Court, a procedural error that falls within the jurisdiction of the Court is set. That replacement judgment involves assessing whether Congress introduced elements that changed what gives identity to the current Constitution in the amendment (Constitutional Court of Colombia 2003).

The Court finally modified several of the questions that would be formulated to the citizens and seemed to place its first limits on the reformist agenda of the Uribe government. After the ruling, the constitutional referendum was held, but the main reform proposals were not approved by the citizens.

The president and the court: reelection, 2005 and 2010

After the "Substitution of the Constitution Doctrine" was settled, the Court faced one of its biggest political and legal challenges when Congress passed the

LA 02 of 2004, which changed the text of the Constitution of 1991 that expressly prohibited presidential reelection. The amendment allowed the immediate reelection of then President Uribe for the next term (2006–2010). Dozens of citizens asked the Court to declare the LA unconstitutional; they argued that there was not an amendment but a substitution of the Constitution, and this violated some principles of the Constitution and generated negative consequences for the constitutional system, especially for the checks and balances (Cajas 2017).

In decision C-1040/2005, the Court declared constitutional the LA 02/2004. According to the Court, the amendment did not replace the essential elements that define the Social Rule of Law model based on human dignity because the people would decide with sovereignty who to choose as president. In addition, the system of checks and balances would remain among the branches of power (Constitutional Court 2005).

Then, by the year 2009, President Uribe had maintained his high popularity ratings in his second mandate, despite scandals such as "parapolitics," where dozens of Congressmen from his ruling coalition were accused of having links with armed groups outside the law, or "paramilitaries." As the LA 02/2004 allowed the presidential reelection for up to one period, supporters of Uribe promoted a referendum to reform the Constitution to allow him to run for a possible third consecutive term.

On February 26, 2010, the Court declared that Law 1354 of 2009 calling the referendum was unconstitutional. For the Court, the adoption of this law had several vices (Constitutional Court 2010): the citizen's initiative for the law, the bill procedure in Congress, and also the "replacing" of the current Constitution. In particular, on the replacement of the Constitution, the Court said the law ignored some structural axes of the Constitution, such as the principle of separation of powers and the system of checks and balances, the rule of alternation and predetermined periods, the right to equality, and the general and abstract nature of the laws. Thus, Congress would have incurred a competence vice because it has the power to amend the Constitution, but not to replace it.

With this decision, the Court stopped a political project that seemed to perpetuate in power, as was the trend in several countries in the region (Venezuela, Ecuador, and Bolivia). In addition, there was another unexpected influence on the Colombian political regime since the new government would give a turn to the armed conflict, which, as will be seen below, would have profound political consequences.

The court and the peace process with Farc

Juan Manuel Santos, formerly Uribe's Minister of Defense, was first elected president in 2010 and then re-elected in 2014. His government conducted a peace negotiation with the guerrillas of Farc, but he received strong opposition from the political bloc led by the senator and former president, Uribe, who always understood the peace process as a "betrayal" of Santos to his political project and a surrender of the country to "terrorism."[11]

As will be seen below, the Constitutional Court and its decisions on the review of constitutional amendments has played a leading role in the peace process with the Farc, and perhaps it will be key in the stage of implementation of the FA signed between the guerrillas and the Colombian government.

Blocking and "unblocking" peace with the Farc

The government of Colombia and the Farc rebels signed the peace agreements (FA) on September 30, 2016, in Havana, Cuba (Karl 2017). The parties decided that the endorsement mechanism of the FA would be a plebiscite. The law that called the plebiscite was previously reviewed by the Constitutional Court and, in its decision C-379/2016, it declared that the nature of the consultation was political, and therefore, it could not produce legal effects. Likewise, Congress approved LA 01 of 2016 ("Special Legislative Act for Peace"), which established an abbreviated procedure to carry out the constitutional and legal amendments required by the FA; in addition, it gave extraordinary powers to the executive to "legislate by decree" everything necessary for its implementation. Finally, the LA conditioned its own validity to the FA to be endorsed by the Colombian people.

At the plebiscite of October 2, 2016, the "No" prevailed over the "Yes" by a difference of 53,894 votes. With this result, the peace agreement seemed to be in a "legal blockade." In addition, the "No" leaders called for a deep renegotiation with Farc. Immediately, thousands of citizens went to the streets in support of the FA. Then, the Santos administration, with political majorities in Congress, reacted by proposing a broad dialogue with sectors in favor of and against the FA. After several weeks of intense negotiations, a new agreement that incorporated some of the opposition's claims was signed with the Farc on November 24, 2016. Then, the government appealed to Congress, which, on December 3, 2016, backed the new and revised FA.

Citizens opposed to the FA challenged LA 01/2016 before the Court on the grounds that it "replaced the Constitution" because of the modification of the procedures of constitutional amendment, the passage of laws, as well as the granting of extraordinary powers to the executive to issue decrees necessary to regulate the FA. They argued that the LA amended substantial aspects of the Constitution, such as the constitutional supremacy and the principle of separation of powers (Cajas 2017).

In decision C-699 of December 13, 2016, with eight votes out of nine, it declared that LA 01/2016 did not replace the Constitution. The Court affirmed that Congress had the "legitimacy" to approve the deal without holding another referendum. In general, the Court took into account that the amendment was framed in a transition process, and that it was necessary to achieve peace, just as the aforementioned amendment was temporary, limited, and with the purpose of implementing the FA (Constitutional Court 2016).

Perhaps the ruling contributed to the opinion of the political opposition which stated that the decision was a deference of the Court to the executive, and also a sign of the loss of its independence in support of the "erroneous policy of peace" (Semana 2016).

Does a "new" Constitutional Court "tighten" its review over peace reforms?

Between the second half of 2016 and the year 2017, six of the nine justices who made up the Constitutional Court finished their terms of eight years, and their replacements were elected by the Senate. The new composition of the Court generated great expectations about the course that could take the review of constitutional and legal amendments related to the FA.

The legal and political controversies around the implementation of the FA kept coming in the next months and years. Three decisions of 2017 showed the landscape. First, on decision C-332 of May 17, the "new Court" decided on the massive petitions of unconstitutionality filed by members of the Congress, opponents of the FA belonging to the rightist Democratic Center Party, against some provisions of LA 01 of 2016. In their opinion, Congress has the full competence to propose new clauses to the constitutional amendments and legal reforms needed to enact the FA in the framework of the aforementioned "Fast Track" process, without prior approval of the executive so that the LA that prohibited it partially "replaced the Constitution." In addition, the prohibition on Congress of voting "en bloc" on the bills also partially replaced the Constitution.

The Court declared that LA 01/2016 partially replaced the Constitution. It stated that the aforementioned congressional ban "distorted the deliberation and effectiveness powers of the vote of Congress, which constitute the axial nucleus of the legislative function." In addition, it argued that such an amendment supposed "an imbalance to the equilibrium between the public powers as well as their independence in favor of the executive, and to the detriment of the functions of the Congress and of the constitutional democracy" (Constitutional Court 2017).

Decision C-332 had immediate effects since most of the proposals of the amendment were delayed in their processing, and some of them even failed to get their approval. The beginning of the preelection period was added to this difficulty, with the aforementioned highly polarized politics, and the executive losing its majorities that require the approval of amendments necessary to comply with the FA.[12] In another unusual issue that accounts for the role of the Courts in the peace, one of the Farc commanders, who had recently demobilized, asked the Constitutional Court to declare null and void its own decision.

The second decision is the C-630 from October 11, 2017. The unanimous full court declared constitutional the LA 02 of 2017, which amended the Constitution in order to give "stability" and "legal security" to the FA. The Court stated that the LA does not replace the constitution when it orders that the governments elected during the next twelve years are obliged to execute the FA but also that the same is a "parameter of interpretation of the state policy in peace by the three branches of power." Moreover, it argued that the FA is a parameter of interpretation and reference of development and validity for the norms and laws that will be implemented.

The Court also said that

> In order to avoid the replacement of the principles of separation of powers, of supremacy of the Constitution, peace, and democracy, the other public

> powers, including the government and the congress, should develop the agreements to the greatest extent possible, following the principle of progressivity, and that they have a margin of appreciation to doing so.

The decision was criticized by the political opposition as they said the Court aligned with the Santos administration in accepting a severe substitution of the constitution, because in their opinion, the LA imposed on future governments the agreements that the people had rejected in a plebiscite, and that it fixed a political agenda which seemed unable to be reversed in the next twelve years (Ramírez 2017).

Finally, on Decision C-674 from November 14, 2017, the Court reviewed LA 01 of 2017, which established the "Peace Special Jurisdiction" creating a system of transitional justice composed by tribunals with jurisdiction to judge those responsible for crimes committed in the armed conflict, and which, according to the parties that signed the FA, Congress approved under serious limitations concerning the peace agreement. The LA was one of the most controversial on the implementation of the FA because it divided the politicians and the public opinion between those who argued for more penalization and those who defended "transitional rules."

The Court declared constitutional LA 01/2017, but under an intense "substitution doctrine," it made several modifications to the text of the amendment (Constitutional Court 2017). The Farc criticized the ruling on the grounds that it partially "modifies" the FA. Voices from the right-wing political opposition stated that the ruling "ignored the will of Colombians, who narrowly rejected the deal in a referendum held just over a year ago, before it was modified and passed through Congress" (Reuters 2018).

Final considerations

This chapter has examined, with a critical perspective, the history of the role of the Courts on the review of constitutional amendments in Colombia. It has shown the different junctures of the political regime in which the constitutional judges have intervened. Thus, the Supreme Court abstained from acting during the times of military rule and the transition to "limited" democracy, but then it stopped constitutional reforms that affected the interests of the judicial branch. A bit later, during times of guerrilla and drug trafficker violence, it allowed the call for a constituent assembly that changed the Constitution of 1886; afterwards, the Constitutional Court tried to curb the constitutional reformism, although it allowed the first presidential reelection and then blocked a second one. Finally, the same Court has had the key role in the peace process with Farc.

In this way, it can be seen how legal doctrine has affected the political regime but also how it has affected the judicial review of constitutional amendments. In short, beyond the debates of the constitutional doctrine and the legal theory on the defense of the Constitution against "unconstitutional amendments," a historical and political reading, contextualized in a country with a complex trajectory of political regime, can contribute to studies in Comparative Legal History.

In short, this chapter has proposed another approach to the field of "limits to constitutional amendments," which usually focuses on constitutional doctrines, on the transplants of the same, or on theoretical debates on the legitimacy of this type of control. Thereby, it has shown an extensive legal history on the review of constitutional amendments, mainly of the Court's creation, as well as a complex political trajectory of amendments and judicial interventions. This undoubtedly demonstrates the importance of the Colombian case as a valuable object of study for the field of Comparative Legal History, in a matter that captures the attention of comparative legal scholars at a global level.

Finally, this history of the role of courts on the review of constitutional amendments is also a way to explore the struggle for judicial independence and the building of the Rule of Law, which has been little studied in Comparative Legal History.

Notes

1 See the F.A.: Oficina del Alto Comisionado para la Paz de Colombia (2018) "Final Agreement to End the Armed Conflict and Build a Stable and Lasting Peace," www.altocomisionadoparalapaz.gov.co/Prensa/Documentos%20compartidos/Colombian-Peace-Agreement-English-Translation.pdf: accessed January 10, 2018.

2 "Colombia is by far the most interesting country in Latin America for the study of judicial review. It introduced in practice two notable innovations which have been widely copied—judicial review by Executive Reference prior to promulgation and the "popular" or public action to declare the unconstitutionality of statutes" (Eder 1960: 589).

3 See my works on this topic: Cajas (2017, 2015, 2008).

4 Some of them were more local, and others had to do with the possibility of reviewing state acts against federal laws or constitutions (Botero 2007; Cajas 2013).

5 The popular action ***in rem*** is more novel. It was developed too early for Colombia to be indebted to Hans Kelsen and his Austrian experiment. If there was any borrowing, it was in the opposite direction… (Grant 1950: 489)

6 "…Save for minor revisions, the present Colombian system was then complete, and its expounders were pointing with pride" alike to its nature and to its scope as proof that Colombia has been "the first of the nations of the world to provide in a practical manner for the defense of the Constitution" in the entire field of public law (Grant 1950: 504).

7 For instance, the LA 04 of September 14, 1954, banned Communism in the country.

8 The amendment was passed amid great political tensions between Liberal and Conservative factions in Congress, to the point that President Carlos Lleras threatened to resign if Congress persisted in blocking the initiative.

9 For instance, in 1985, a command of the M-19 guerrilla group took over the Palace of Justice, where the Council of State and the Supreme Court operated. In the takeover and the retaking of the building by the Colombian Army, eleven magistrates died, including the entire Constitutional Chamber.

10 On the "transformations" of the Constitution, see Botero (2017).

11 Tensions between President Santos and former president Uribe reached the point that in 2015, the coalition of government in Congress approved a constitutional amendment that expressly prohibited presidential reelection. The reform sought to stop any attempt to reelect Uribe, given the possibility that he could seek his return to power. Only a popular referendum or constituent assembly could reverse the amendment. See: LA 01, 2015, Article 9.

12 The approximately 7,000 fighters in the group are in a holding pattern in twenty-six rural camps. Those suspected of war crimes are waiting for their cases to be handled by transitional courts. Most rank-and-file fighters have been granted amnesty and could leave the camps this month. The process has been slow (...). Fast-track procedures to approve legislation in Congress were struck down by the constitutional court, stalling laws for land reform, political participation, and a truth commission (...) (The New York Times 2017).

References

Albert, R. (2018) "Constitutional Amendment and Dismemberment," *Yale Journal of International Law* 43: 1.

Arboleda, E. (1981) *La reforma constitucional de 1979: Su inexequibilidad*, Bogotá: Dintel.

Bernal Pulido, C. et al. (2018) "The State of Liberal Democracy," *Global Review of Constitutional Law*, edited by David E. Landau et al, Eds, Iconnect: 59–62.

——— (2013) "Unconstitutional Constitutional Amendments in the Case Study of Colombia: An Analysis of the Justification and Meaning of the Constitutional Replacement Doctrine," *International Journal of Constitutional Law* 11(2): 339–357.

Botero, A. (2017) "Balance de los 25 años de la Constitución de 1991: la Constitución de los dioses y la Constitución de los hombres," *Universitas* 134: 59–92.

——— (2007) "Haciendo memoria de la defensa judicial de la Constitución," *Pensamiento Jurídico* 20: 91–101.

Cajas Sarria, M. (2017) "Judicial Review of Constitutional Amendments in Colombia: A Political and Historical Perspective 1955–2016," *The Theory and Practice of Legislation* 5(3): 245–275.

——— (2015) *La historia de la Corte Suprema de Justicia de Colombia, 1886–1991*, Volumes I–II, Bogotá: Universidad de los Andes and Universidad Icesi.

——— (2013) "De juez de la regeneración a juez constitucional: La Corte Suprema de Justicia de Colombia, 1886–1910," *Historia Constitucional* 14: 425–465.

——— (2008) *El control judicial a la reforma constitucional: Colombia, 1910–2007*, Cali: Universidad Icesi

Cárdenas, E. & Corredor, F. (2018) "El juez constitucional y la reelección presidencial en América Latina," *Revista de Economía Institucional* 20(38): 45–70.

Cepeda, M. J. (2005) "The Judicialization of Politics in Colombia: The Old and the New," *The Judicialization of Politics in Latin America*, edited by Rachel Sieder et al., Palgrave: 67–104

Colon, J. (2014) "Constitutionalism and Democracy in Latin America," *New Zealand Association for Comparative Law* 20: 155–167.

Congress of Colombia, LA 01 of 1968, article 71, *Diario Oficial* 32673, December 17, 1968.

Constitutional Court of Colombia, Decision C-551, July 9, 2003, Opinion of Justice Eduardo Montealegre Lynett.

——— Decision C-1040 of October 19, 2005. Opinion of Justice Manuel J. Cepeda and others.

——— Decision C-141 of 26, February, 2010, Opinion of Justice Humberto Sierra Porto.

——— Decision C-699 of December 13, 2016. Opinion of Justice María Victoria Calle Correa.

——— Decision C-332 of May 17, 2017. Opinion of Justice Antonio J. Lizarazo.

——— Decision C-674 of November 14, 2017. Opinion of Justice Luis Guillermo Guerrero.

——— Press Release of October 11, 2017: www.corteconstitucional.gov.co/comunicados/No.%2051%20comunicado%2011%20de%20octubre%20de%202017.pdf.

Eder, P. J. (1960) "Judicial Review in Latin America," *Ohio State Law Journal* 21: 570–615.

Grant, J. A. C. (1954) "Judicial Control of Legislation," *American Journal of Comparative Law* 3.

——— (1950) "Judicial Control of the Constitutionality of Statutes and Administrative Legislation in Colombia: Nature and Evolution of the Present System," *California Law Review* S. 23: 484.

Karl, R. (2017) "The Politics of Peace in Colombia: Peace Was Supposed to Save Colombia's Democracy, But Democracy Must Perhaps First Save the Basis of Peace," *NACLA Report on the Americas* 49, www.tandfonline.com/doi/full/10.1080/10714839.2017.1409010.

Landau, D. et al. (2018) "Terms Limits and the Constitutional Unconstitutional Amendment Doctrine: Lessons from Latin America" (Forthcoming in Alexander Baturo and Robert Elgie eds., *Politics of Presidential Terms Limits*, Oxford University Press). https://papers.ssrn.com/sol3/papers.cfm?abstract_id=3208187: 1–20.

——— (2017) "Democratic Erosion and Constitution-Making Moments: The Role of International Law," *UC Irvine Journal of International, Transnational and Comparative Law* 2 (87).

Oficina del Alto Comisionado para la Paz de Colombia (OACP) (2018) "Final Agreement to End the Armed Conflict and Build a Stable and Lasting Peace," www.altocomisionadoparalapaz.gov.co/Prensa/Documentos%20compartidos/Colombian-Peace-Agreement-English-Translation.pdf: accessed January 10, 2018.

Ramirez, G. (2017) "The Colombian Constitutional Court Rules That the Peace Agreement is Mandatory for Three Presidential Terms," *I-CONnect, Blog of the International Journal of Constitutional Law*, October 27, 2017, www.iconnectblog.com/2017/10/the-colombian-constitutional-court-rules-that-the-peace-agreement-is-mandatory-for-three-presidential-terms/.

Semana (2016) "Las seís críticas del uribismo al fallo del Fast Track ["Six Critics of the Uribism to the Decision on Fast Track"], December 15, 2016, www.semana.com/nacion/articulo/centro-democratico-critica-fallo-de-la-corte-constitucional/509609: accessed January 10, 2018.

Supreme Court of Colombia, Decision of October 28, 1955. Opinion of Justice Luis Enrique Cuervo, *Gaceta Judicial* 2159.

——— Decision of January 30, 1956. Opinion of Justice Ignacio Gómez Posse, *Gaceta Judicial* 2163/2164.

——— Decision of November 28, 1957. Opinion of Justice Guillermo Hernández Peñaloza, *Gaceta Judicial* 2188.

——— Dissenting Opinion of Justices Alejandro Cordoba et al., Decision of April 16, 1971, *Gaceta Judicial* 2340–2342.

——— Decision of May 5, 1978. Opinion of Justice José María Velasco Guerrero, *Gaceta Judicial* 2397-104.

——— Decision No. 7 of 1981. Opinion of Justice Fernando Uribe Restrepo, *Gaceta Judicial* 2405.

——— Decision 138 of October 9, 1990. Opinion of Justices Hernando Gómez Otálora and Fabio Morón Díaz.

——— (1993) Gaceta Especial Sala Constitucional: La reforma constitucional de 1991, Tomo I, Santafé de Bogotá, D.C: Imprenta Nacional de Colombia.

The Guardian (2016) "Farc Peace Deal: Rebels and Colombian Government Sign Accord to End War," August 25, 2016, www.theguardian.com/world/2016/aug/24/colombia-government-farc-rebels-peace-deal-52-year-war: accessed December 20, 2017.

The Guardian (2018) "Colombia's Polarized Elections Tears for Fragile Peace," June 16, 2018, www.theguardian.com/world/2018/jun/16/colombias-election-peace-ivan-duque-gustavo-petro: accessed June 17, 2018.

The New York Times (2017) "How to Keep the Farc Guerrillas Out of the Fight," August 3, 2017, www.nytimes.com/2017/08/03/opinion/farc-colombia.html.

Uprimny, L. (1957) "¿Puede una reforma constitucional ser inconstitucional? ["Can a Constitutional Reform be Unconstitutional?"] *Revista de la Academia Colombiana de Jurisprudencia* 174: 19–37.

Valencia, A. (2011) "El juicio a Rojas Pinilla y la construcción de la memoria colectiva de los años cincuenta en Colombia" ["The Trial of Rojas Pinilla and the Construction of a Collective Memory on the Fifties in Colombia"], *Universitas humanística* 72: 15–36.

Yaniv, R. (2017) *Unconstitutional Constitutional Amendments: The Limits of Amendment Powers*, Oxford: Oxford University Press.

——— (2013) "Unconstitutional Constitutional Amendments: The Migration and Success of a Constitutional Idea," *The American Journal of Comparative Law* 61(3), 657–719.

6 The revolutionary constitution of 1917 in Mexico

From individual guarantees to social rights, 1917–1928

Humberto Morales Moreno

"Reforming congressmen" in the 1917 Constituent Assembly and individual guarantees: the birth of the new authoritarian Mexican state

The Constituent Assembly was formed during the Mexican Revolution with an eye toward updating the country's constitution. Counted among the "renewal faction" (*bloc renovador*) among the deputies, Luis Manuel Rojas and José Natividad Macías engaged in discussions to move from reform to elaboration of a new political constitution in Mexico. They proposed a doctrinal modification to the philosophical basis expressed in Article 1 of the new Constitution of 1917.[1] When Deputy Martinez de Escobar suggested that the rights to be protected in Articles 27 and 123 should be called social rights, his suggestion was not accepted because the spirit of the new chapter was to protect individual guarantees and not social rights. Although the deputies incorporated relative rights into the new charter, these became *social guarantees* arbitrated by the state.

Pastor Rouaix, a civil engineer and trusted protege of Venustiano Carranza, head of the Constitutionalist Revolution in Mexico, provided an interesting report on the development of the reforms. Rouaix reviewed the two dominant interpretations of the constituent debate, that of Djed Bojórquez, the deputy close to the movement of General Álvaro Obregón, and that of Carrancista Félix Palavicini. Rouaix concluded that

> [t]he broad divergence of opinion concerning the two books that have been written about the history of the Constituent Congress of Queretaro (which produced the glorious Constitution that now governs us), makes the publication of this work more useful. It has been written with complete impartiality and without any prejudice. As I have said before, my role in Congress was that of an independent deputy who served as a link between the two extremes.[2]

Both chroniclers of the Constituent Assembly recognized that Rouaix had acted impartially in his efforts with regard to the commissions entrusted to the

Constituent Assembly. Rouaix had emphasized the crucial role that Victorio Góngora, a lawyer close to the Catholic ideas of *Rerum Novarum*, played in the formation of the new Article 123, thanks to his knowledge of the European concept of a "social issue" with regard to the protection of the laboring classes. Rouaix himself took the position that of many of the corrections made to both Articles 123 and 27 the Christian-Catholic language actually added to those that came from the socialist-anarchist language of strong Magonista inspiration (Adame 1981). Jorge Adame explains it this way:

> Pastor Rouaix, the head of the commission responsible for drafting article 123, explained in the book he wrote later, while discussing the origin of the concept of a "maximum workday," that the deputies in charge of preparing the project "were going to reform the social institutions of the country through articles 123 and 27 of the Constitution, so that the theoretical principles of Christianity, which had been so many times extolled there [in the episcopal palace of Querétaro, where the commission met] were realized in practice. This frank statement, which contains an implicit complaint against the Church, cannot be taken literally, especially since Pastor himself indicated what he understood by "Christian principles": that "the meek were blessed to possess the land and the humble were raised up to dispossess the powerful of the inveterate privileges they enjoyed."[3]

The Encyclical of Leo XIII on Capital and Labor, issued on May 15, 1891, was published in the Catholic newspapers of Mexico, *El País* and *La Nación*, between 1910 and 1913. But the "social question" was discussed in Europe long before the Catholic Church officially responded to the perverse effects of liberal capitalism. The Prussian Empire of Bismarck was the first European state that sought to address the impoverishment of working-class living conditions, but as a strategic response to defuse the demands of the socialists, who were already a very strong party at the time. Social security, retirement, and compensation for sickness or unemployment were part of the package of reforms between 1883 and 1889, which were intended to prevent the strengthening of workers' associations in the heart of the German Empire. After the British New Liberalism and the proposal in the Third French Republic for an intervention by the state in solidarity with the dispossessed classes, a debate commenced regarding obligatory state intervention in the protection of social rights, due to the fact that liberal individualism had failed to sustain them. In Spain, the conservative government of Antonio Canovas del Castillo determined in 1890 at the Ateneo de Madrid that there was an urgent necessity to legislate the intervention of the state in the protection of rights of the working classes. This proposal met with strong opposition even within their own political party because the liberals refused to regulate working days. At the same time, the Catholic Church always viewed state interventionism in the protection of social rights with distrust, and when the encyclical went to protect workers' rights, the basis was always moral and social rather than economic.[4]

In the New World, it was in Chile, around 1876, where the debates written by politicians and intellectuals about the Chilean "social issue" began, with a very strong *Fourierist* influence. This point of view, based on a strongly individualist liberalism, did not allow for the legislation of protection beyond worker's associations and emerging unions. The conservative diatribes of Zorobabel Rodríguez, published in the magazine *El Independiente* at the end of 1876, with the title of "The Workers Question," promoted protective policies that would lead to the creation of savings banks, in direct opposition to the corporate pressure supported by the later speech of the mutualist leader Fermín Vivaceta, in 1877, that was closer to the cooperative unions.

The creation of the boards of conciliation and arbitration seems to reflect a great influence of Catholic ideas since *El Pais* proposed them on April 29, 1908 (Adame 1981). In the spirit of conciliation and assistance suggested by the encyclical, it was proposed to give to these boards full power to mediate between the interests of owners and those of the working classes, without attacking private property because it was argued that workers had their own properties and could make additional income revenue.[5] In section 33, the encyclical provides,

> There is another and deeper consideration which must not be lost sight of. As regards the State, the interests of all, whether high or low, are equal. The members of the working classes are citizens by nature and by the same right as the rich; they are real parts, living the life which makes up, through the family, the body of the commonwealth; and it need hardly be said that they are in every city very largely in the majority. It would be irrational to neglect one portion of the citizens and favor another, and therefore the public administration must duly and solicitously provide for the welfare and the comfort of the working classes; otherwise, that law of justice will be violated which ordains that each man shall have his due. To cite the wise words of St. Thomas Aquinas: "As the part and the whole are in a certain sense identical, so that which belongs to the whole in a sense belongs to the part."(27) Among the many and grave duties of rulers who would do their best for the people, the first and chief is to act with strict justice – with that justice which is called distributive – toward each and every class alike.[6]

The encyclical thus promoted a kind of Rule of Law (equity) between unequal people. Section 37 of the encyclical stated,

> Rights must be religiously respected wherever they exist, and it is the duty of the public authority to prevent and to punish injury, and to protect every one in the possession of his own. Still, when there is a question of defending the rights of individuals, the poor and badly off have a claim to especial consideration. The richer class have many ways of shielding themselves, and stand less in need of help from the State; whereas the mass of the poor have no resources of their own to fall back upon, and must chiefly depend upon the assistance of the State. And it is for this reason that wage-earners, since

> they mostly belong in the mass of the needy, should be specially cared for and protected by the government.

This type of welfare statement regarding the poor and weak actually had older roots in America. Néstor de Buen reminds us that Law VI of Title VI of Book III of the *Recopilación de Leyes de Indias* of 1593 was the first labor law in America to have a notable theoretical impact, independent of its practical reliability. This law already stipulated a working day of eight daily hours, weekly rest, and payment on the seventh day. Regarding salary, a minimum was already mentioned for Indians in labors and mines, "setting it as one *real* and a half per day, or one *real* and enough food and hot meat with cooked corn tortillas (called *pozole*)."[7] In 1790, by a special statement added to *La Novísima Recopilación* reprinted in 1775, criteria were established for the protection of pregnant women's work, health, and hygiene; medical attention; minimum working age; and hygienic housing.[8]

In nineteenth-century Mexico, Ignacio Ramírez predicted the future of fair distribution of the fruits of labor if the legislation had opened a chapter of working social protection in the 1857 Constitution:

> The great and real social problem is to emancipate the day laborers from the capitalists: the answer is simple and may be reduced to making work into capital. This change, strictly demanded by justice, will assure to the laborer not only the salary that will provide him with subsistence, but a right to proportionally divide the profits with the employer. The economic school is right to proclaim that capital in cash ought to produce a return, like capital in mercantile goods and in real estate; but the economists will complete their work, anticipating the aspirations of socialism, on the day in which they grant to labor capital the unquestionable rights to revenue. Gentlemen of the commission, you will proclaim the sovereignty of the people in vain while depriving the everyday laborer of all the fruits of his labor...[9]

The Provisional Statute of the Mexican Empire of Maximilian of Habsburg, April 10, 1865, evidently had in the statutory law of Articles 58–60 an advanced code in labor matters:

> More clearly related to labor law is the so-called Law on Workers, issued on November 1, 1865, issued as a regulation of articles 58, 69 and 70 of the Organic Statute of the Empire relating to working hours, weekly rest and compulsory holidays, child labor, cash payment, personal debts, free transit from work centers, establishment of schools under the care of managers, housing of farm workers, medical treatment of workers, the abolition of corporal punishment, etc. This legislation is more advanced from the social point of view than what was in force during the years after the fall of the Empire and even before the 1917 Constitution. It is clear that the legislation in force during the regime of General Díaz did not have such a scope.[10]

In accordance with this tradition of statutory protection of worker's rights, Ricardo Flores Magón and the Mexican Liberal party, in their manifesto of 1906, raised the other doctrinal influence of social constitutionalism in labor matters when they stated that

> [t]he establishment of an eight-hour workday is a benefit for all workers without the need for modifications for specific cases. The same is not true of a one-peso minimum wage. Living conditions are not the same throughout the Republic. There are regions in Mexico where the cost of living is much higher than in the rest of the country. In those regions the wages may be higher, but the workers are just as miserable.... It is therefore necessary to prevent such injustice, and when the labor law is formulated in detail, the exceptions for the application of the minimum wage of $1.00 must be expressed, establishing a higher minimum salary for places where the cost of living is higher. It must be ensured that all workers obtain the benefits of this law in equal proportion. The other protections proposed for labor legislation are of obvious necessity and justice. Hygiene in factories, workshops, accommodations and other places where dependents and workers would spend a lot of time; guarantees of the worker's life; the prohibition of child labor; the Sunday rest; compensation for accidents and pensions for retired workers; the prohibition of fines and discounts; the obligation to pay with cash; the annulment of the day laborers' debt; the measures to avoid abuses in piecework and to protect sharecroppers. All this is demanded by the sad conditions of work in our country, and its necessity needs no demonstration. The obligation imposed on urban landlords to compensate tenants who leave improvements in their homes or fields is of great public utility. In this way, unscrupulous landlords who never make repairs in the slums they rent out will be forced to improve their properties to the advantage of the public. In general, it is not fair for a poor man to improve the property of a rich man, without receiving any compensatory benefit.[11]

Returning to the proposals of labor courts or conciliation boards, the most significant developments occurred during the administration of Victoriano Huerta, when the National Congress engaged on the law reform project of September 17, 1913, to revise sections VII and XII of Articles 75 and 309 of the Commercial Charter then in force. In this proposal, the civil character of the labor contracts did not disappear (Remolina Roqueñí 1976: 37–38), but conciliation boards were introduced to settle the conflicts between workers and employers and set the minimum wages in each state of the union. The project was not a success.

The pre-constitutional Labor Laws of Cándido Aguilar in Veracruz emerged through this legislative project, which was drafted by José Macias on October 19, 1914, and created a civil administration board for labor disputes. A law of Salvador Alvarado in Yucatan, enacted May 14, 1915, with an amendment on December 11, created industrial tribunals to avoid the long civil process of the ordinary courts. Another example was the Berlanga Law of Jalisco of January

1, 1916, which contained special provisions to protect welfare conditions and promote reconciliation between capital and labor with state referees in each municipality.

In addition to these various efforts, a little-known project to which Pastor Rouaix made a remarkable contribution is mentioned very modestly in his book *Génesis de los Artículos,* and helps one better understand his role in the founding nucleus of the Commission that created the future Article 123 of the new 1917 Constitution. On January 28, 1915, apparently by an order of President Carranza, Rouaix, Macias, and Rojas published in the newspaper *El Pueblo* a "Minimum Wage Law and Board of Agreements," a direct antecedent of what was legislated in the constituent commission (Remolina Roqueñí 1976: 38).

The new SCJN and its initial jurisprudence on "social guarantees," 1918–1928

The jurisprudential criteria that the *Suprema Corte de Justicia de la Nación* (SCJN) adopted following the first labor resolution of March 20, 1918, were very important. By the express mandate of Article 123, state labor codes went into force, beginning with the key codes of Campeche, Veracruz, and Yucatan between December 1917 and October 1918. However, there were also state-level labor laws during the Porfirian and revolutionary periods, which should be noted here because they had an important impact on legal practice in civil and labor matters in many Mexican states leading up to the Federal Labor Law of 1931. First of all, we have the Labor Law of Bernardo Reyes in Nuevo León of November 9, 1906, which for the first time fixed the compensation criteria for work accidents and the legal burden of proof that might exculpate the employers when the workers were responsible for their injuries. It was provided in these state codes that workers would be compensated at 50 percent for up to two years for labor accidents that resulted in total work disability on a temporary basis and proportionally in cases of partial disability. A 100 percent payment for two years was given in case of permanent disability, and employers were forced to pay death expenses. According to Mario de la Cueva, this law was based on the French law on work accidents of 1899 (Cueva 1949: 95).

After Nuevo León led the way with its statute during the Porfirian period, a significant amount of labor legislation followed during the revolutionary period. These laws took the form not of codes, but of decrees.[12] Porfirio Marquet reminds us that with the prerogative of legislating state labor codes between 1918 and 1929, twenty-five states of the Republic had elaborated those codes.[13] As the Federal District of Mexico City and the territories did not have conciliation boards, Carranza issued the law published on December 3, 1917, on the conciliation and arbitration boards, which intensified the academic and jurisprudential debates in the SCJN. There would be oral, three-day trials, and illegal lockouts by employers would justify confiscations (precautionary seizures in support of laborer demands). The debate in the court was whether these boards were administrative conciliation tribunals or judicial courts.

Between the judicial resolution of the "Cabrera" case of March 8, 1918, and the case of the "La Corona" factory of February 1, 1924, the SCJN changed its position. Accepting in the first case that boards were administrative bodies, in the second case, the SCJN gave them jurisdictional attributes. In 1926, the *Juntas de Conciliación* of the Federal District (Mexico City) of 1926 granted them arbitration powers. Without discarding the civil procedural model, the Supreme Court recognized them as judicial boards. We transcribe the recitals of the legal resolution "Cabrera" to understand better the way in which this first revolutionary Supreme Court understood the conciliation in labor matters:

> Amparo by Guillermo Cabrera. Volume II of the *Semanario Judicial*, page 773. Mexico, March 8, 1918.
>
> First. Pursuant to article 123, section 20 of the Federal Constitution, differences or conflicts between capital and labor shall be submitted to the decision of a Conciliation and Arbitration Board, formed by an equal number of representatives of the workers and of the employers and one representative of the Government. This process applies when there is an actual dispute concerning current work, stemming from a deed or inaction of one of the contracting parties that is out of compliance with its commitments. When disputes arise involving claims that concern the consequences of a contract that has expired or that should be required, they should be raised before the ordinary courts, and not before the conciliation and arbitration boards.
>
> Second. The established interpretation is corroborated with the provisions of section 21 of the same Article 123, which declares that if an employer refuses to submit its differences to arbitration, or to accept the damages pronounced by the board, its right to the worker's labor will be terminated and it will be obliged to compensate the worker with a sum equal to three months' salary, in addition to the losses resulting from the dispute. If it is the worker who refuses to submit to arbitration, the work contract will be terminated. This was the clear intent of the legislation: that the board mediate conflicts regarding fulfillment of an employment contract, in execution, as occurs in the cases of strikes, work stoppages, sabotage, boycotts and other means of reprisal used, both by the management and by the workers referred to in sections 14 and 19 of Article 123 of the aforementioned Constitution. These disputes have a direct effect on social order and the development and prosperity or ruin of the industries, and the board therefore provides the interested parties with a prompt and effective means of remedying their difficulties.
>
> Third. If the interpretation given by the Board of Conciliation and Arbitration of Yucatan were accurate, in the sense of being entitled to hear civil or commercial lawsuits arising from an employment contract, giving executive character to its resolutions, the board would cease to be a Board of Conciliation and Arbitration, as it is titled, and it would unduly extend its powers, usurping a jurisdiction not assigned to it by the Fundamental Charter. This jurisdiction is limited to the judicial authority of the Federation

or of the States, by virtue of the federal pact. It is inconceivable that the Constituent Assembly sanctioned this, since that would require an ignorance of the powers that the Assembly itself assigned to the judicial authorities."[14]

With these resolutions and the case of *La Corona* factory cited above, the conciliation boards acquired definitively their status of judicial labor tribunals. The history of the separation of civil procedural law in labor lawsuits thus began on its own, but did not see the light, academically speaking, until the publication of Manuel Martínez Pastor's text on the jurisprudence of the SCJN in labor matters of 1935 and Octavio Trigo's 1939 manual on procedural labor law.[15]

1925–1928

In a second period of SCJN labor law jurisprudence between 1925 and 1928, the corporate control of the federal executive power and the states over labor disputes increased, so the court had to justify the grant of judicial power to authorities other than the judicial ones in the administration of justice although the *amparos* (Mexican judicial protection according to the reform of 1908) had a civil and administrative source. Despite several years having passed since the enactment of Article 123 of the Constitution, there were still conflicts over the validity of the decisions of the conciliation boards that belonged to the executive power and not to the judicial tribunals. The SCJN validated this administrative procedure.

Timothy James, perhaps following the warnings of Bassols himself, explains how many of the social reforms promulgated in the Constitution of 1917 required legislation to implement them before they could be executed. In this sense, the new labor provisions had to be developed at the local or state level (Article 123). This was immediately and fully done in some states but not entirely in others. In the first case, obstacles arose such as resistance from their own courts and even the SCJN.

In 1917, three new ministers (Alberto M. González, José María Truchuelo, and Enrique Colunga) who were former constitutional deputies had the responsibility to oversee the safeguarding of social guarantees at the constitutional level. The Constitution of 1917 largely preserved the *amparo* system since it had taken shape before the revolution. As noted by James, "[t]he most important innovation was the creation of direct amparo, or amparo of a single instance, in cases filed against judicial decisions" (James 2013: 55, 72). In this way, the Supreme Court admitted and decided the *amparos* starting from May 1917, despite the evident absence of new regulatory legislation.

Direct *amparo* served in many ways as a counterpoint to the defense of social guarantees in general and against the new labor law in particular. Like the previous regulations governing the *amparo*, legislation adopted in 1908 established that this would be an option in two cases: first, at the level of district judges, and second (mandatory), review of the decision by the Supreme Court in full. In regions where there was no district judge, an *amparo* could be initiated before a local judge of first instance, or in urgent cases of life and liberty, any "justice of the peace" or other person empowered to provide administrative justice, provided that the relevant federal judge (district judge) was notified immediately. But this new judicial figure offered the only opportunity to owners or workers to call on the Supreme Court as referee when individual and social or economic rights were violated by resolution of the Juntas de Conciliación.

Statistics of the new labor matter in the SCJN between 1921 and 1928: ambiguities and protection of social guarantees

What follows is a brief analysis of the litigation of labor issues in the SCJN since the year 1921, using the most reliable data available. From 301 selected case files that included labor disputes, 291 allude to *amparo* judgments reviewed or direct *amparo* by the Supreme Court. Five dealt with general pleadings by individuals or company representatives requesting direct intervention from the SCJN, two dealt with court jurisdiction issues, two dealt with appeals before the SCJN of the decisions of local authorities, and one did not provide adequate information (Table 6.1).

As can be seen from the table above, most of the *amparos* under review by the SCJN were due to majority resolutions of district courts or state courts of justice, by virtue of which the companies or workers did not accept the "friendly composition" of the local boards upon formation. The civil and/or administrative nature of the resolutions was evident. Through the direct *amparo*, we have resolutions on local laws of distribution of working utilities, and finally the resolutions appealed due to the issuance of local working laws and/or erection of conciliation boards of the federal states.

As for *Amparos* promoted by individuals or small family companies, as well as trade unions, these constituted the majority in this period, with a total of 207 files (Table 6.2).

Table 6.1 Labor matter litigation in SCJN from 1921 to 1924: amparos (private and public companies)

Total files	*State codes and local Juntas de Conciliación*	*Local rules of utilities working rights*	*Judicial local and federal resolutions*
84	14	18	51

Table 6.2 Labor matter litigation of the SCJN 1921–1924: *amparos* (individuals, small family companies, and trade unions)

Total files	*State codes and local Juntas de Conciliación*	*Local rules of utilities working rights*	*Judicial local and federal resolutions*
207	49	76	82

Individuals who hired workers and resorted to direct *amparo* or review by the Supreme Court, due to resolutions of a federal jurisdictional court or of the local boards of the states, usually represented small family partnerships or trade unions. A faithful reflection of a new national working class expanded on the basis of small companies compared to stock firms. The litigation of labor *amparos* shows that these small companies were very vulnerable to the new laws of working rights utilities and to a greater extent, the resolutions that the district courts made on the application of the new state laws derived from Article 123, in particular protection from unemployment, illnesses, accidents, or death, and guarantees of Sunday rest or a seventh free paid day. The demands for protection against the new laws and the erection and/or attributions of the conciliation boards were not of greater weight in this observed group, except for the obligatory nature of appointing representatives of the small employers to integrate the local boards. However, attention must be paid to the case of the resolutions that the Central Board of Conciliation and Arbitration of Xalapa issued for a special compensation of three months, plus one month of additional salary, in favor of a former employee of a small employer. An appeal was evidently sent to the District Court in Veracruz, dated August 16, 1923, ratifying in the SCJN the suspension of "claimed act" by incidental route. In general, the parties preferred to go to the courts to resolve labor disputes, when the resolutions of the boards did not meet their demands. The employer could demonstrate that the original resolution was contrary to the rule of Article 123.

Finally, it is worth noting the first *amparo* brought to the District Court of Mazatlán on November 21, 1924, in favor of a small company, "Echeguren y Cía," against the new federal income tax law of February 21, 1924, better known as the "Tax Law on salaries, profits and emoluments and its regulations." Here, the SCJN was close to the legal interpretation of 1917 and tried to protect many small companies against federal resolutions contrary to the liberal spirit of the Mexican revolution.

From a total of 780 cases between 1925 and 1928, 291 applications for direct *amparo* or review at SCJN were presented by companies. The full recognition of the conciliation and arbitration boards as labor judicial courts is already observed here. Their resolutions could be challenged through direct *amparo* at the Supreme Court or in review by the same SCJN when the origin of the challenge came from a district court (Table 6.3).

Despite the recognition of the local boards as judicial tribunals, the weight of the litigation of labor cases in this third period of the revolutionary SCJN was

Table 6.3 Litigation in labor matter of the SCJN 1925–1928: *Amparos* (companies)

Total files	*Direct amparo. Full plenary and first court's room*	*Review amparo. Full plenary and 1,2,4 court's room*	*Amparo and suspension incidents. Full plenary and first court's room*
291	8	199	84

supported to a large extent by the resolutions of the district courts. The performance of these federal courts deserves further study, in terms of the criteria used to confirm or reject resolutions then coming from the conciliation boards. In this third period, we find *amparos* against resolutions on unjustified labor dismissals, compensation of three months' salary, reinstatement of workers, validity of collective bargaining agreements, and compensation for workplace accidents. The first twelve cases of the new Federal Board of Conciliation and Arbitration that began operating in 1928 are highlighted. The mining, oil, and railroad companies, including the National Railways of Mexico (owned by the Federal State), were the first to be covered in resolutions by the Federal Board of 1928. In accordance with the spirit of social constitutionalism at the core of Article 123, the protection of workers did not distinguish, except for the specific categories of "special and strategic work," between contractual relations and the right to strike between private and state companies and organizations. Only with the constitutional reforms of 1928–1929, and with the Federal Labor Law of 1931, did the revolutionary state reverse the stage of radical demands of Mexican working classes (Table 6.4).

Relative to the previous period, the weight of an *amparo* in labor litigation was stronger in large companies than the small family ones, civil associations, and trade unions. Again, each *amparo* reviewed by SCJN carried a huge weight. However, other new categories may be discerned in this period, as shown in Table 6.5.

Under the heading of "several matters," we find writings to the SCJN, especially by trade unions requesting that labor resolutions coming from the boards should be executed or carried out to the district courts. Here, we find an interesting request of the Federation of Trade Union Workers of the Federal District (Mexico City) made in 1926 demanding that the SCJN set the precedent that resolutions of the conciliation boards should not give rise to an *Amparo*.

Table 6.4 Litigation in labor matters of the SCJN 1925–1928: *amparos* (individuals, small family companies, civil associations, and labor unions)

Total files	*Direct amparo. Full plenary and first court's room*	*Review amparo. Full plenary and 1,2,4 court's room*	*Amparo and suspension incidents. Full plenary and first court's room*
409	17	314	78

Table 6.5 Labor matter files addressed to the full plenary of SCJN in the period 1925–1928

Several matters	*Judicial complaint*	*Judgment impulse incidents*	*Judicial excuses*	*Judicial competences*	*Economic affairs*
7	21	2	4	39	2

As for judicial complaints, the plaintiffs are individuals and companies that were complaining about the performance of the boards or of the district courts in the execution of Resolutions. The judgment impulse incidents were not important, nor were the excuses or impediments. The economic matters refer to a Union of Workers and Customs Employees and to a demand of *amparo* filed by Mr. Jorge McDonald. Conflicts over judicial jurisdictions were the most important here.

Conclusion

The social constitutionalism inaugurated by the political generation of Pastor Rouaix and the Constituent Assembly of Queretaro had the foresight to realize the importance of the protection of social guarantees in the context of human rights. They also managed to determine the role of the new state, not only as an arbitrator between the factors of production, typical of the economic liberalism of the previous era, but they also endowed the revolutionary state with the power to implement a state-led production model. The precocious norm of the constitutional minimum wage is a clear statement of this new role. Rouaix, whom his contemporaries, like Luis Cabrera, considered to have been unjustly relegated to private life in his Granja Viena and later his Centenario house in Coyoacán (Mexico City), left a silent, discreet,[16] but fundamental legacy in the architecture of social protection. Rouaix was convinced that land provision for the new agricultural worker was absolutely necessary, even if it brought the federal state into the patriarchal axis of property in land. Like many comrades of his generation, Rouaix believed in a social state of law: liberal, inclined to redeem the dispossessed from centuries of prostration to turn them into free citizens, with individual rights gradually driven by a necessary state paternalism to avoid abuse and enslavement by the upper classes who had inherited a tendency to oligarchic domination from the old Spanish regime.

The labor law of the new revolutionary SCJN, in its three great revolutionary periods: 1917–1919, 1920–1924 and 1925–1928, soon showed that the constituent legislative balance had failed to notice a huge contradiction between individual guarantees and protection of new social rights at the level of the administration of justice. This contradiction was embedded in a constitutional doctrine that on the one hand proclaimed the private property and the safeguard of individual rights, and on the other, the conversion of these rights into prerogatives limited by the Constitution itself, due to the ideological imperative to satisfy the demands of the agrarian and laboring classes coming from a majority indigenous and mestizo population. It was on the backs of these workers that, as General Diaz was aware, modern Mexico had been built. Constitutional protection in labor issues would promote the delicate flowering of the future federalization of labor laws and the consolidation of the federal and local conciliation boards with greater interference by the federal executive power, leading to the corporate control of the laborer and peasant, especially under the constitutional reforms of 1928–1929.

Archives

Archivo Histórico de la SCJN. Actas del Pleno y Salas. Series: Amparo. Conflictos de Competencias. Súplicas. Varios. Years 1921–1928.

Notes

1 See Cabrera Acevedo (1994). Natural law was not restricted according to the 1857 charter. Instead, social guarantees could be limited in a new authoritarian rule that restricted social rights in articles 5, 27, and 123 of the new 1917 charter.

2 "*Esta extrema divergencia de criterio de los dos libros que se ha escrito sobre la historia del Congreso Constituyente de Querétaro del que brotó la gloriosa Constitución que nos rige ahora, creo que hace de mayor utilidad la publicación de este trabajo, que ha sido redactado con la más completa imparcialidad y ayuno de cualquier prejuicio, pues como antes lo dije, mi actuación en el Congreso fue la de un diputado independiente que tuvo la satisfacción de haber servido de lazo de unión entre exaltados extremos....*" Capítulo VIII. La labor personal de los diputados en la formación de la Carta Magna, in Rouaix (1945: 223), quoting *Palavicini* (1938) and Bojórquez (1938).

3 "*Pastor Rouaix, el jefe de la comisión encargada de redactar el proyecto de artículo 123, comentó en el libro que escribió posteriormente acerca del origen de este precepto, (jornada máxima de trabajo) que los diputados encargados de elaborar el proyecto: 'iban a reformar las instituciones sociales del país con los artículos 123 y 27 de la Constitución, para conseguir con ello que los principios teóricos del Cristianismo, que tantas veces habían sido ensalzados allí (en el palacio episcopal de Querétaro, donde se reunió la comisión) tuviera una realización en la práctica.' "Esta declaración franca, que contiene una queja solapada contra la Iglesia, no puede entenderse a la letra, máxime que el mismo Pastor indicó a continuación lo que entendía por 'principios cristianos': que 'fueran bienaventurados los mansos para que poseyeran la tierra y elevados los humildes al desposeer a los poderosos de los privilegios inveterados de que gozaban.*" Adame (1981: 55)

4 For a brief summary in Spanish of Europe's "social issue," see Suárez Cortina (2006) as well as Grez Toso (1995). In Mexico, Jesuit priest Alfredo Méndez Medina wrote a classic text, *La Cuestión Social*, in 1913, as a consequence of the "Dieta de Zamora" of the Circulo de Obreros Católicos of México that convened around 1909. His text was published in *Conferencia del Episcopado Mexicano-Comisión Episcopal de Pastoral Social* (1988: 65–81). Méndez's ideas were supported by those of German priest Franz Hitze (1880; 1921: 41–70). See the overview by Ceballos Ramírez (2000). On the side of anarchism, see Flores Magón (1912).

5 http://w2.vatican.va/content/leo-xiii/en/encyclicals/documents/hf_l-xiii_enc_15051891_rerum-novarum.html 22-10-2015.

6 http://w2.vatican.va/content/leo-xiii/es/encyclicals/documents/hf_l-xiii_enc_15051891_rerum-novarum.html 22-10-2015

7 See Ley VI, Libro III, Título VI under the decree of Felipe II ("*...fijándolo en real y medio por día o un real y comida suficiente y bastante carne caliente con tortillas de maíz cocido que se llama pozole*"). Néstor de Buen took the original quotation from Pedro Larrea Peñaherrera, 1964.

8 See the evolution of these statements in De Buen and Mario de la Cueva (1949), and also Marquet Guerrero (2014: 243–280).

9 "*El grande, el verdadero problema social, es emancipar a los jornaleros de los capitalistas: la resolución es sencilla y se reduce a convertir en capital el trabajo. Esta operación exigida imperiosamente por la justicia asegurará al jornalero no solamente el salario que conviene a su subsistencia, sino un derecho a dividir proporcionalmente las ganancias con el empresario. La escuela económica tiene razón al proclamar que el capital en numerario debe producir un rédito, como el capital en efectos mercantiles y en bienes*

raíces; pero los economistas completarán su obra, adelantándose a las aspiraciones del socialismo, el día en que concedan los derechos incuestionables a un rédito, al capital trabajo. Señores de la comisión, en vano proclamaréis la soberanía del pueblo mientras privéis a cada jornalero de todo fruto de su trabajo...." (Tena Ramírez 1978: 1311)

10 "*Más claramente relacionada con el derecho del trabajo, se encuentra la llamada Ley sobre Trabajadores, expedida el 1o. de noviembre de 1865, la cual se ostenta como reglamentaria de los artículos 58, 69 y 70 del Estatuto Orgánico del Imperio y entre cuyas disposiciones se encuentran la regulación de la jornada de trabajo, el descanso semanal, los días de descanso obligatorio, el trabajo de los menores, el pago en efectivo, el carácter personal de las deudas, el libre tránsito de los centros de trabajo, el establecimiento de escuelas a cargo de los patrones, el otorgamiento de habitaciones en las fincas a los trabajadores, el otorgamiento de asistencia médica en caso de enfermedad de un jornalero, la abolición de los castigos corporales, etcétera. Puede afirmarse, sin embargo, que esta legislación es más avanzada desde el punto de vista social que la que estuvo vigente en los años posteriores a la caída del Imperio y hasta antes de la expedición de la Constitución de 1917; resulta claro que la legislación vigente durante el régimen del general Díaz no tuvo estos alcances.*" (Marquet Guerrero 2014: 255)

11 "*El establecimiento de ocho horas de trabajo es un beneficio para la totalidad de los trabajadores, aplicable generalmente sin necesidad de modificaciones para casos determinados. No sucede lo mismo con el salario mínimo de un peso, y sobre esto hay que hacer una advertencia en extremo importante. Las condiciones de vida no son iguales en toda la República: hay regiones en México en que la vida resulta mucho más cara que en el resto del país. En esas regiones los jornales son más altos, pero a pesar de esto el trabajador sufre allí tanta miseria como la que sufren con más bajos salarios los trabajadores en los puntos donde es más barata la existencia .... Por tanto, si se aplica con absoluta generalidad el salario mínimo de $1.00 que no los salvan de la miseria, continuarían en la misma desastrosa condición en que ahora se encuentran sin obtener con la ley de qué hablamos el más insignificante beneficio. Es, pues, preciso prevenir tal injusticia, y al formularse detalladamente la ley del trabajo deberán expresarse las excepciones para la aplicación del salario mínimo de $1.00, estableciendo para aquellas regiones en que la vida es más cara, y en que ahora ya se gana ese jornal, un salario mayor de $1.00. Debe procurarse que todos los trabajadores obtengan en igual proporción los beneficios de esta ley. Los demás puntos que se proponen para la legislación sobre el trabajo son de necesidad y justicia patentes. La higiene en fábricas, talleres, alojamientos y otros lugares en que dependientes y obreros deben estar por largo tiempo; las garantías a la vida del trabajador; la prohibición del trabajo infantil; el descanso dominical, la indemnización por accidentes y la pensión a obreros que han agotado sus energías en el trabajo; la prohibición de multas y descuentos; la obligación de pagar con dinero efectivo; la anulación de la deuda de los jornaleros; las medidas para evitar abusos en el trabajo a destajo y las de protección a los medieros; todo esto lo reclaman de tal manera las tristes condiciones del trabajo en nuestra Patria, que su conveniencia no necesita demostrarse con ninguna consideración. La obligación que se impone a los propietarios urbanos de indemnizar a los arrendatarios que dejen mejoras en sus casas o campos es de gran utilidad pública. De este modo, los propietarios sórdidos que jamás hacen reparaciones en las pocilgas que rentan serán obligados a mejorar sus posesiones con ventaja para el público. En general, no es justo que un pobre mejore la propiedad de un rico, sin recibir ninguna compensación, y sólo para beneficio del rico.*" www.ordenjuridico.gob.mx/Constitucion/CH6.pdf 21-10-2015.

12 Marquet Guerrero lists them as follows: "La Ley de Sirvientes de Chiapas del 14 de diciembre de 1912; la Ley del Descanso Dominical de San Luis Potosí del 13 de enero de 1913; la Nueva Ley del Descanso Dominical de San Luis Potosí, del 6 de mayo de 1913; la Ley sobre el Descanso Dominical de Puebla del 30 de enero de 1914; la Ley del Descanso Obligatorio de Jalisco del 2 de julio de 1914; la Ley sobre Descanso Semanal de Veracruz del 9 de octubre de 1914; la Ley de Cándido Aguilar del Estado

de Veracruz del 29 de octubre de 1914; la Ley de Obreros de Chiapas del 31 de octubre de 1914; la Ley sobre Jornaleros y Arrendatarios del Campo de Zacatecas del 21 de noviembre de 1915; la Ley de Asociaciones Profesionales de Veracruz del 14 de diciembre de 1915; la Ley del Trabajo de Yucatán del 15 de diciembre de 1915; la Ley sobre Accidentes de Trabajo de Hidalgo del 25 de diciembre de 1915; la Ley del Trabajo de Jalisco del 1o. de enero de 1916; Ley del Trabajo de Aguascalientes del 8 de febrero de 1916; la Ley sobre Asociaciones Profesionales de Veracruz del 8 de febrero de 1916; la Ley sobre Accidentes del Trabajo de Zacatecas del 24 de julio de 1916, y la Ley del Trabajo de Coahuila del 27 de octubre de 1916" (Marquet Guerrero 2014: 260). See Remolina Roqueñí (1976) for full text.

13 "...Además de Campeche y Veracruz, (...) expidieron leyes laborales en este periodo: el Estado de México en 1918; Sonora en 1918 tres veces y una más en 1919; Nayarit en 1918 en dos ocasiones y una en 1929; Yucatán en 1918 y en 1926; Sinaloa dos veces en 1920; Coahuila en 1920 y 1926; Guanajuato en 1921, 1922, dos en 1923 y dos en 1924; Michoacán en 1921; Puebla en 1921; San Luis Potosí en 1922, 1923, 1925 y 1926; Chihuahua, Durango y Querétaro en 1922; Jalisco en 1923; Nuevo León en dos ocasiones en 1924; Hidalgo dos leyes en 1925 y una en 1928; Tamaulipas en 1925; Oaxaca y Tabasco en 1926; Chiapas y Zacatecas en 1927, así como Aguascalientes en 1928." (Marquet Guerrero 2014: 263)

14 *Semanario Judicial*, p. 773. México, ocho de marzo de mil novecientos dieciocho. Amparo de Guillermo Cabrera. Tomo II. *Considerando primero*. Que, con arreglo al artículo ciento veintitrés, fracción veinte, de la Constitución Federal, las diferencias o conflictos entre el capital y el trabajo se sujetarán a la decisión de una Junta de Conciliación y Arbitraje, formada por igual número de representantes de los obreros y de los patronos y uno del Gobierno; lo que supone un conflicto actual, de trabajo presente, en que la dificultad surge por hecho o la negativa de una de las partes contratantes, que no cumple con sus compromisos; sin que la disposición legal referida pueda extenderse a demandas que atañen a las consecuencias de un contrato que haya expirado y que deben exigirse, en casos de disidencia entre las partes, ante los tribunales ordinarios, y no ante las Juntas de Conciliación y Arbitraje.

Considerando segundo. Que la interpretación establecida se corrobora con lo preceptuado en la fracción veintiuna del mismo artículo ciento veintitrés, la cual declara: que si el patrono no se negare a someter sus diferencias al arbitraje, o a aceptar el laudo pronunciado por la Junta, se dará por terminado el trato de trabajo y quedará obligado a indemnizar al obrero, con el importe de tres meses de salario, además de la responsabilidad que le resulte del conflicto. y si la negativa fuere de los trabajadores, se dará por terminado el contrato de trabajo; lo que de una manera clara y terminante revela el pensamiento del legislador, que no fue otro que el que las mencionadas Juntas mediasen en los conflictos que ocurren sobre el cumplimiento de un contrato de trabajo, en ejecución, como ocurre en los casos de huelgas, paros de trabajo, sabotaje, boycotajes y otros medios de represalia usados, tanto por los patrones como por los obreros a que aluden las fracciones catorce y diecienueve, del artículo ciento veintitrés de la Constitución citada, que quiso, en esos casos, que ordinariamente trascienden al orden de la sociedad y desarrollo y prosperidad o ruina de las industrias, proporcionar a los interesados un medio pronto y eficaz de remediar susdificultades.

Considerando tercero. Que si la interpretación dada por la Junta de Conciliación y Arbitraje de Yucatán fuera exacta, en el sentido de estar facultadas para conocer de las demandas civiles o comerciales, que derivaran de un contrato de trabajo, dando carácter ejecutivo a sus resoluciones, dejaría de ser Junta de Conciliación y Arbitraje, como se titula, y extendería indebidamente sus facultades, invistiéndose de una jurisdicción que no le confiere la Carta Fundamental, y que sólo atribuye a los poderes del orden judicial de la Federación o de los Estados, en virtud del pacto federal; hipótesis que es inconcebible que sancionara el Constituyente, puesto que ellas importaría el desconocimiento de las facultades que él mismo reconoció en las autoridades judiciales."

15 Martínez Pastor et al. (1935) and Trigo (1939).
16 Dr. Cuauhtémoc Calderón Villarreal explains in an interview that, when Leon Trotsky arrived as an exiled to live as Rouaix's neighbor in the street of Viena, Coyoacán, many conversations took place between them with total discretion. Rouaix confessed his wife once, and she told that her sister, Dr. Calderón's mother, that Trotsky had no future in México and probably would be killed by Stalin.

References

Adame Goddard, Jorge (1981) *El pensamiento político y social de los católicos mexicanos 1867–1914*, México, IIJ-UNAM.

Bojórquez, Juan de Dios (1938) *Crónica del Constituyente*, México, Botas.

Cabrera Acevedo, Lucio (1994) *La Suprema Corte de Justicia, la Revolución y el Constituyente de 1917 (1914–1917)*, México, Suprema Corte de Justicia de la Nación.

Ceballos Ramírez, Manuel y Alejandro Garza Rangel (eds.) (2000) *Catolicismo social en México. Teoría, fuentes e historiografía*, Monterrey, Academia de Investigación Humanística.

Conferencia del Episcopado Mexicano-Comisión Episcopal de Pastoral Social, 90 años de pastoral social en México (1988) *Anexos*, México, CEPS-Cáritas Mexicana.

Cueva, Mario de la (1949) *Derecho Mexicano del Trabajo*, México, Editorial Porrúa.

Flores Magón, Ricardo (1912) *La cuestión social en México*, Regeneración, Feb. 10.

Grez Toso, Sergio (1995) *La "Cuestión Social" en: Chile. Ideas y Debates precursores (1804–1902)*, Fuentes para la Historia de la República, Vol. VII. Santiago de Chile, Biblioteca Nacional.

Hitze, Franz (1880) *Die Quintessenz der Sozialen Frage*, Paderborn, Schöningh, ed.

——— (1921) *Kapital und Arbeit und die Reorganisation der Gesellschaft*, Deutsche Arbeit 6, 41–70.

James, Timothy M. (2013) *Mexico's Supreme Court: Between Liberal Individual and Revolutionary Social Rights, 1867–1934*. Albuquerque, University of New Mexico Press.

Larrea Peñaherrera, Pedro (1964) "La legislación del trabajo en la Audiencia de Quito", en: *Cultura Hispánica*, Vol. III, No. 7. Quito.

Marquet Guerrero, Porfirio (2014) *Fuentes y antecedentes del derecho mexicano del trabajo*, in Patricia Kurczyn Villalobos (ed.), *Derechos humanos en el trabajo y la seguridad social. Liber Amicorum in honor of Jorge Carpizo*, México, IIJ-UNAM, 243–280.

Martínez Pastor, Manuel, Raúl Berrón Mucel and Jorge Morfín Delorme (eds.) (1935) *Actual jurisprudencia de la Suprema Corte de Justicia, en materia de trabajo*, México, Antigua Imprenta de Murguía.

Palavicini, Félix (1938) *Historia de la Constitución de 1917*, México, Botas.

Remolina Roqueñí, Felipe (1976) *Evolución de las Instituciones y del Derecho del Trabajo en México*, México, Junta Federal de Conciliación y Arbitraje.

Rouaix, Pastor (1945) *Génesis de los artículos 27 y 123 de la Constitución politica de 1917*. México, Gobierno del Estado de Puebla.

Suárez Cortina, Manuel (2006) *La España Liberal (1868–1917). Política y sociedad*, Madrid, Síntesis.

Tena Ramírez, Felipe (1978) *Leyes fundamentales de México, 1808–1978*, México, Porrúa.

Trigo, Octavio M. (1939) *Curso de derecho procesal mexicano del trabajo*, México, Botas.

7 Presidential impeachments in Brazil

Lessons from the past and challenges for the future[1]

Rafael Mafei Rabelo Queiroz

Introduction

Several disputes fuel practical and academic discussions on accusations and trials in presidential impeachment cases. One of the most difficult, and perhaps the most important, is the distinction between their legal and political aspects. It is true that impeachment processes are both legal and political, but if we can't determine the moments in which one aspect or the other should prevail, invoking their "legal and political" nature comes down to a useless truism.

The unfolding of this inquiry leads into two specific debates on presidential impeachments. The first, which has received greater attention, regards the nature of impeachable offenses: are they a type of general criminal offense (i.e., indictable offenses) or something else – a substantially political fault? Most scholars, notably after President Richard Nixon's impeachment (1974), have concluded that criminality is not a mandatory requisite of impeachable delicts (Staff of the Impeachment Inquiry 1974; Labovitz 1978; Gerhardt 1996; Sunstein 2017). In Brazil, although this debate resurfaced during President Dilma Rousseff's accusations and trial in 2016, writings predating Nixon (Brossard 1965: 65–70) and more recent scholarship (Queiroz 2017) have pointed to the same conclusion.

Another inquiry has received less attention, even though it was one of the main concerns of the framers regarding impeachments (Hamilton 2001a; 2001b). If impeachments are to take a form akin to a trial, how should the competent body – the Senate – exert its power of trying impeached officials? Possibly because the design of presidential impeachments has been around for so long, and because no institution other than the Senate appears to be an obvious substitute for trying impeachments, we have naturalized this power given to the Senate. We have paid little attention – in Brazil at least – to the *conditions and procedures* that impeachment trials must observe in order to accomplish what the original design of presidential impeachments intended. Those important issues involve not only the fine line separating attributions of the upper and lower houses of Congress in accusing and trying a president but also the proceedings of the trial in the upper house, where a court-like process is expected.

A historical and comparative analysis must take into consideration the reasons why the impeachment and trial of presidents was a role assigned to the

Legislative branch, and why the competence of each of the two houses was allocated the way it was. This historical background is important for the critical appraisal of present-day impeachment procedures in Brazil. Surveying this history is the main goal of this chapter.

I will argue that the authority for presidential impeachment trials, given to the Senate, presupposed several factors that have been mitigated over time. I will also argue that Brazil's current constitution (1988), with the interpretation it has received from the country's paramount court (*Supremo Tribunal Federal* – STF) in the trials of presidents Collor (1992) and Rousseff (2016), has widened the gap between theory and practice and made things worse.

This chapter is structured as follows. In Section "Impeachments in Anglo-American law: origins and adaptations," I present the origins of impeachment in English law. Section "The Senate as a tribunal" concentrates on the debates in the U.S. constitutional convention of 1787 regarding the proper role of the Senate as a court to judge presidential impeachments. In Section "Impeachments in Brazil before the 1988 constitution," I explain the adaptation of presidential impeachments in Brazil and its combination with our legal definition of impeachable offenses ("*crimes de responsabilidade*"), which, during the greater part of the nineteenth century (1827–1889), regulated the legal responsibility of agents of the Imperial Executive Power. In Section "The trial of presidential impeachments: between legal and political," I address the role of presidential impeachment in the 1988 Constitution, as well as how the Federal Senate's power to try impeachments was interpreted in the cases of presidents Fernando Collor, in 1992, and Dilma Rousseff, in 2016. I conclude with suggestions for constitutional and legal reforms in the impeachment procedure.

Impeachments in Anglo-American law: origins and adaptations

Impeachments, defined broadly as the accusation and trial of relevant authorities by representative political bodies, have their origins in late Medieval English law. Treason trials in the fourteenth century held before the early Parliament were part of early efforts to make royal agents legally accountable.[2] The direct relationship between English impeachments and later presidential impeachment in the U.S. Constitution comes from seventeenth-century practice in English law, when Parliament used impeachment against crown agents and "claimed anew the power to declare ministerial acts treasonable retrospectively" (Berger 1973: 7). It was then that the House of Commons claimed the right to accuse, and the House of Lords to ultimately convict, royal agents via a trial-like procedure. In the background of this development was the modern struggle to make government officials accountable to Parliament more than to the Crown. This made impeachments remarkably different from bills of attainder, which allowed for the conviction of accused people in more expedited ways.

The central concept of "treason" involved an effective or planned attack against the person of the king – hence its origins in the great treason statute of Edward

III (1350). However, Parliament progressively enlarged the concept to make it applicable to other forms of abuse of power which, while not affecting the person of the king directly – or even being practiced with the king's consent – were breaches of the kingdom's fundamental laws. These were treason in a broader sense: a betrayal, by attempted subversion, of the pact governing the crown's relations with its subjects, especially regarding the freedoms of Parliament.[3]

English practice bequeathed to the North American settlers the rough outline of impeachment design – an accusation by the lower house followed by a trial in the upper house – as well as the core meaning of impeachable offenses: betrayals against the nation's fundamental interests (treason), venality (bribery), and other grave violations of public duties (high crimes and misdemeanors). The exact phrase "impeachment for treason, bribery, or other high crimes and misdemeanors," which would appear in the final draft of the U.S. Constitution, was used and had a relatively determinable content in English law at the time (Berger 1973: 54).

Impeachment was used in the colonial assemblies in English North America since the seventeenth century. As Hoffer and Hull's research revealed, the colonial leaders sought to provide solemn condemnation, with removal from office, of English authorities accused of contempt against the rights of locally elected officials. Print materials and scholarly texts provided information in several colonies on the practice of English impeachments. Well before 1787, colonial political elites had a broadly shared practice revealing an "ideology of legislative privilege," whose legitimacy rested on their "understanding of the English precedent" (Hoffer & Hull 1979: 68). This ideology legitimized punishments of public authorities decided in court-like procedures that mimicked criminal trials, whenever abuse of public powers resulted in serious attacks against the fundamental laws of the community. Certain pieces of colonial legislation, in Massachusetts for instance, specifically mentioned the power to "impeach" criminals (Hoffer & Hull 1979: 53).

Delegates in Philadelphia were therefore aware of impeachments of public officials: they were involved in political action in the colonies. Many had formal legal training and experience, which must have made them familiar with analogous English laws. Additionally, Warren Hastings, the general governor of India, was being tried for impeachment by the British Parliament while the U.S. constitutional convention was being held. His case was brought up during the conventional debates by delegate Mason (Labovitz 1978: 15). Thus, the framers were informed not only by English precedents and colonial cases of trials of public authorities by local political bodies but also by an ongoing trial pending in the English Parliament.[4]

In adapting impeachments into the structure of the U.S. Constitution, the framers went through an itinerary which covered the following questions: (1) *Who* may suffer impeachments? (2) Under *what grounds*? (3) Which bodies shall have the *power to accuse and try* them? and (4) What shall be the *consequences* of a guilty verdict?

The "who" question received a broad answer: the President, the Vice-President, and "all civil officers."[5] As Cass Sunstein (2017: 18–19) points out, the impeachment clause in the constitution is akin to the "no titles of nobility" clause:[6] they were both central to the goal of making accountable "officials who abused their authority" and "avoiding a return to the monarchical heritage." Monarchical heritage implied that the paramount political figures – i.e., the King and his most direct delegates – were not legally accountable. The drafters of the U.S. Constitution, by contrast, worked under the precaution that the "chief magistrate" could very well do wrong, and that his gravest wrongs could risk the integrity of the republic and of all institutions. According to Hamilton (2001c: 355–356), this full accountability by another political institution was in fact the key difference between a president and a monarch. The single-person head of the executive branch, as opposed to multi-person cabinets or councils, was also part of the plan for facilitating accountability for unlawful decisions.[7]

The "under what grounds" answer drew straight upon English law. Impeachment was to be admitted upon cases of "Treason, Bribery, or other high Crimes and Misdemeanors," an expression with specific meaning and currency in the common law of England. "Treason" was defined in the constitution itself.[8] "Bribery" implied a violation of specific public duties.[9] "High Crimes and Misdemeanors" were the most difficult to define, thus leading to the great disputes in the convention. "Treason" and "bribery" were taken to be too narrow, and "High Crimes and Misdemeanors" was preferred over the alternative of "maladministration," which was too vague. Although somewhat imprecise, the phrase conveyed the central idea of impeachments: they should be restricted to "great injuries" and "great misdemeanors" (Berger 1973: 88), which could, however, take the concrete form of countless different acts that could not be specifically defined in legal formulae.

As far as the consequences of a conviction on impeachment, the framers departed significantly from English precedent. In England, impeachments often led to the criminal punishment of convicted officials – even death. The framers did not want to go that far: Benjamin Franklin, who had seen impeachment cases in Pennsylvania,[10] warned that political disputes with an "obnoxious" leader should not lead to "assassinations" (Gerhardt 1996: 8). The consequences for impeachment were thus limited to political remedies: removal from office and future incapacity to perform public functions.[11] Although the consequences of impeachment do hold a "residual punitive aura" (Berger 1973: 81),[12] they are substantially different from ordinary criminal sanctions.

Finally, regarding the institutions empowered to accuse and try impeachments, the English formula was preserved (as it would in Brazil's republican constitution of 1891). The power to accuse was vested in the lower house,[13] while the power to try was given to the upper house of the Legislative branch.[14] The legitimacy of the House of Representatives in accusing the President came from the fact the Representatives were then the sole national institution directly elected by the people (Labovitz 1978: 20; Sunstein 2017: 150). In the following section, I will explain in detail the choice of the Senate as the appropriate forum for impeachment trials.

The Senate as a tribunal

In the U.S. Constitution, the Senate was the institution most akin to the English House of Lords, the ultimate court for impeachment trials in England. Berger points to records from as early as the thirteenth century that document the participation of "prelates, earls, barons, magnates and other learned men" in the task of "dispens[ing] justice and determin[ing] doubts regarding judgment" (Berger 1973: 18–19).

The choice of the Senate as the tribunal for impeachments in the U.S. constitution was the product of careful reflection. As seen in the famous sixty-fifth essay of *The Federalist*, the framers considered, but ultimately rejected, the alternative of the Supreme Court: it was envisioned to be too small a body and its members were directly appointed by the President (albeit with life tenure and Senate confirmation), which caused concerns regarding its independence. The role of the Judiciary was preserved for trials of civil and criminal matters against the expelled president. A special court for trying impeachments was dismissed for being too costly (in the case of a permanent body) or too impractical (in the case of an *ad hoc* tribunal) (Hamilton 1788a). The Senate seemed to be the best choice: the parallel with the English design made it an obvious pick, and its large size and expected quasi-aristocratic composition made it seem well suited for the task.

Gouverneur Morris, the New York representative in Philadelphia, assured his fellow framers that no other institution should be awarded such sensitive attributions. Nevertheless, he suggested a further check: that senators, when sitting in for impeachment trials, should take a special impartiality oath (Labovitz 1978: 15). This shows how they were expected to act as "judges and not politicians" in these occasions (Sunstein 2017: 150). The requisite of a two-thirds majority for convictions would help mitigate the threat of frivolous accusations, according to Hamilton (1788b: 343).

It was also expected that the Senate's composition would make it more temperate than the House of Representatives. Senators were not elected by popular vote in the original design of the U.S. Constitution: they were chosen by state legislatures. It was thought that this indirect option would favor the election of men of prestige within local political elites rather than political adventurers or demagogues who might seduce the common folk with malice and populism. Senators were not electorally accountable to the same audience as the House of Representatives. They had also to be older (at least thirty), and their terms were longer (six years). All of these factors made the Senate seem reliable and independent for the trial of presidential impeachments.

One last historical circumstance is relevant of notice: the framers did not foresee the involvement of political parties that developed in later years. Political philosophy at the time "did not recognize that ongoing and organized party opposition was a legitimate, indeed an indispensable, part of democratic life" (Ackerman 2005: 22). On the contrary, the view of interest groups that seized public positions was quite negative. Many feared these groups would get bogged down in parochial disputes, and posed a risk for national interests in the event that the national government got captured by their provincial agendas. Political philosophy at the time of the framers was wary of political parties. For example, James Madison (2001) argued for a strong central power that would guarantee the prevalence of national policies over petty local interests. This spirit remained after the enacting of the Constitution: George Washington's farewell speech, in 1796, appealed to the conscience of politicians of the time against the prevailing of regional over national interests: "The name of American, which belongs to you in your national capacity, must always exalt the just pride of patriotism more than any appellation derived from local discriminations" (Washington 1796).

All these circumstances were decisive in choosing the Senate as the appropriate body to try impeachment accusations. Keeping them in mind is most helpful in evaluating the design of presidential impeachments in Brazil.

Impeachments in Brazil before the 1988 Constitution

During most of the nineteenth century, while the U.S. Senate were holding their first impeachment trials, including one against the country's president,[15] Brazil functioned as an independent monarchy. As was then standard in monarchies, the king was immune from all legal prosecution. Article 99 of the Imperial Constitution of 1824 stated, "The Person of the Emperor is inviolable, and Holy: He is not subject to any form of responsibility."

For all other agents of the Emperor, a statute was made to regulate their legal accountability. The Law of October 15th, 1827 defined functional crimes (*crimes de responsabilidade*) of ministers of state, who served the Emperor in exercise of the Executive Power, and counselors of state, who served him in exercise of properly royal power (*Poder Moderador*).[16] Though aimed primarily at high-ranking officials, archival evidence has shown this statute was used to punish lower-ranking public employees.[17] Analogous to the English case, and in contrast to the United States, these functional crimes were indictable offenses leading to criminal punishments: fines, dismissal from public service, and prison. The accusation of ministers and counselors was entrusted to the House of Representatives; the trial was left to the Senate.[18]

Although Paulo Brossard claims the 1827 statute as the beginning of impeachment in Brazil,[19] we should keep in mind that central aspects of current-day impeachments were then absent: the country's highest political authority (the Emperor) could not be held accountable in legal trials; and the consequences of the conviction were criminal sanctions, not mere removal from office.[20]

This is not to say that analogous questions were not at stake in Brazilian Public Law *in illo tempore*: the accountability of ministers of state for private acts of the Emperor[21] was a major debate nineteenth century in Brazilian public law. Since Brazil's 1824 Constitution opted for an institutional design that grave primacy to the Monarch by naming him both the head of the executive branch[22] and the sole bearer of royal moderating powers,[23] there was notable concern regarding how accountability was to be enforced in the exercise of those important attributions. Some authors claimed imperial actions should only be accountable directly to the national public opinion (via criticism of the press, for example), but never to other political institutions or authorities, as the Emperor embodied national sovereignty himself (Pimenta Bueno 1857); others claimed that no imperial actions were made effective in practice without the collaboration of cabinet members, who were fully accountable and should be so held if they chose to enforce imperial orders flagrantly contrary to statutes, to the Constitution, or to the nation's high interests (Vasconcellos 1862).

Defenders of a sharper distinction between monarchy and government were mollified by an 1847 Imperial decree that created the office of President of the Council of Ministers[24] – a prime minister, in other words. Although the letter of the 1824 Constitution stated the Emperor could freely appoint (*nomear livremente*) all cabinet members (art. 101, VI), this new statute provided that all cabinet members would be chosen by the President of the Council and merely approved by the Emperor (Barbosa 2007). In practice, this brought Brazil closer to the ideal of a parliamentarian monarchy in the second half of the nineteenth century. The missing piece of the puzzle were clean elections: fraud was widespread and the political party running the government was able to use all sorts of illicit mechanisms to guarantee electoral victories. As a result, the Emperor often resorted to the prerogative of dissolving the chamber of deputies and appointing a cabinet chief of the opposing party in order to avoid one party from perpetrating itself in power. This practice came to be known as "upside down parliamentarianism" (*parlamentarismo às avessas*) since electoral victory was the end, and not the beginning, of the formation of a new government (Carvalho 2003: 401). In these cases, political accountability was promoted based on each party's capacity to approve legislation and to implement policies desired by the Emperor. Failure to approve the necessary legislation often caused the Crown to dissolve the lower house and alternate the party in charge of government, hoping they would succeed in overcoming political hurdles that stopped the other party – after new elections that the new party in power would most likely manipulate to ensure the necessary majority in parliament.[25] This mechanism of imperial arbitration dissipated political crisis without the need for trial-like procedures. They would only become necessary when Brazil abolished monarchy in 1889, resorting to fixed-term presidentialism.

Brazil's first republican constitution was enacted in 1891. It contained clauses on presidential impeachments,[26] retaining the term *crimes de responsabilidade* from the 1827 statute. The logic, however, was altered: the president was not immune to legal prosecution; the nature of those functional crimes was no longer criminal; and the consequence of conviction was mere removal from office, with an eventual incapacity to hold public office. It was all much like the U.S. model, but Brazil's impeachment design had a unique trait: following the legal tradition of previous imperial law, functional crimes of the president were not left open by a broad definition such as "high crimes and misdemeanors." The 1891 constitution mandated Congress to pass a statute defining impeachable offenses. Decree 30, in 1892, did just that.

Decree 30 had, however, a major flaw for a statute that was meant to define anything: several of its clauses were vague and imprecise. For example, article 43 defined the crime of "misuse of authority, committing excesses and abuses not defined in the present statute." This vagueness was deemed dangerous to the independence of the executive branch by President Deodoro da Fonseca. He vetoed several articles of the bill approved by Congress. The president claimed that the vetoed parts would put the presidency in risk of retaliation when exercising checks on the legislature.[27] But Congress overruled his veto: the statute came into effect with its original text.

After the long rule of president Getulio Vargas (1930–1945), Brazil's 1946 constitution repeated the same institutional design: presidential impeachments were named in the constitution, but impeachable offenses themselves – still *crimes de responsabilidade* – were delegated to a specific statute, which came to be Federal Law 1079/1950. The consequences of conviction were removal from office and incapacity to hold public office for a certain period.

Much like Decree 30/1892, this new statute – which is still partly in effect in the present – defined impeachable offenses quite vaguely.[28] Paulo Brossard's *O impeachment* (1965), the most prestigious Brazilian book on the matter to this day, reinforced vagueness in interpreting that statute. According to Brossard, impeachable offenses defined by Law 1079 were mere examples of conducts that could lead to impeachments.[29] For this reason, despite Federal Law 1079's long list of impeachable offenses, most of the doctrine holds that impeachable offenses are not indictable crimes, but political wrongs committed through the grave abuse of public trust in the president's powers.[30] This same understanding predominates among U.S. impeachment scholars.[31]

In addition to this indefinite characterization of impeachable offenses, Brazil's impeachment design in 1946's constitution and Federal Law 1079/1950 preserved another trait of the classic impeachment scheme: combined action of both houses of Congress was necessary for the effectiveness of impeachments. According to Federal law 1079, the House of Representatives was to decide whether an accusation against the president was to lead to his impeachment. If so, the House should draft a libel of accusation against the president, describing his conducts and the functional crimes he committed. This accusatory libel would be sent to the Senate for trial. Senators were expected to act impartially, in judicial manner. This was true since the enactment of the previous statute, Decree 30/1892, which ordered the Senate to act as "tribunal."[32] Defending the approval of Federal Law 1079 in congress, in 1948, congressman Raul Pilla referred to the senate as a "judging trial" (*tribunal julgador*) when voting on impeachment accusations (Congresso Nacional 1948: 285 ff.).

Despite several efforts, all attempted presidential removals through impeachments in twentieth-century Brazil failed, until 1992. This led to general frustration among Brazilian scholars regarding the possibility of holding presidents accountable for their actions. Lauro Nogueira, a law professor in the state of Ceará, put things bluntly in his 1947 book: "it's true that the Constitution establishes presidential responsibility. It's also true that a law has been passed, with detailed provisions on presidential impeachments. Everyone feels, however, that it all amounts to comedy" (Nogueira 1947: 130). Raul Chaves, likewise, claimed impeachments were a trait of "ingenuity" of Latin American constitutionalism and were predestined to ever-growing irrelevance (Chaves 1960: 102).

The ineffectiveness of impeachments stems partly from the fact that until the 1990s, conflicts between presidents and other political actors in Brazil were handled in expedited and informal ways. They led to short- or long-term institutional breakdowns – temporary constitutional suspensions (as was the case in Brazil in 1955) or lasting coups (as was the case in the 1964–1985 military dictatorship).[33] Since in Brazil impeachments are restricted to very few high-ranking public officials – unlike the United States, where all civil officers are impeachable – there was no actual practice of impeachments until president Collor's case, in 1992. Only then did Brazil's legal community face the challenges of the actual practice of an impeachment trial. For the most part, the history of impeachments in twentieth-century Brazil is limited to Brazilian scholars reproducing the lessons of U.S. academics, and mourning their inefficacy among us. While specific obstacles in each case have helped shape the material concept of "high crime and misdemeanors" in U.S. impeachment law, nothing analogous helped refine Brazilian doctrine during the twentieth century.

After Brazil's re-democratization (1985) and the enactment of the current constitution (1988), this scenario changed sharply: the country entered the era of "failed presidencies," as did the rest of the continent (Hochstetler and Edwards 2009). In this period, Brazil went through two impeachments, and practice forced scholars and practitioners to reflect on the country's own challenges for its procedure. In the following section, I argue that Brazil's current design of impeachment, built after the Collor and Rousseff trials, falls short of awarding defendants with something that deserves to be called a "trial," as ordered by our constitution.

The trial of presidential impeachments: between legal and political

Brazil's 1988 constitution apparently preserved the basic logic of impeachment design: a president's removal requires accusation and conviction by a specific kind of illegality (*crimes de responsabilidade*);[34] additionally, carrying the process through requires combined action by the House of Representatives and the Senate, by a vote of two-thirds of each of the houses.[35]

Brazil's 1988 Constitution established symmetrical, though not interchangeable,[36] procedures for political accountability (through impeachments) and criminal accountability (through ordinary criminal trials) of the president. For ordinary indictable offenses, the Supreme Court has the power to try the president for crimes relating to presidential functions committed during his term in office. For impeachable offenses (*crimes de responsabilidade*), the sole power to try the president belongs to the Senate. In both cases, an "accusation,"[37] consisting of one or more imputations of violation of criminal law or the constitution, is made against the president. Both types of accusation should lead to a "trial" (*julgamento*). Trials require tribunals (STF, in ordinary indictable offenses) or another institution that can function likewise (the Senate, in case of impeachable offenses).

If the procedure carried out in the Senate is to function as a "trial" – a not a mere measure of the president's political support in Congress – it should observe certain requisites that make it substantially different from average political voting. This precaution is also mandatory according to the Brazilian Senate's house rules, that order the house function as a "judiciary body" (*órgão judiciário*) in impeachment trials.[38] It seemed that this division would hold after the 1988 constitution: in president Collor's 1992 trial, the part of the procedure that took place in the House of Representatives was defined as the *judicium accusationes*, which was not to be mixed up with the *judiciam causae* of the Senate.[39]

It would have been good if this had been the case. In the original logic of impeachment procedure, as the historical inquiry in parts 2 and 3 above has shown, the distinct roles of the two houses of Congress were crucial in its design. The Senate's role was to preserve a minimum amount of impartiality and fairness in a trial in which political tensions would always be elevated. The House of Representatives, on the other hand, would function more as a political thermometer of the accusations against the president, with the additional role of building up a trial-like accusation by the end of its performance.

These roles ought to be reflected in aspects of each house's procedural rules on the matter. The House of Representatives must work towards building an accusation against the president that is able to indicate his proven conduct and the breaches of duty that amount to impeachable offenses. That may be achieved via a committee, which should ideally be assisted by experienced trial lawyers: they know how to make a case that stands before a tribunal, building a coherent narrative supported by convincing pieces of evidence. In the United States, the final product of this work leads to the articles of impeachment. If approved in the Judiciary Committee and on the House of Representatives floor, these articles are brought to the Senate by specially designated managers that will plea for the president's conviction on all articles (Gerhardt 1996: 26–31). The Senate jumps in to hold a trial only once the accusations have been settled by the House of Representatives.

In Brazil, this clear distinction of the roles of both houses, and of the preservation of the Senate as an impartial judgment body, has been lost. Brazil's Supreme Court clung onto the literal meaning of the word "admit," in article 86 of the Constitution ("If two thirds of the House of Representatives *admit* the accusation against the President, he will be tried by [...] the Federal Senate for functional crimes") and ruled that the current constitution removed the power to accuse from the House of Representatives. In a meeting behind closed doors preparing for the Collor case, Brazil's Supreme Court held that this was the current law.[40] This interpretation was revalidated in the 2016 trial of President Dilma Rousseff (case *ADPF 378*), when the court understandably chose to follow the Collor precedent as strictly as possible.

Representatives are limited to a single vote – "yes" or "no" – to authorize an accusation by any Brazilian citizen to follow through to the Senate. It is no longer the role of the House of Representatives to make the case and build the accusation against the president. This has caused the actual content of the accusation to become rather irrelevant in impeachment procedures in the House of Representatives in Brazil, as the case against Dilma Rousseff (2016) clearly revealed: the original accusations against her were presented in three different pieces by a varying group of lawyers who accused her of impeachable offenses that ranged from supporting dictatorships in Latin America to not exercising proper control over wrongdoings in the country's national oil company.[41] The Speaker of the House of Representatives accepted only part of the accusations, in a very questionable decision that made it even harder to specify what she would be tried for.[42] In the middle of the process, a legislative court that issues recommendations on financial compliance by political agents disapproved the government's financial statements for the previous year. This gave momentum to the specific accusations of breach of financial control mechanisms. That was the accusation that eventually led to her downfall. Accusations against Mrs. Rousseff were formed in snowball fashion, increasing in size as they gained political momentum, until one of them finally stuck to her administration. An evolving economic crisis and Mrs. Rousseff's plummeting popularity helped to create the perfect storm.

In the U.S. House of Representatives procedure, the accusations may also shift. The Judicial Committee uses specific techniques to limit facts and legal issues, and the final articles may diverge from the original accusations presented to the Speaker of the House. But these shifts all occur within the House of Representatives, and are part of the accusation-building process: once articles of impeachment are defined and approved by the proper majority in the House, the accusation is fixed for the Senate trial. The House determines the scope of the Senate's work; the Senate knows precisely what to try; the president knows what to defend himself of.

In Brazil, the final terms of the accusation – i.e., that which senators will vote on – is, in practice, built during the impeachment committee phase in the Senate. It is only then that senators will go back to the original accusations presented to the House and choose, based on current political momentum, what charges might stick. By this time, however, the President will have been forced to step down: Brazil's constitution determines preventive removal from office once the case is accepted by the Senate. Therefore, in practice, all sorts of coalition rearrangements for the *de facto* new government are going on at the same time as the process reaches its closing moments.

The special impeachment committee in the Brazilian Senate has twenty-one members (out of eighty-one total senators). Its places are distributed *pro rata* in accordance with the parties' representation in the house, as with all other committees. The Brazilian Supreme Court reinforced this logic when it decided that party representations in the Senate are the relevant actors in impeachment committees.[43] Therefore, this committee functions like any other committee in Congress: senators are there conditionally and are expected to follow party guidelines. The committee reflects leadership strategies regarding the desired outcome of the case. There is no room for individual deliberations based on evidence and legal interpretation. By the time the Senate committee drafts its report, the initial accusation presented to the Speaker of the House, months before, is nothing but a distant memory. The report of the Senate committee gets all the attention in the days just before the trial takes place.

While the existence of a committee in the Senate is acceptable and even necessary, this committee should perceive its role as judicial (or quasi-judicial): describing facts and elements of evidence, as well as the relevant statutes and the key arguments of each of the contending parties. In the United States, since the impeachment of judge Harold Louderback in 1933, impeachment committees have also existed in the Senate. However, their reports are mostly factual and do not advance any suggestion regarding the guilt or innocence of the accused persons. They are limited to a "neutral statement of facts, and a summary of the evidence that the parties have introduced on the contested issues of fact" (Gerhardt 1996: 34).

In the U.S. Senate, for the trial proper, all senators take a special oath – as Governeur Morris, in the Philadelphia convention, suggested they ought to – by which they solemnly swear that "in all things appertaining to the trial of the impeachment [...] now pending," they will do "impartial justice according to the Constitution and laws."[44] In both presidential impeachments that have been tried by the U.S. Senate, the accused presidents were acquitted with votes from opposing parties: seven Republican Senators voted to acquit Andrew Johnson in 1868 (Benedict 1973: 181); in the Clinton trial, ten Republicans voted for acquittal on charges of perjury, and five on charges of obstruction of justice (Sunstein 2017: 104). Partisanship played a role, of course; but hat it been dispositive, the outcome of both cases would have been different.

In Brazil, senators of opposing parties were announcing their verdicts in the press[45] prior to Mrs. Rousseff's testimony and her lawyer's oral defense on the Senate floor. The claim was that she would be convicted in a "political trial" based on a general disapproval of her government – and therefore, the accusations and the evidence in her trial were superfluous. Parties with a history of identifiable political action upon certain principles stood entirely for or against the president. Others, with a history of support and opposition to both right- and left-wing governments, bargained their support up to the last moment. When senators allow themselves to act that way, it becomes difficult to distinguish presidential removal based on convictions for specific impeachable offenses from government rearrangements for political motives.[46]

Final remarks: the legal future of constitutional impeachments in Brazil

Presidential impeachments in Latin America have turned into a damage-control mechanism for resolving conflicts between the legislative and the executive branches. Impeachments have allowed grave impasses to be solved by changing governments without having to do away with the whole political regime (Pérez Liñàn 2007: 40–44). Nevertheless, impeachments do not acquire legitimacy simply because they are named in a country's constitution. Carefully considered logic lies behind it's the procedure, upon which its legitimacy partially depends.

The history of impeachment's institutional design reveals how impeachments balance the authority and independence of the executive branch versus the possibility of holding law-breaking presidents accountable for their gravest wrongs. This balance is key to the integrity of democratic institutions at risk. One of the cornerstones of this balance lays in the distinct roles of the House of Representatives and the Senate in the impeachment process. The House should accuse, and the Senate should try impeachments. The House might me impetuous and biased; the Senate, however, will act to cool off excesses, and guarantee the least bit of impartiality and fairness in the president's trial.

The 1988 Brazilian Constitution blurred this distinction by giving the lower house of Congress the power to merely "authorize" an impeachment process against the President. The House was left with too little, and the Senate with too much power: senators alone remove *pro tempore* the president by merely opening the case against him, and are free to use the initial accusation as raw material for the report of the Senate's impeachment committee.

There are now two impeachment precedents (Dilma Rousseff and Fernando Collor) and one STF case (ADPF 378) that uphold the interpretation of this unbalanced distribution of power between both Houses of Congress. At this point, restoring a better impeachment design requires legal and constitutional reforms that restore the lower house's sole power to accuse, and the upper houses sole power to try, impeachment accusations in the specific terms formulated by the lower house of Congress. Additionally, complex accusations should be broken down into simplified articles that give more clarity to the general public on the terms, the debates, and the evidence supporting each one of them, as jury trials do. Brazilian jurists have been too lenient with the abuse of a solemn legal ritual – a trial – as a *façade* for partisan dispute that harms credibility in both electoral democracy and the law's capacity to deliver procedural fairness in the face of intense political divisions.

Notes

1 The research that led to this chapter was partially conducted at the Center for Latin American and Latino Studies (CLALS), at the American University in Washington, DC, with funding from *Fundação de Amparo à Pesquisa do Estado de São Paulo* (FAPESP).

2 Berger (1973: 59–60), *inter alia*, singles out the accusation and trial of the Earl of Suffolk, in 1386, as the first proceeding to have the characteristics of an impeachment. This is not to say, of course, that the political significance of impeachment trials did not vary over time: while the early cases were more of a struggle between the early English Parliament and ordinary courts, modern impeachments embodied a struggle between a more independent Parliament and the Crown.

3 This was the essence of the accusation made against the Earl of Strafford, in 1642. According to parliamentary leader John Pym, Strafford had committed the "crime of subverting the laws, and introducing an arbitrary and tyrannical government," which was "contrary to the pact and covenant between the King and his people" (Berger 1973: 33). For reasons not entirely known, Parliament ceased to try the impeachment of Strafford and went for a bill of attainder. Shortly after, however, other accusations coming from Parliament were made against several royal agents (Earl of Clarendon in 1663; Earl of Danby in 1678; and Justice Scroggs in 1680, among others).

4 According to Labovitz (1978: 14–15), the Warren Hastings case led some participants of the constitutional convention, such as George Mason, to suggest that impeachments should not be limited to "treason and bribery," but should be allowed against any "attempt to subvert the Constitution." See, likewise, Berger (1973: 172) and Gerhardt (1996: 104). Hastings was accused of 22 crimes, for having submitted the authority of the General-Government of India to the mercantile interests of the East India Company, in exchange for personal gains (Volcansek 1990: 49–51).

5 U.S. Constitution art. II, § 4: "The President, Vice President and all civil Officers of the United States, shall be removed from Office on Impeachment for, and Conviction of, Treason, Bribery, or other high Crimes and Misdemeanors."

6 U.S. Constitution art. I, § 9: 8:

> No Title of Nobility shall be granted by the United States: And no Person holding any Office of Profit or Trust under them, shall, without the Consent of the Congress, accept of any present, Emolument, Office, or Title, of any kind whatever, from any King, Prince, or foreign State.

7 The delegates of the Constitutional Convention "explicitly rejected a plural executive, despite the arguments that they were creating 'the foetus of monarchy', because a single person would give the most responsibility to the office" (Staff of the Impeachment Inquiry 1974: 8).

8 U.S. Constitution, art. III, § 3, 1: "Treason against the United States, shall consist only in levying War against them, or in adhering to their Enemies, giving them Aid and Comfort."

9 As Berger (1973: 176) points out, bribery refers to the receiving of something of value as the determinant motive for the practice of an act inherent to one's public duty.

10 See Hoffer e Hull (1979: 62 ff.).

11 U.S. Constitution, art. I, § 3, 7:

> Judgment in Cases of impeachment shall not extend further than to removal from Office, and disqualification to hold and enjoy any Office of honor, Trust or Profit under the United States: but the Party convicted shall nevertheless be liable and subject to Indictment, Trial, Judgment and Punishment, according to Law.

12 Brossard (1965:128) acknowledges that punishments for impeachment are indeed *punishments*. However, they are "political penalties" that follow from a "constitutional disciplinary power" [*"poder disciplinar de natureza constitucional"*] that aims at "preserving constitutional integrity." This is a classic understanding among Brazilian jurists: Galdino Siqueira defended the same idea five decades prior to Brossard (Siqueira 1912: 4–5).

13 US Const., art. I, § 2, 5: "5: The House of Representatives shall choose their Speaker and other Officers; and shall have the sole Power of Impeachment."

14 US Const., art. I, §3, 6:

> 6: The Senate shall have the sole Power to try all Impeachments. When sitting for that Purpose, they shall be on Oath or Affirmation. When the President of the United States is tried, the Chief Justice shall preside: And no Person shall be convicted without the Concurrence of two thirds of the Members present.

15 The best work still written about the Johnson impeachment is that of Michael Les Benedict (1973). Benedict situates the two attempts to impeach Andrew Johnson within the broader scenario of the reconstruction plans after the Civil War.

16 The Political Constitution of the Empire [*Constituição Política do Império*] concentrated the executive and royal powers [*Poder Executivo, Poder Moderador*] in the Emperor. In doing so, it weakened the distinction between head of state and head of government, which was quite clear in English constitutional practice by the early nineteenth century. A clearer separation of both functions was instituted only in the so-called second reign, from 1840 on, under the rule of D. Pedro II, Brazil's second constitutional monarch. This was achieved through the creation of the office of "President of the Ministers' Council" – the equivalent of a First Minister – by Imperial Decree 523 (July 20, 1847).

17 Documents held by the National Archive in Rio de Janeiro prove the existence of several lawsuits against public agents during the second half of the nineteenth century, all of them classified under the category of *crimes de responsabilidade*. The accusations range from corruption to murder. The defendants were agents of the executive branch but also local and appellate judges.

18 Political Constitution of the Brazilian Empire, art. 37: "The House [of Representatives] has the sole power to decree accusations against Ministers of State, and Counselors of State"; and art. 47: "The Senate has the sole power to: [...] II. Acknowledge [*conhecer da*] the responsibilities of Ministers and Counselors of State."

19 "Impeachment, however, was not born with the Republic. Its first configuration among us is found in the 1824 Imperial Constitution" (Brossard 1965: 13).

20 Brossard himself acknowledges, later in his work, the limits of the analogies of the *crimes de responsabilidade* in the 1827 statute in comparison the republican impeachable offenses, despite the retention of the same name (Brossard 1965: 21–33).

21 The central debate, in later nineteenth-century Brazil, was between a broader or narrower responsibility of ministers of state for their actions regarding royal powers of the Emperor. The best example of a defender of the broader interpretation is Zacarias de Góes e Vasconcellos in his *Da Natureza e Limites do Poder Moderador* (1862); for a defender of the narrower responsibility, see Pimenta Bueno (1857: 215–216).

22 Political Constitution of the Brazilian Empire, art. 102: "The Emperor is the Chief Executive, acting through his Ministers of State."

23 Political Constitution of the Brazilian Empire, art. 98, invested in the Emperor the sole exercise of the *Poder Moderador*. Inspired by Benjamin Constant's observation of the engines of mixed government in eighteenth-century England, this power was to be invested in the Monarch, while at the same time keeping him rather distant from everyday political affairs in order to preserve his neutrality, which should be exercised only in cases of grave political conflicts. Brazil's 1824 Constitution, however, blurred that distinction by making the Emperor Head of the executive branch as well. The *Poder Moderador* allowed the Emperor to appoint senators, to sanction statutes in order to give them legal efficacy, to approve or suspend provincial statutes, to dissolve the lower house of parliament and call new elections, to suspend judges for disciplinary motives, and to grant pardons, among other powers. It was often exercised during the monarchical period.

24 Decree nº 523 de 20 de julho de 1847.

25 José Murilo de Carvalho (1993: 40–41) mentions the example of the statutes that progressively abolished slavery in Brazil to prove this point. Successive rotations between liberal and conservative cabinets promoted by the Emperor were effective in passing the necessary legislation.

26 Constitution of the United States of Brazil (1891), art. 54 and art. 57 § 2º: "Functional crimes ['*crimes de responsabilidade*'] and the process for their trial were defined in decrees approved during the first republican legislature": Decree 27, January 7, 1892; and Decree 30, January 8, 1892.

27 The justification and a summary of the parliamentary debates on the bill can be found in Barbalho (1924: 290–291).

28 For example, art. 9, 7, of Federal Law 1079/1950: "acting in a manner incompatible with the dignity, honor and respectfulness of office."

29 Brossard (1965: 141). It is worth mentioning that Brossard relies on the lessons of J. N. Pomeroy and J. Story in this passage. Pomeroy and Story, however, are obviously referring to "high crimes and misdemeanors" in the constitutional law of the United States, where – unlike in Brazil – no special statute exists to define them.

30 Among classical works, see Brossard (1965: 57–70;) for a contemporary argument, that takes into account the Dilma Rousseff precedent, see Queiroz (2017). For an opposing opinion, see Galuppo (2016: 40 ff.).

31 Among US impeachment scholars, the majority opinion is that impeachable offenses need not be indictable offenses. As Gerhardt points out, the real debate "is not whether imnpeachable offenses should be strictly limited to indictable crimes, but rather over the range of nonidictable offenses on which na impeachment may be based" (Gerhardt 1996: 103).

32 Decree 27/1892, art. 23:

> [...] the president shall write a brief report of the evidence and grounds of accusation and defense and shall ask if the defendant has committed the crime or the crimes of which he is accused, and if the *Tribunal* is to convict him to lose his office.

33 For the concepts of short- and long-term presidential breakdowns, including an analysis of Brazilian political history in the twentieth century up to 2007, see Pérez Liñàn (2007: 55–57).

34 Constitution of the Federative Republic of Brazil, art. 85:

> Those acts of the President of the Republic which attempt on the Federal Constitution and especially on the following, are functional crimes (*crimes de responsabilidade*): I – the existence of the Union; II – the free exercise of the Legislative Power, the Judicial Power, the Public Prosecution and the constitutional Powers of the units of the Federation; III – the exercise of political, individual and social rights; IV – the internal security of the country; V – probity in the administration; VI – the budgetary law; VII – compliance with the laws and with court decisions. Sole paragraph. These crimes shall be defined in a special law, which shall establish the rules of procedure and trial.

35 Id., art. 86:

> If charges against the President of the Republic are accepted by two thirds of the Chamber of Deputies, he shall be submitted to trial before the Supreme Federal Court for common criminal offenses or before the Federal Senate for functional crimes (*crimes de responsabilidade*).

36 Marcelo Galuppo understands that the authorization given for a criminal lawsuit against the president cannot be used to authorize an impeachment process and vice versa (Galuppo 2016: 133).

37 See n. 36, retro.

38 Federal Senate Resolution No. 93 (1970), articles 377 to 382, updated in accordance to the 1988 Constitution.

39 Congresso Nacional. Diário Oficial, 08 de outubro de 1992. Seção I, 14246–14247.

40 For the Brazilian Supreme Courts administrative decision, see the oral testimony of former Chief Justice Sydney Sanches, who presided over the Collor impeachment trial in the Senate (Fontainha 2015: 118–121).

41 The accusers – lawyers Hélio Bicudo and Janaína Paschoal, originally, and Miguel Reale Jr. later on – made successive accusations against Dilma Rousseff. The final accusation is available at: http://bit.ly/2z50PNx (accessed December 20, 2017).

42 For the decision of the Speaker of the House of Representatives, who accepted only partially the accusations against President Dilma Rousseff, see Câmara dos Deputados 2015. There are doubts as to whether the Speaker had powers to reject part of the accusation by himself since neither the Constitution nor any other statute authorize his doing so (Pereira 2017).

43 According to the leading opinion expressed by justice Luís Roberto Barroso in ADPF 378:

> In accordance with Congress rules, committees must be understood as being formed by parties or party blocks. These parties and blocks hold the right, as much as possible, to be proportionally represented in the committees, in accordance to the proportion of their representation in the totality of each house.

44 U.S. Senate 1986, Rule 125.2.

45 See Jereissati 2016.

46 This alert was made by the Staff of the Impeachment Inquiry for the Nixon impeachment in the House of Representatives: the purpose of impeachment is not to criminally punish an individual, but it is also not a mechanism to rearrange departments of government in a moment of severe political disorientation (Staff of the Impeachment Inquiry 1974: 16).

References

Ackerman, Bruce. *The Failure of the Founding Fathers: Jefferson, Marshall, and the Rise of Presidential Democracy.* Cambridge (MA): Belknap/Harvard, 2005.

Barbalho, João. *Constituição Federal Brasileira: Comentários. 2ª ed.* Rio de Janeiro: F. Briguiet & Cia., 1924.

Barbosa, Silvana Mota. "O Conselho de Ministros no Império do Brasil." *Locus: Revista de História 13 (1)*, 2007: 52–62.

Benedict, Michael Les. *The Impeachment and Trial of Andrew Johnson.* New York (NY): W. W. Norton & Co., 1973.

Berger, Raoul. *Impeachment: the Constitutional Problems.* Cambridge (MA): Harvard, 1973.

Brossard, Paulo. *O Impeachment.* Porto Alegre: O Globo, 1965.

Câmara dos Deputados. "Decisão da Presidência. Recebimento de denúncia de crimes de responsabilidade contra a Presidente Dilma Vana Rousseff." *Câmara dos Deputados.* 2015. www.camara.gov.br/internet/agencia/pdf/Decis%C3%A3o_sobre_impeachment_CD.pdf (accessed December 20, 2017).

Carvalho, José Murilo de. *A Construção da Ordem: A elite Política Imperial. Teatro de Sombras: A Política Imperial.* Rio de Janeiro: Civilização Brasileira, 2003.

Chaves, Raul. *Crimes de Responsabilidade.* Salvador: S. A. Artes Gráficas, 1960.

Congresso Nacional. "Discussão do PLS 22/1948." *Anais do Senado.* Brasília: Imprensa Nacional, jun. 1948.

Fontainha, Fernando de Castro, Marco Auérlio Vanucchi Leme Mattos, and Leonardo Seiichi Sasada Sato. *História oral do Supremo (1988–2013), v.5: Sydney Sanches.* Rio de Janeiro: FGV Direito Rio, 2015.

Galuppo, Marcelo Campos. *Impeachment: o que é, como se processa e por que se faz. 2ª ed.* Belo Horizonte: D'Plácido , 2016.

———. *Impeachment: o que é, como se processa, por que se faz.* Belo Horizonte: D'Plácido, 2016.

Gerhardt, Michael J. *The Federal Impeachment Process: A Constitutional and Historical Analysis.* Princeton (NJ): Princeton, 1996.

Hamilton, Alexander. "Federalist No. 65." In *The Federalist*, by George W. Carey and James McClellan. Indianapolis: Liberty Fund, 2001a: 337–341.

———. "Federalist No. 66." In *The Federalist*, by George W Carey and James McClellan. Indianapolis: Liberty Fund, 2001b: 342–346.

———. "Federalist No. 69." In *The Federalist*, by George W. Carey and James McClellan. Indianapolis: Liberty Fund, 2001c: 355–361.

Hochstetler, Kathryn, and Margaret E. Edwards. "Failed Presidencies: Identifying and Explaining a South American Anomaly." *Journal of Politics in Latin America 1 (2)*, 2009: 31–57.

Hoffer, Peter C., and Natalie E. H. Hull. "Power and Precedent in the Creation of an American Impeachment Tradition." *The William and Mary Quarterly 36 (1)*, Jan. 1979: 51–77.

Jereissati, Tasso. "A justiça do impeachment." *Folha de S. Paulo* (96), August 29, 2016: A3.

Labovitz, John R. *Presidential Impeachment*. New Haven (CT): Yale, 1978.

Madison, James. "Federalist No. 45." In *The Federalist*, by George W Carey and James McClellan, 237–242. Indianapolis: Liberty Fund, 2001.

Nogueira, Lauro. *O impeachment: especialmente no Direito brasileiro*. Fortaleza: S. E., 1947.

Pereira, Thomaz. "Quais os poderes de Eduardo Cunha no Impeachment." In *Impeachment de Dilma Rouseff: entre o Congresso e o Supremo*, by Joaquim Falcão, Diego Werneck Arguelhes and Thomaz Pereira, 206. Rio de Janeiro: FGV Direito Rio, 2017.

Pérez Liñàn, Aníbal. *Presidential Impeachment and the New Political Instability in Latin America*. Cambridge: Cambridge University Press, 2007.

Pimenta Bueno, José Antônio. *Direito Público Brazileiro e Analyse da Constituição do Império*. Rio de Janeiro: J. Villeneuve E. C., 1857.

Queiroz, Rafael Mafei Rabelo. "A natureza jurídica dos crimes de responsabilidade presidencial no Direito Brasileiro: lições a partir do caso Dilma Rousseff." *E-Pública - Revista on line de Direito Público 4 (2)*, 2017: 220–245.

Rehnquist, William H. *Grand Inquests: The Historic Impeachments of Justice Samuel Chase and President Andrew Johnson*. New York (NY): William Morrow & Co., 1992.

Siqueira, Galdino. *O impeachment, especialmente no direito brasileiro*. São Paulo: Minerva, 1912.

Staff of the Impeachment Inquiry. *Constitutional Grounds for Presidential Impeachment*. Report to the Judiciary Committee of the House of Representatives, Washington, DC: U.S. Govt. Printing Office, 1974.

Sunstein, Cass R. *Impeachment: A Citizen's Guide*. Cambridge (MA): Harvard, 2017.

U.S. Senate. "Rules of Procedure and Practice in Senate When Sitting on Impeachment Trials (Revised ed.)." Washington, DC: U.S. Govt. Printing Office, 08 15, 1986.

Vasconcellos, Zacarias de Góes e. *Da Natureza e Limites do Poder Moderador*. Rio de Janeiro: Typ. Laemmert, 1862.

Volcansek, Mary L. "British Antecedents for U.S. Impeachment Practices: Continuity and Change." *The Justice System Journal 14 (1)*, 1990: 40–62.

Washington, George. *Farewell Address, 1796*. From The Avalon Project from Yale Law School. http://avalon.law.yale.edu/18th_century/washing.asp (accessed August 13th, 2018).

Part III

History of judicial experiences

8 Exclusion and inclusion of the French law on neighboring plots of land in the civil codes of francophone Switzerland, Louisiana, and Quebec

Reflections on the relation between law and society

Asya Ostroukh

Abbreviations

C.C.C.F.: Civil Code of the Canton of Fribourg
C.C.K.S.: Civil Code of the Kingdom of Sardinia
C.C.L.C: Civil Code of Lower Canada
C.C.R.C.N: Civil Code of the Republic and the Canton of Neuchâtel
C.C.S.L.: Civil Code of the State of Louisiana
C.C.C.Vd.: Civil Code of the Canton of Vaud
C.C.C.Vs.: Civil Code of the Canton of Valais
C.N.: Code Napoléon

Introduction

It is well known that local legislators in the nineteenth century used the French Civil Code of 1804 (known historically as *Code Napoléon*) as the model for their territorial codifications while drafting the civil codes of the Swiss cantons of Vaud, Fribourg, Valais, and Neuchâtel, as well as the civil codes of Quebec and Louisiana. Sometimes, they merely reproduced corresponding provisions of the French Code.[1] It is also well known that the second book of the French Code *of Property and the Different Modifications of Ownership* was received more successfully. However, in the civil codes of the jurisdictions in question substantial differences from the French model can be found, even in the area of property law.

This chapter examines some examples of the transplantation of the French legal provisions concerning certain restrictions on the use of neighboring plots of land in Francophone Switzerland, Quebec, and Louisiana in the nineteenth century. These examples are the rules concerning common walls and ditches, plants bordering neighboring estates, the distance and the intermediate works required for certain structures on the boundaries of two plots of land, and the right of view over neighboring property. In civil law countries, such legal provisions are normally contained in the law of servitudes. More specifically, in French law, such restrictions are considered as servitudes established by law.[2]

Even though such matters may seem to be of minor importance within the scope of property law, it is exactly in this area—legal provisions concerning neighboring plots of land—where there is the highest level of deviation from the French model. The striking feature of the newly codified property law in nineteenth-century Francophone Switzerland, Quebec, and Louisiana was that the respective civil codes often incorporated not French rules but provisions of their old customary law, rules borrowed from other jurisdictions, or newly designed provisions that would better suit their societies. Those provisions are also more detailed than their French equivalents.

Every landowner will agree with the statement by Frederic Walton, the Dean of the Faculty of Law at McGill University in 1897–1915:

> Acts of trespass or supposed trespass, questions of boundaries, questions about trees which overhang boundaries, and so forth, give rise to quarrels between neighbours which are sometimes fought out in the courts with as much passion as if the interests of humanity were at stake.
>
> (Walton 1916, 102)[3]

Thus, it is not surprising that the population of the territories in question was more concerned with plants, walls, buildings, and other structures between two neighboring estates rather than general principles and definitions and classifications of property, which adhered predominantly to the French Civil Code.

During the codification process, Swiss, Quebec, and Louisiana legislators filtered the provisions of the French law through local needs, customs, geography, lifestyle, and circumstances. These decisions were not easily made.[4] In jurisdictions with records regarding the history of the debates about drafting of the civil codes, the records show how meticulously the politicians discussed at what distance should be planted different types of trees on the border of two contingent plots of land; what the time period should be that bars a neighbor's claim to cut the trees that are planted at a shorter distance from his plot than required by the law; what the distance should be between a window and the wall of the neighbor's house or the distance between the hedge and the neighboring plot; whether a neighbor is entitled to make a construction that would obstruct another neighbor's right of view or the right to receive light, and so on. Such debates challenge the opinion that transplanting or receiving legal rules is socially easy and that legal rules travel easily from one jurisdiction to another (Watson 1974, 21–30). At least in the area of law of neighborhood, local societies resisted a complete transplantation of French provisions.

Common walls and ditches

The first Swiss jurisdiction that challenged the local applicability of the French law of servitudes was the Canton of Vaud whose Civil Code was promulgated in 1821. As the first codification of civil law in Francophone Switzerland, the Civil Code of the Canton of Vaud naturally became another model (after the *Code Napoléon*) for the Civil Codes of Fribourg, Valais, and Neuchâtel. It was also used by Quebec codifiers as a secondary model for their codification.

Article 653 of the French code, concerning common walls and ditches, says:

> in towns and in the country, every wall serving for separation between buildings up to the extent of the lower building, or between yards and gardens and even between enclosures in the fields, is presumed to be common, if there be no title or mark to the contrary.[5]

The Civil Code of the Canton of Vaud substantially reproduces the rules of the French Code, but modifies them with the notions of immovable "of the same level" (*de niveau*) and "of the same nature" (*de la même nature*). Thus, article 441 of the Civil Code of the Canton of Vaud says in the first paragraph:

> in town and country, walls serving for separation between buildings up to the to the extent of the lower building, or between courts and gardens, and also between plots of land of the same nature, if these plots are of the same level, are presumed to be common, if there be no title or mark to the contrary.

The next paragraph stipulates that if two immovable properties are of the same level but not of the same nature, the wall belongs exclusively to the owner of the more valuable land, as determined by the law. The Vaud legislator also gives a few examples of this: a garden is more valuable than a hemp-field, a hemp-field is more valuable than a vine-yard, a vine-yard more valuable than a meadow, a meadow more valuable than a field, and a field more valuable than a forest. The third paragraph provides that if two properties are not of the same level, and the wall supports a higher property, then the wall is considered to belong exclusively to the owner of the supported property.

Later, these new rules of the Vaud Code were almost exactly reproduced in the Civil Code of the Canton of Fribourg of 1834–1850 (article 477) with the only exception that the hierarchy of different types of land (hemp-field, vine-yard, meadow, etc.) was slightly different.

The Civil Code of the Canton of Valais of 1843–1855 upholds the same notion of buildings of the same level from article 441 of the Vaud Code, but not buildings of the same nature. Thus, the hierarchy of lands in the codes of Vaud and Fribourg is absent from the Code of Valais, which only stipulates that if two immovable properties are of the same level, then the wall is presumed to be common (if there be no title or mark to the contrary). If the properties are not of the same level and a wall supports a higher property, then the wall is considered to belong exclusively to the owner of the land supported by the wall (article 493 C.C.C.Vs.).

Section 1 of the title on servitudes in the Valais Code – "Of common walls and ditches" – also contains provisions that are absent from the *Code Napoléon* and that are aimed at the limitation of the rights of co-owners to use common walls in a way prejudicial to other co-owners (articles 497–499 and 502 C.C.C.Vs). These provisions were entirely borrowed from the 1838 Civil Code of the Kingdom of Sardinia (articles 375, 376, and 380). In the Civil Code of the Canton of Neuchâtel of 1853–1855, the provisions concerning common walls were similar, although not identical to the French Code.

Although most provisions of the 1825 Civil Code of the State of Louisiana about common walls were similar to the French Code, some of them were not borrowed from the French model. Article 671 stipulates,

> He who first builds in the cities, towns, or suburbs of this State, in a place which is not surrounded by walls may rest one half of his wall on the land of his neighbor, provided he builds with stones or bricks at least as high as the first story, and not in frame or otherwise; and provided the whole thickness of this wall do not exceed eighteen inches, not including the plastering, which must not be more than three inches.

However, this person cannot compel his neighbor to contribute to the raising of this wall. If the neighbor is willing to contribute for his half to the building of the wall raised, then this wall becomes a common wall of the two owners. Even if the neighbor has refused to contribute to the raising of the wall, he still preserves the right of making it a wall in common by paying half of the value to the person who has made the wall (article 672). The origin of such bulky provisions that defy the clear and concise style of the French Code is unclear. Professor Yiannopoulos suggests the origin of these provisions is in the Custom of Orleans (Yiannopoulos 1975, 1253–4). However, it seems that the similarity of the codal provisions with article 236 of the Custom of Orleans is quite remote.

The provisions of the 1866 Civil Code of Lower Canada concerning common wall and ditches (articles 510–527 C.C.L.C.) reproduce the provisions of the French Code with minor modifications most of which concern distances.

Thus, in the jurisdictions studied, the French law concerning common walls was carefully revised and modified to varying degrees to make the French model more suitable to the local needs and customs.

Plants bordering neighboring land

The French Code in article 671 stipulates that the distances between plants and the neighboring plot of land should be prescribed by special regulations or by consistent and recognized usages. In the absence of such regulations and usages, the distance should be 2 meters from the separation line for trees with tall trunks (*haute tige*) and a half-meter for other trees and quickset hedges (*haie vive*). In most codes studied, this rule was modified. The provisions of article 458 of the Civil Code of the Canton of Vaud are more specific than the French law in relation to the types of trees and distances between them. Initially, the Vaud codifiers intended to include rules on distances based not only on the types of trees but also on their orientation, which were based on cantonal customs (*Code d'Aigle* and *Loix* and *Statuts de Payerne*). These rules were eventually rejected because distance for trees varied in different local customs (Guignard 1976, 93–4). Ultimately, the cantonal legislator chose a solution that considered the interests of all owners, did not significantly depart from previous law and contained more practical round figures (Guignard 1976, 96–7). Thus, article 458 prescribes distances longer than those in the French Code: the distance of 20 feet from the separation line for trees with tall trunks if they are not fruit trees, sweet chestnut or walnut trees, and 10 feet for fruit trees. In addition to the difference in distance, article 458. C.C.C.Vd. contains another rule absent from the French Code, stipulating that if two plots are separated by a stream, a road, or a path belonging to the public, the separation line is considered to pass in the middle of such stream, road, or path.

Article 459 C.C.C.Vd. reproduces the provision of article 672. C.N. that gives every neighbor a right to require that any trees and hedges, which are planted at a lesser distance, be uprooted, but the Vaud Code gives the owner of those trees or hedges a right to prove that they were planted more than ten years prior (in which case they cannot be uprooted). This new important rule was reproduced in the Civil Code of the Canton of Fribourg (article 472).

During the drafting of the Civil Code in Fribourg, local politicians meticulously debated at what distance different types of trees should be planted on the border of two contingent plots of land (the figures for the distance were borrowed from the law of the Canton of Berne, to which bilingual Fribourg had been politically and culturally close). They also discussed why espaliers are excluded from the list of such plants (article 471) (Archives de l'Etat de Fribourg, Fonds Législation et variétés. Séance du 9 avril 1829, 583). Additionally, there were debates about the time period that bars a neighbor's claim to cut the trees that are planted at a shorter distance from his plot than required by the law (article 472) and the distance between the hedge and the neighboring plot (article 501) (Archives de l'Etat de Fribourg, Fonds Législation et variétés. Séance du 16 septembre 1830, 652).

Similarly to the Canton of Fribourg, the provisions on the distance between plants and neighboring property were the subject of a heated discussion in the legislative commission of the Canton of Neuchâtel. Deputy Perrot said the distances prescribed by the French Code were less considerable, and because Neuchâtel was very small and divided, nothing could be exaggerated. Deputy Piaget responded the trees there were harmful in the same way to neighboring plots as in France, even though their country was smaller. Deputy Philippin added that the French Code reserved the question of distances for plants to local usages, and only legislated it in the absence of those usages and ancient regulations. Meanwhile, in Neuchâtel, they did not have ancient regulations or usages and needed to create new rules *(Bulletin de la discussion du Code civil de la République et canton de Neuchâtel* 1857, 369). However, Philippin was not correct in saying that there were no rules at all concerning plants in Neuchâtel. Henri-Pierre Jacottet, a famous Neuchâtel lawyer and legal scholar, indicates that the *Ordonnance des Ligues* of 1523 prescribed the distance for walnut trees, while a 1788 "Act Concerning Paths through Vines" (*Loi concernant les sentiers de vignes*) prescribed distances from vines although those provisions were clearly insufficient (Jacottet 1879, 475).

As a result of this discussion, the Neuchâtel Code incorporated rules concerning the distance between plants and neighboring property that were different from the corresponding French provisions, but that were borrowed from the Vaud Code. The first paragraph of article 522 C.C.R.C.N. reproduces the rules of the first paragraph of article 458 of the C.C.C.Vd. The legislative commission also discussed whether to include provisions on the distance at which a vine should be planted, and eventually the second paragraph of article 522 of the C.C.R.C.N. incorporated rules concerning distances for hedges and vines that were not found in either the French or the Vaud codes.

The Canton of Valais also rejected the French provisions on the distance at which trees and plants are allowed to grow near neighboring land. Article 515, which prescribes such distances, reproduces in substance Article 603 of the Civil Code of Sardinia, whereas article 8 of the "Transitional Act on the Coming into Force of the Civil Code" (Code Civil du Canton du Valais 1895, 559) prescribes that these provisions should not apply to the trees planted before January 1, 1844 (the date when the book on property entered into force) with the exception of trees planted on a common boundary (article 509 C.C.C.Vs.).

Article 516, also borrowed from the Code of Sardinia, stipulates that local usages should be observed when growing plants inside forests, on the board of canals, or along common roads and that, only in the absence of such usages, should the provisions of article 515 be applied. It is an important article, as it introduces the possibility of applying ancient customary law in Valais, which, in this particular case, overrules provisions of the Civil Code.

The Civil Code of Lower Canada, like the French Code, relegates the prescription of distances to special regulations or consistent and recognized usages, but in their absence it prescribes that distances should be determined according to the nature of the trees and their situation, so as not to injure the neighbor (article 528). The Quebec codifiers explain that such a provision complies with the Custom of Paris, which does not fix the distance for plants, making it dependent on the nature of the trees and their situation (*Civil code of Lower Canada: [reports]*, Third Report 1865, 395). Article 531 contains special rules about the trees planted on uncleared land, which is contiguous to the land in a state of cultivation, taken from s.17 of "An Act respecting Abuses Prejudicial to Agriculture" (*The Consolidated Statutes for Lower Canada* 1861, Cap. 26, s. 17).

Similarly to all four Swiss cantonal codes and the Code of Quebec, the Louisiana Civil Code amended the provisions of the French Code on the distance between plants and neighboring property. Unlike the codes of other jurisdictions that either included the distances known to their customary law, borrowed from other jurisdictions, or created from scratch, the Louisiana Code simply prohibits planting of trees that may be of any injury whatsoever to the neighbor on the boundary line separating two estates (article 687).

Thus, none of the jurisdictions in question borrowed the French provisions on the distance between plants on neighboring plots of land. Instead, each jurisdiction adopted a solution that reflected local needs.

The distance and the intermediate works required for certain structures

In the French Civil Code, if someone wanted to have a well, a water tank, a privy, a forge, an oven, a stable, a store for salt or other corrosive substances, a chimney, or a hearth near a common wall or wall belonging to his neighbor, he was obliged to leave the distance prescribed by the regulations and usages or to do the works prescribed by the same regulations and usages to avoid nuisance to the neighbor (article 674 C.N.). This provision was also modified in all the jurisdictions studied.

The Civil Code of Vaud contains specified distances for construction of a well, a water tank, a privy, a forge or an oven, without references to regulations or usages, similarly to the provisions on the distances required for planting trees on neighboring plots. No one could have a well, a water tank or a privy near the common wall or a wall belonging to his neighbor except at a distance of 6 feet, unless he erects on his land a wall or a counter-wall sufficient to prevent those constructions from damaging the neighbor (article 462). A similar rule is provided by article 463 for the construction of a forge or an oven, but the distance was reduced to 3 feet. According to article 464, someone who wishes to have a stable or a store for salt or other corrosive substances near a common wall or wall belonging to his neighbor is obliged to make on his plot of land a wall or counter-wall sufficient to avoid damage to the neighbor. Article 465 prohibits the building of a chimney or a hearth against a wall that totally belongs to a neighbor. All these rules are different from the French legislation. This set of provisions of the Vaud Civil Code was almost completely reproduced in the Civil Code of the Canton of Neuchâtel. The Civil Code of Valais copies the provisions of the Vaud Code, but complements them with one more article, stipulating that the owner of a plot cannot make on it a ditch or an aqueduct unless he reserves a distance equal to the depth of the ditch or an aqueduct from the separation line or take other necessary precautions to avoid disturbance to his neighbor (article 514).

The Fribourg Code also contains provisions different from the French model. According to article 490, no one can have a well, a water tank, or a privy, dig near a neighboring plot, wall, or building or remove earth supporting the superior plot, but on a distance required so that such structures or works do not disturb the neighbor (a decision to be determined by experts). Alternatively, one could construct on his plot a wall or a counter-wall sufficient to prevent any damage. Article 491 C.C.C.F, concerning having a stable or a store for salt or other corrosive substances, was borrowed from the Vaud Code. Article 492 C.C.C.F introduces a rule absent from both the French and the Vaud Code, according to which constructions requiring precautions against fire and those located along public roads, streets, and places are regulated by legislative acts or special regulations.

The corresponding section of the Civil Code of Louisiana is entitled "Of Cases Where it is necessary to have Double or Counter Walls" and not "Of the distance and the intermediate works required for certain structures," as it is found in the French Code. Provisions in articles 689–691 of the C.C.S.L. do not have corresponding provisions in the French Code. Article 689 declares that someone who wishes to build a chimney or hearth against a wall held in common is bound to make a double wall of brick or other proper materials 6 inches thick. Article 690 reads that someone who wishes to build an oven, a forge, or a furnace against a wall held in common is bound to leave half a foot interval and vacancy between such wall and that of his oven, forge, or furnace, and this last wall must be 1 foot thick. Article 691 provides that someone who wishes to dig a necessary or a well against a wall, whether held in common or not, is bound to build another wall 1 foot thick; when there is a well on one side and a necessary on the other, there shall be 4-foot masonry between the two, including the thickness on both sides, but between two wells a 3-foot interval is sufficient. In his book of concordances between the French Civil Code and foreign codes, Antoine Fortuné de Saint-Joseph erroneously classifies these articles of the Louisiana Code the same as articles 688–691 of the C.N. (Saint-Joseph 1856, 34). Rodolfo Batiza correctly identifies the source of these provisions as the Custom of Paris (Batiza 1971, 70).

Similarly to Louisiana, Quebec provisions on the distance and the intermediate works required for certain structures are substantially different from the corresponding section in the French Code (article 674), which the Lower Canadian codifiers found "very meagre" (*Civil code of Lower Canada: [reports]*, Third Report 1865, 397). In their reports, the Quebec codifiers recall that the provision of article 674 C.N. (that relegates the regulation of the construction of such structures to regulations and usages) was criticized during the discussion of the Code in France as it did not establish a general and uniform rule. The response to this criticism was that it was impossible to establish such a uniform rule because the same materials had not always been used in building, nor had the same principles been followed in different localities (*Civil code of Lower Canada: [reports]*, Third Report 1865, 397). The Quebec commissioners highlight the inapplicability of this discussion to Quebec's conditions:

> If that reason were valid in France, it is less so in this country, where walls are almost everywhere constructed with the same materials (stone, brick and wood.) It was perhaps necessary in France, where so many different customs and usages prevailed, to allow the subject to be regulated in the different localities, by such usages and customs; but for us the same reason

> does not exist; the Custom of Paris is the guide which has always been and must continue to be followed on this kind of servitude — it was then necessary to express its dispositions... But although guided by the Custom of Paris, the Commissioners have made to its dispositions rather serious changes considered necessary to adapt its system to our particular usages and circumstances.
>
> (*Civil code of Lower Canada: [reports]*, Third Report 1865, 397)

One of the changes to the provisions of the Custom of Paris was that the rule proposed by the commissioners applied to a common wall and a wall belonging to a neighbor, while the Custom only spoke about the common wall.

The Quebec codifiers also criticized the French Code and the Custom of Paris because they "truly indicate the works to be made and the distance to be observed in making them, but say nothing about the distance beyond which they are no longer required" (*Civil code of Lower Canada: [reports]*, Third Report 1865, 399). To fill in this gap, the commissioners introduced into the third paragraph of article 532 a rule, which was neither in the Custom of Paris nor in the French Code, that the distance beyond which counter-walls were no longer required was to be determined by regulations of municipal authorities, and in default of such regulations, by established and recognized usages, and in default of both, the distance should be 3 feet. According to the codifiers,

> The necessity of such distance varying according to places, the declivity of the ground, the nature and depth of the work, the quality of the soil and many other circumstances, it has been thought proper to leave to corporations and municipalities the power of making regulations to provide for this object and for others of the same kind, being of a local and particular character...
>
> (*Civil code of Lower Canada: [reports]*, Third Report 1865, 399)

Thus, the drafters of the Quebec Code deliberately rejected the provisions of the French Civil Code and replaced the uniform rule of the Custom of Paris by one that took into account local circumstances.

Likewise, paragraph 4 of article 532 of the C.C.L.C. that obliges the person, who wants to construct a chimney, a hearth, a stable, or a store for salt or other corrosive substances near a common wall or a wall belonging to his neighbor, or to raise the ground or heap earth against it, to build a counter-wall or other work does not provide for any specific thickness of the wall or other work as in the Custom of Paris. Instead, this article declares that the sufficiency of the wall or other work shall be determined by municipal regulations, by established and recognized usage, and, in default of regulations or usages, by the courts in each case. Thomas McCord, one of the secretaries of the Lower Canadian Codification Commission, lists article 532 among the five that changed the law of property during the codification (McCord 1880, xx).

It can be seen that, similarly to the provisions on the distances required for planting trees on neighboring plots, in all jurisdictions studied, the French rules on the distance and the intermediate works required for certain structures were substantially modified and explicated, reflecting local needs better. Relegating the determination of distances required for certain structures to experts, legislative acts, or municipal regulations (as it was done in Fribourg and Quebec), however, contributed to the process of de-codification that became endemic in civil law countries in the twentieth century.[6]

The right of view over neighboring property

The French Code in articles 676 and 677 allows an owner of a non-common wall, joining an estate of another, to make in it openings or windows with iron gratings and fixed glass (*fenêtres à fer maillé et verre dormant*) and prescribes their size, structure, and precise location. These provisions are also different from the French Code in most of the jurisdictions in question. The Code of Vaud did not retain the provision of articles 676 and 677 C.N. that speak about windows with iron gratings and fixed glass (*fenêtres à fer maillé et verre dormant*). During the discussion of this provision, the Vaud legislator rejected it on the following grounds:

> It is a complete derogation from our actual law...We could expect that, after the promulgation of the Code, a thousand of windows would be open over the possession of neighbours, and that the next month three quarters of them would be blocked by constructions.
>
> (Observations de la deuxième commission de jurisconsultes présentées au Conseil d'État le 15 janvier 1819, as cited in Guignard, 1976, 120)

It is worth noting that the provision was not retained in Fribourg, Neuchâtel, and Louisiana, and that it was substantially changed in Valais. In Quebec, it was kept with minor modifications.

The section of the Vaud Code on the right of view onto the property of a neighbor also contains a provision absent from the French Code. Article 470 of this Code provides that, if direct or oblique views were acquired by title or prescription, the neighbor (servient owner) can only build on a distance no less that 18 feet from the opposite building if the views are direct or from 6 feet if the views are oblique. Pierre-Henri Guignard believes this provision is typically local. It differs greatly from French provisions and is based on *Loix et Statuts du Pays de Vaud* of 1616 and the Custom of Grandson of 1703. In relation to the approach of the Vaud codifiers to the right of view over neighboring property, Guignard justly highlights that "while in our country the emphasis was put on the prohibition to watch the neighboring plot, in France it was aeration that was the criterion for differentiation" (Guignard 1976, 117). This clearly explains the rejection of the French rules in Vaud.

The provisions of articles 676 and 677 C.N. were not retained in the cantons of Fribourg and Neuchâtel either and were substantially changed in Valais. In the Valais code, openings or windows may not be equipped with metal bars shaped in a cross unless there is a 9-foot distance from neighboring land. This prohibition does not operate if there is a servitude in this respect or there is a path or a small street between the two properties, although the actual distance is less than 9 feet (article 521 of the C.C.C.Vs.).

Some provisions of the Neuchâtel Code concerning the right of view onto the property of a neighbor were also absent from the French model. Formulated in articles 531–533, these provisions are more restrictive than those in the French Code. Article 528 reduces the distance imposed by the French Code for having windows with direct views or prospects, balconies, or other like projections overlooking the fenced or unfenced land of the other to that of 3 feet. During the discussion of the draft of the Code, Deputy Wavre admitted that the 3-foot distance was in the ancient custom, but proposed to increase it for reasons of health, indicating that in the French Code the distance was 6 feet (article 678), while in the codes of Vaud and Fribourg it was 9 feet (articles 467 and 493, respectively). Wavre argued for keeping the 6-foot distance found in the French Code but did not receive support and the commission kept the distance found in the Custom of Neuchâtel (*Bulletin de la discussion du Code civil de la République et canton de Neuchâtel* 1857, 377–8).

The report of the Neuchâtel *Conseil d'État* says that the drafters preserved the ancient right acquired by prescription that prohibited the obstruction of lights onto the property of a neighbor by construction, but the codifiers established exact limits to this right, as this servitude had been frequently abused (*Bulletin de la discussion du Code civil de la République et canton de Neuchâtel* 1857, 42). The theoretical justification for this proposal of the *Conseil* is that servitudes, especially those acquired by prescription, are always of strict law (*droit étroit*), which means that they can neither be extended by analogy, aggravating the position of the servient land, nor to impose a new burden on it (*Bulletin de la discussion du Code civil de la République et canton de Neuchâtel 1857*, 42). As the result of such considerations, article 531 of the C.C.R.C.N. introduces the principle according to which the right of light does not give a right to have new lights or to extend existing ones. It also stipulates that this right cannot prevent the servient owner from building against the part of the wall that does not have windows, under the window (light), or even before the light (in this last case, the servient owner should leave a distance of 3 feet from each side of the light). Article 532 restricts the right of view to the window itself; there is no right to have blinds or other exterior objects protruding onto the neighboring land or to make any other projections unless such a servitude was acquired by title or prescription. In any case, article 533 proscribes oblique views to be a servitude over neighboring land. In this respect, the Neuchâtel Code is different from the French and Vaud codes that allow oblique views as servitudes but prescribe a certain distance to be respected (2 feet in article 679 C.N. and 3 feet in article 468 C.C.C.Vd.).

Meanwhile, the Louisiana codifiers copied the provisions of the French Code concerning the right of view in the Digest of Civil Laws of 1808 (articles 43 and 44, section III chapter III title IV book II), but decided to repeal them while drafting the 1825 Civil Code. They write in their commentaries:

> We have thought we ought to suppress these two articles which proved, that the owner of a wall, not held in common immediately adjoining the estate, must not make apertures or windows in the wall, but at a certain elevation and then secured by iron bars and immovable frames. We have thought it best to permit the owner to do what he pleases with his property, and to open such windows as he thinks proper in his wall, leaving to his neighbour the right of building up walls or enclosures opposite thereto.
> (*A Republication of the Project of the Civil Code of Louisiana* 1937, 73)

Such approach gives to the Louisiana law on the right of view a more liberal dimension when compared to the French Code. Instead of fixing specific rules on windows facing neighboring property, the Louisiana codifiers delegated this to the neighbors to decide among themselves, which is different not only from the French Code but also from the Code of Vaud where such right to makes windows in the wall adjoining neighboring property equipped with iron gratings and fixed glass was prohibited at all.

Besides, such an amendment to the provisions of the Digest of 1808 shows that in 1825 the Louisiana codifiers took their task of revising the Civil Code seriously enough to revise relatively minor provisions on the right of view so as to ensure that new Code properly reflects local needs, customs, and practices.

In Quebec, the French provisions were kept with minor modifications. Possibly, these provisions were based on French customs that were not relevant to other jurisdictions, except for Quebec, while the Louisiana legislator just decided to change the law in 1825. Thus, with the exception of Quebec, the civil codes of all other jurisdictions rejected the French provisions on the right of view over neighboring estate as not reflecting local law and replaced them by those that would better reflect local circumstances.

Conclusion

The four examples given in this chapter (rules on common walls and ditches, on plants bordering neighboring land, on the distance and the intermediate works required for certain structures, and on the right of view over neighboring property) demonstrate that legal rules concerning two neighboring estates vary in different jurisdictions, even if these jurisdictions may share the same legal history and may have a common textual source that inspired their legal provisions (the French Civil Code of 1804 in this case). While doing this exercise of inclusion or exclusion of the French law on neighboring plots of land into their local civil law, the legislators in all these jurisdictions were sensitive to the expectations of the society and tried to provide solutions that, hopefully, did not separate neighboring landowners and provoke conflicts between them, but rather united local communities. Quite often French provisions were rejected in favor of provisions from ancient customary law of respective territories or from civil codes of other territories (the Civil Code of the Canton of Vaud, of Berne, or of Sardinia). At times, completely new provisions had to be formulated and incorporated into a civil code. Many of these solutions are not just historical, as they became the foundation of the contemporary civil law of these jurisdictions.[7]

When the legislators in these territories rejected or amended provisions of French law, they did so because the French provisions did not match the local geography, agriculture, lifestyle, customs, and practices. This fact demonstrates that in all the jurisdictions studied the codification of the civil law was well thought-out enterprise that took into account local particularities and interests, as well as historical sources of local law. Codifiers were not afraid of rejecting certain provisions of the French law if they found them unsuitable for their society, and the French Code had always been tested against the sources of local law and other comparative sources.

Notes

1 For the influence of the French Civil Code on the codification in Francophone Switzerland, Quebec, and Louisiana see Dunand (2005), Haldy (1986), Halpérin (2003), Patry (1994), Poudret (1991), Batiza (1971), Palmer (2003), Cairns (2015), Dargo (2009), Young (1994), and Brierley (1968).

2 For more about servitudes in the French law, see Terré (2006), Mazeaud (1994), and Larroumet (2006).

3 For more about Walton and his scholarship, see Cairns (2013: 688–93).

4 See *Bulletin de la discussion du Code civil de la République et canton de Neuchâtel (1853-1855)* (1857); *Code civil du Bas Canada: [rapports] = Civil code of Lower Canada: [reports]* (1865); Archives de l'Etat de Fribourg; Archives cantonales vaudoises as cited by Guignard, *Les servitudes foncières dans le Code civil vaudois* (1976).

5 Known as "party walls" in common law jurisdictions. "Common wall" is a literal translation of *mur mitoyen*.

6 For more about the process of de-codification, see Cabrillac (2002: 114–35).

7 For instance, article 688b of the Swiss Civil Code stipulates that cantonal legislation may determine the distances that owners shall observe for their plants, depending on different types of plants and immovables. It may also oblige neighbors to tolerate branches and roots of fruit trees to advance on their properties, as well as establish or abolish the right of an owner on the fruits overhanging his plot.

References

A Republication of the Project of the Civil Code of Louisiana of 1825 (1937). New Orleans: T.J. Moran's Sons.

Archives cantonales vaudoises, Fond K VII: préparation du Code civil vaudois, Code de procédure civile, lois sur l'état civil, lois diverses as cited by Guignard (1976).

Archives de l'Etat de Fribourg, CH AEF, Fonds Législation et variétés, Code civil: 74, Vol. 1.

Batiza, Rodolfo (1971) "The Louisiana Civil Code of 1808: Its Actual Sources and Present Relevance." *Tulane Law Review* 46: 4–165.

Brierley, John E.C. (1968) "Quebec's Civil Law Codification. Viewed and Reviewed." *McGill Law Journal* 14: 521–89.

Bulletin de la discussion du Code civil de la République et canton de Neuchâtel (1853–1855) (1857). Neuchâtel: n.p.

Cabrillac, Rémy (2002) *Les Codifications*. Paris: Presses Universitaires de France.

Cairns, John W. (2013) "Watson, Walton, and the History of Legal Transplants." *Georgia Journal International and Comparative Law* 41: 637–96.

——— (2015) *Codification, Transplants and History: Law Reform in Louisiana (1808) and Quebec (1866)*. New Jersey: Clark.

Code Civil du Bas Canada: [rapports] = Civil Code of Lower Canada: [reports] (1865). Quebec: G.E. Desbarats.

Code Civil du Canton du Valais et annexes (1895). Sion: F. Aymon.

Dargo, George (2009) *Jefferson's Louisiana: Politics and the Clash of Legal Traditions (Revised edition)*. New Jersey: Clark.

Dunand, Jean-Phillippe (2005) "Le géant et les nains Le Code Napoléon comme modèle des codes civils des cantons suisses" romands." *Forum historiae juris, premiere revue electronique d'histoire du droit* www.forhistiur.de/zitat/0510dunand.htm (last visited 3 March 2018).

Guignard, Pierre-Henri (1976) *Les servitudes foncières dans le Code civil vaudois*. Yverdon: Imprimerie des Remparts.

Haldy, Jacques (1986) "Les limites du modèle français sur les codes romands en matière de succession ab intestate." In P. Caroni (ed.) *L'unification du droit prive suisse au XIXe siecle: méthodes et problèmes*, pp. 153–60. Fribourg: Éditions universitaires.

Halpérin, Jean-Louis (2003) "L'exportation en Suisse des institutions politiques et juridiques françaises." In A. Dufour, Till Hanisch &Victor Monnier (eds.) *Bonaparte, la Suisse et l'Europe*, pp. 39–52. Bruylant: Berliner Wissenschafts-Verlag & Schulthess.

Jacottet, Henri-Pierre (1879) *Le droit civil neuchâtelois. Cours professé à l'Académie de Neuchâtel*, Vol. 1, *Droit des personnes et des choses. Droit des successions*. Neuchâtel: Sandoz.

Larroumet, Christian (2006) *Droit civil. Les Biens. Droits réels principaux*, 2nd ed, Vol. 2. Paris: Economica, 471–563.

Mazeaud, Henri, Léon, Jean & Chabas, François (1994) *Leçons de droit civil*, V.2, *Biens. Droit de propriété et ses démembrements*, 8th ed. Paris: Montchrestin, 424–50.

McCord, Thomas (1880) "Synopsis of the Changes in the Law Effected by the Civil Code of Lower Canada." In *The Civil Code of Lower Canada: Together with a Synopsis of Changes in the Law, References to the Reports of the Commissioners, the Authorities as Reported by the Commissioners, a Concordance with the Code Napoléon and Code de Commerce: Special References for Notaries, Clergymen, Physicians, Merchants, Real Estate Owners, and Persons Out of Lower Canada, and a Complete Index*, pp. i–xxx. Montreal: Dawson Brothers.

Palmer, Vernon V. (2003) "The French Connection and the Spanish Perception: Historical Debates and Contemporary Evaluation of French Influence on Louisiana Civil Law." *Louisiana. Law Review* 63: 1067–126.

Patry, Robert (1994) "Rapport suisse." In *La circulation du modèle juridique français, travaux de l'association Henri Capitant*, Vol. 14, pp. 467–94. Paris: Litec.

Poudret, Jean-François (1991) "Les limites de l'influence du Code Napoléon sur les codifications romandes du XIXe siècle." *Revue historique de droit français et etranger* 69: 41–61.

Saint-Joseph, Fortuné Antoine (1856) *Concordance entre les codes civils étrangers et le Code Napoléon: deuxième édition entièrement refondue et augmentée de la concordance de la législation civile de plus de quarante pays*. Paris: Cotillon.

Terré, François & Simler, Philippe (2006) *Droit civil. Les biens*, 7th ed. Paris: Dalloz.

The Consolidated Statutes for Lower Canada (1861). Quebec: S. Derbishire and G. Desbarats.

Watson, Alan (1974) *Legal Transplants: An Approach to Comparative Law*. Edinburgh: Scottish Academic Press.

Walton, Frederick P. (1916) "Civil Codes and Their Revision. Some Suggestions for Revision of the Title "Of ownership." *Southern Law Quarterly* 1: 102.

Yiannopoulos, Athanassios N. (1975) "Common Walls, Fences, and Ditches: Louisiana and Comparative Law." *Louisiana Law Review* 35: 1253–4.

Young, Brian J. (1994) *The Politics of Codification: The Lower Canadian Civil Code of 1866*. Montreal: McGill-Queen's University Press.

9 A legal-historical chronicle of Rule-of-Law narratives in Hong Kong

Andra le Roux-Kemp

Introduction

The Rule of Law is often evoked as the foundation of modern legal systems; yet little consensus exists on its content and scope of operation. Zumbansen explains,

> [I]t conjures community as well as insists on authority and emphasizes rule-boundedness as well as promises enforceability, [but] it does not say very much outright as to its stakeholders and its constituents, those who give it legitimacy and those who are affected by it. Whose Rule of Law are we speaking of, which values are enshrined in its concrete instantiation in a particular place and time? Which processes of legitimation and execution does it require or presuppose? Which actors are considered central or peripheral to the optimal operation of the [Rule of Law]? Which norms can the [Rule of law] not do without, and what is their place in the Rule of Law's system? Does the [Rule of Law] require a hierarchy of norms, and does the concept itself allow for an identification of the values for that hierarchy?
>
> (Zumbansen 2017: 4)

This seeming existential crisis of the Rule of Law is indeed not novel (Belton 2005; Nachbar 2009). The Rule of Law has always been a composite concept, containing multiple dimensions, considered by scholars working on vastly different phenomena relating to its conceptual, theoretical, and empirical being, and utilized in equally diverse contexts and settings in achieving an array of objectives. Historical expositions on the Rule of Law exemplify what Møller and Skaaning refer to as "thin" definitions of the concept Rule of Law and what Tamanaha refers to as the "formal" version of the Rule of Law (Møller & Skaaning 2014: 16; Tamanaha 2004). "Thin," or "formal" definitions of the Rule of Law refer to those expositions that emphasize the role of the law as an instrument of government action, explain individual rights and obligations, and serve a legitimizing function of the law and legal action vis-a-vis its subjects (e.g. Rawls 1971: 51, 180, 207–208). Black's Law Dictionary contains such a "thin" or "formal" definition of the Rule of Law, which is described in terms of

> [t]he supremacy of regular as opposed to arbitrary power...the supremacy of the law...[t]he doctrine that every person is subject to the ordinary law within the jurisdiction; the equal subordination of all citizens and classes to the ordinary law of the law...[and] [t]he doctrine that general constitutional principles are the result of judicial decisions determining the rights of private individuals in the courts....
>
> (Garner 2014: 1531–1532)

"Thick" or "substantive" definitions of the Rule of Law became prevalent after World War II, when Rule of Law discourse was invoked by the international community as "a principle of desirable political (international order) ... a historical 'achievement' of Western liberalism, human rights and democracy" (Ruskola 2013: 12; Zumbansen 2017: 18). Møller and Skaaning explain that by the late 1990s, the Rule of Law had "been construed as a universal cure for almost any political, economic, or social disease" (Møller & Skaaning 2014: 2). This normative turn in the Rule of Law discourse was further perpetuated by the end of the Cold War, which provided the

> historical moment for a long-harbored normative closure: human rights could and, indeed, should not be defended, fought for and fought over in every corner of the world, now that their previous ideological ambiguity had given way to universal recognition.
>
> (Zumbansen 2017: 18)

Such "thick" or "substantive" definitions of the Rule of Law therefore go beyond the "thin" or "formal" conceptual edifice that power ought to be exercised via positive law, and rather insists on certain norms and political ideals that are assumed/suggested to be universal/inherent.

Finding a definition for the rule of law that addresses both its legalistic function and its higher pursuits remains vexing in the absence of an agreed-upon *numerus clausus* of characteristics and/or standards against which this concept should be evaluated. Perhaps easier than defining and typifying the Rule of Law may be to identify those instances where it is absent. In this regard, the Rule of Law and China have always existed in an antithetical relationship; "There is no discourse of rule-of-law that is not at the same time a discourse of legal Orientalism – a set of usually unarticulated cultural assumptions about that which is not law, and about those who do not have it" (Ruskola 2013: 4 & 10). While "the ubiquitous pressure of the multistate system"[1] that spurred the creation of the first tenets of the Rule of Law in the form of medieval constitutionalism in the West was also present in China and also produced a consolidation of the various independent or separate political units, the consequences for Rule of Law development were completely opposite (Møller & Skaaning 2014: 140). In Western Christendom in the Middle Ages, the development of the Rule of Law discourse followed a "bottom-up" approach, while the Warring States period (656 BC–221 BC) in China saw a "top-down" approach, with rulers augmenting their power using positive law as an instrument to exercise power and not as a check on the arbitrariness of power (Hui 2005; Von Falkenhausen 2006; Møller & Skaaning 2014: 140–141; Bell 2017). Thus, "the same trigger (geopolitical pressure) had a mix of almost completely parallel and almost completely opposite effects. In Warring States China and later in Russia, it produced political rationalization, including a centripetal strengthening of the state apparatus. But it did not produce any lasting sort of constitutionalism.

The aim of this chapter is not to add to what is already a rich body of literature on the legal-political development of China versus the "West" (e.g. Ruskola 2013; Zhang 2017; Smith 2018). The primary objective here is rather to steer the focus more concretely to a geopolitical zone that represents both the "East" and the "West," where the Rule of Law discourse can be observed in both its "thin" and "thick" conceptualizations. Hong Kong is a particularly interesting locus for such an investigation, as it is caught between various cultures of contestation that present dichotomies for comparison, i.e., "East" versus "West," common law versus civil law, and Western-style democracy versus the Chinese one-party socialist system.

The methodology of this chapter is premised on the notion that an exclusively legal positivist analysis of the Rule of Law precludes a proper understanding of how the law and its subjects participate in the (legal) fabrication and contestation of this concept and its discourse. Thus, in order to ensure a context-sensitive and utility-informed understanding of the progression of Rule of Law discourse in Hong Kong a survey and analysis of popular English news media referring to the concept "Rule of Law" was selected as the primary basis of this inquiry. The data collected from this survey and analysis is then used, in conjunction with more traditional legal resources and commentary, in tracing the contours of the historical progression of Rule of Law discourse in Hong Kong. It is ultimately shown that the Rule of Law is a social practice and in the context of Hong Kong, has developed as a constitutive ideology or rhetoric, used to represent a particular "way of being" in the world, and distinguishing that "way of being" from those of others. The chapter concludes with an argument in favor of a more legal-pluralist Rule of Law discourse which will better serve the legal, social, and political development of Hong Kong.

Rule of Law discourse in the Hong Kong Special Administrative Region of the People's Republic of China

The territory known as Hong Kong was acquired by the British Empire as a product of the First Anglo-Chinese War (1839–1842), also known as the "Opium War" (Tsang 2004: 3). Of this, Steve Tsang explains as follows:

> Sharing little in outlook or core values in the handling of international relations, and increasingly tangled in expanding commercial and other relations that gave rise to conflicts and misunderstandings, the British and the Chinese empires behaved like all empires had previously done. They sized

> each other up, with the more powerful one moving towards a contest for supremacy when the furtherance of its perceived interests made this desirable. The scene for a major confrontation was set.
>
> (Tsang 2004: 4–5)

With the end of the first of these wars, Hong Kong Island was ceded to the British Empire "to be possessed in perpetuity by Her Britannic Majesty, her Heirs and Successors, and to be governed by such laws and regulations as Her Majesty the Queen...shall see fit to direct" (Treaty of Nanking 1842, article III; Tsang 2004: 14 & 18). The Crown Colony of Hong Kong formally came into existence following the exchange of ratification in June 1843 (Tsang 2004: 14 & 18). This territory was later expanded upon with a small area of the peninsula of Kowloon in 1860 (Convention of Peking 1860, article VI), and with the New Territories in 1898 (Endacott 1958; Siu 1989: 391; Tsang 2004: 29 & 38).

The legal system so established in Hong Kong under British rule is a direct transplantation of British law, the contours of which have largely remained the same during the 153 years of British sovereignty to date. The political system of Hong Kong, on the other hand, can be described as a negotiated truce, the product of protracted negotiations between the People's Republic of China and Britain from September 1982 to July 1, 1997, when Hong Kong was finally retroceded back to the Chinese Empire (Tsang 2004: 18). In terms of the Sino-British Joint Declaration, which was formally signed on December 19, 1984, and ratified in May 1985, both powers agreed that Hong Kong be transferred from Britain to the PRC on July 1, 1997, that Hong Kong is a Special Administrative Region of the PRC under the slogan "one country two systems," that it enjoys a high degree of autonomy, except in foreign and defense affairs, and that the laws in force at that time in Hong Kong are to remain basically unchanged (Tsang 2004: 226). It was also agreed that Hong Kong would enjoy the free flow of capital and freely convertible currency, and that these (and other) commitments on the part of the Chinese government be pledged under a Basic Law for Hong Kong, which would remain unchanged for a period of fifty years, up to 2047 (Tsang 2004: 226).

The focus of the remainder of this Chapter is on *how* the Rule of Law discourse have been conceptualized and utilized in the Hong Kong Special Administrative Region from its recession to the PRC (July 1, 1997) to date. In order to ensure a context-sensitive and utility-informed understanding of the historical progression of Rule of Law discourse in Hong Kong, the analysis is based on a survey of popular English news media referring to the concept "Rule of Law." For this purpose, the news articles and opinion pieces published in arguably the oldest leading English newspaper in Hong Kong, the *South China Morning Post*, were surveyed. This newspaper was first published on November 6, 1903, and was known as *Nam Ching Jo Bo* (South Qing Morning Post) from its founding during the Qing dynasty until the establishment of the Republic in 1912 (Yuen 2009). The newspaper has since become a hallmark of English language news in Hong Kong, and was only briefly forced to close its doors to make way for the *Hong Kong News* during the Japanese occupation in the early 1940s (Yuen 2009).

Rule of Law discourse in Hong Kong popular English news media prior to July 1, 1997

The concept of "Rule of Law" featured in the *South China Morning Post* and its affiliated publications from 1905 to 1999 a total of 3,474 times. A survey of these newspaper articles and opinion pieces reveal an almost exclusive use of the concept "Rule of Law" in terms of its a "thin" or "formal" definition, i.e., referring to a specific rule of the law, or the law in a legalistic sense. Newspaper articles preceding and immediately after the end of World War I (from 1910 to 1919) reveal a different trend. A number of articles published towards the end of World War I used the concept Rule of Law in terms of its "thick" or more "substantive" meaning. In an article entitled "False Gods and True: 'The weightier matters of the law,'" an unknown author states "[t]he tradition of England is the rule of law. The tradition of Prussia is necessity of state. The glories of our English blood are Magna Charta and the Bill of Rights. The glories of Prussia are organizations of armies and annexations of territories" (SCMP 1916: 11). And in another article written by a French journalist on America it is stated that "...the United States proclaims the Rule of Law the judicial state permanently and definitely established between equals, respect alike for the individual personality and the collective personality" (Rodrigues 1919: 11). More specifically with regard to China, and the territory of Hong Kong/Canton, a translation of a telegram written by ten citizens to the Acting President Feng in Peking said the following about the Rule of Law in the People's Republic of China at that time:

> It is now seven years since the establishment of the Republic. Monarchical despotism has disappeared and the political conception of the people has undergone a complete change. Upon what can the foundation of the country rely if there is no rule of law? While it is recognized that law alone cannot rule without the right person to administer it, yet the administrator and the rule of law must go hand in hand and the latter must not be disregarded so as facilitate the former. Furthermore, it is highlight improper that in regard to the same law certain provisions are obeyed because they are profitable while other provisions are disregarded because they are unprofitable...The attempt is now more of pursuing self-convenience in reality under the veil of the Constitution, of concealing right and wrong in the heart while doing service to law with the lips.
>
> (SCMP 1918: 6)

These references to Rule of Law in terms of its "thick" or more "substantive" meaning remained fairly consistent for the period 1920–1929, but increased exponentially from 1930 onwards. Of the 3,428 newspaper articles, opinion pieces, and other reports that were published from 1930 to 1999 in the *South China Morning Post* and its affiliates, the concept "Rule of Law" was increasingly and almost exclusively invoked in terms of its "thick" or "substantive" meaning, and was manifestly used to juxtapose British governance and Anglo-American law against a perceived absence of any Rule of Law in China (Figure 9.1).

For example, in a 1934 reprint of an article from a British newspaper *Truth*, it was stated that

> [t]he trouble with Chinese judicature is that the notion of rule of law as understood in the West simply does not exist. Chinese Judges are looked on as servants of the executive, whose orders it is their duty to carry out, regardless of inconvenient technicalities or tight and wrong.
>
> (SCMP 1934: 15)

And in 1965 a Hong Kong barrister reportedly said that he attributed, "as [a] fundamental weakness to the rule of law in Southeast Asia, the lack of any 'rule of law' in Chinese philosophy..." (SCMP 1965: 6). Conversely, it was reported of Hong Kong in 1936 that the Governor of Hong Kong "is subject to that universal characteristic of British civic life – the rule of law" (SCMP 1936: 14). And in 1949, it was reported that the Attorney General of Hong Kong had said that the Rule of Law

> was the eternal desire of human beings to conduct themselves, their affairs and their relations with others along lines of decency and decorum and so distinguish themselves from animals. It is an instinct which has been repressed betimes by tyranny and despotism but which had nevertheless survived. Gradually it took definite shape in the civilization of the Medi-terranean countries, in the culture that was born of Jerusalem, Athens and

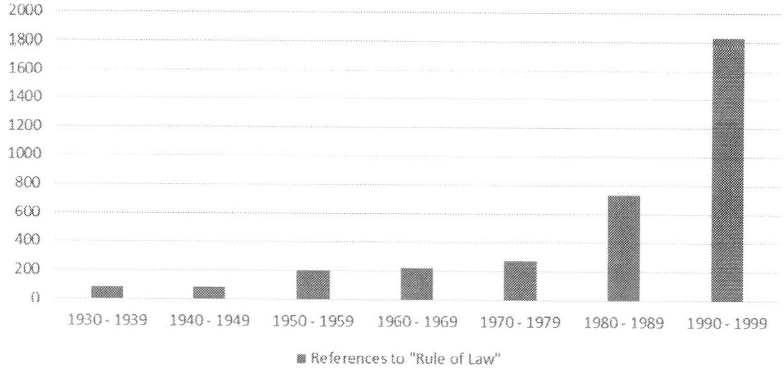

Figure 9.1 References to "Rule of Law" in the South China Morning Post and its affiliate publications, 1930–1999.

> Rome. Finally it was fixed in the mold of set rules in the conjunction of the two greatest systems: Roman Law intertwined with the rationalizing influence of Christianity. This system gradually spread over the Mediterranean lands, over Europe to Britain. ...The desire and demand for the rule of law became inherent and innate.
>
> (SCMP 1949: 4)

From the 1960s to approximately the early 1980s, the surveyed news media predominantly reported on Rule of Law matters in the international community more generally, as well as in other jurisdictions like, for example, South Africa (e.g. Uys 1972: 2; Hartman 1978: 2; Slambrouck 1984: 2). This "outward" trend in Rule of Law discourse – at least from the perspective of the Hong Kong news media – waned in the years immediately preceding and prior to the signing of the Sino-British Declaration in 1984/1985 and has remained predominantly "inward" looking ever since. Similar to much of the news media reporting on Rule of Law matters in Hong Kong today, the media in 1984/1985 reflected anxiety for the Rule of Law in Hong Kong being under threat. In a news article of 1983, Henry Litton described the Rule of Law in Hong Kong as "one aspect of the 'Hongkong miracle'" (Litton 1983: 2), bankers urged for the preservation of the Rule of Law as being "vital" to Hong Kong maintaining its economic prosperity (MacCallum 1983: 23; Yeung 1988: 2; Lococo 1995: 26), and various other stakeholders added their voice to the defiant posturing for the safekeeping of the Hong Kong Rule of Law (Gilchrist 1983: 1; Choi 1985: 13; Ing, 1991; Moir & Li 1996: 6). Indeed, news reports representing a more optimistic view of Hong Kong's future were few and far between (e.g. Barton 1987: 14; Thatcher 1992: 11).

Rule of Law discourse in Hong Kong popular news media post-handover on July 1, 1997

The relatively sudden and disproportionate increase in reporting on the Rule of Law and related matters in the news media in Hong Kong from the mid-1980s up to the years immediately after handover (July 1, 1997–December 31, 1999), and which was described above, dissipated as quickly as its onset. Over the past seventeen years (from 2000 to June 15, 2017), a total of 1,390 newspaper articles, opinion pieces, and other reports referring to the concept "rule of law," were published in the *South China Morning Post* and its affiliate media. These 1390 media reports average at about 60 to 65 per year, except for a slight increase in 2003–2005, and again in 2012–2014. These increases coincide with local political anxieties about Hong Kong's relationship with the People's Republic of China. The second increase is particularly significant and came about with the promulgation of the decision by the Chinese National People's Congress Standing Committee (NPCSC) on the model for the election of Hong Kong's Chief Executive in 2017 (Chen 2017: 65–83). Such local political events generate an anxiety about the future of Hong Kong's Rule of Law similar (but to a lesser extent) to that which prevailed in 1997 immediately prior to the handover of Hong Kong (Figure 9.2).

For example, in 2003, Elsie Leung Oi-sie, the then Secretary for Justice for the Hong Kong Special Administrative Region wrote in the *South China Morning Post* that "the rule of law is one of the strengths of Hong Kong. Allegations that there is a regression in Hong Kong's rule of law may mislead investors into believing that this is true, and hamper their willingness to invest in Hong Kong" (Leung 2003: 13). In the same year Vincent Duhamel, the then chief executive of the State Street Global Advisers Asia said that "Hong Kong...has probably one of the best rule of law histories..." (Seawright 2003: 2). It was reported that Edward Snowden chose to flee to Hong Kong due to it being "the best place in the region... [for its] strong rule of law and independent judiciary" (Chowdhury 2013: 4; Ng 2013: 4). In 2012, Cheung Simpson reported that "Mainland China has no rule of law now" and if the Hong Kong system was to be brought in line with that of China it would mean the end of the Rule of Law in Hong Kong (Cheung 2012: 3).

Thus, by 2013, a hallmark of the Rule of Law discourse in Hong Kong has become its goal of "othering" Hong Kong from the People's Republic of China; in that Hong Kong has the Rule of Law, the Rule of Law is absent in the People's Republic of China, and that this is a threat to Hong Kong. On July 1, 2007, exactly ten years after Hong Kong was receded back to the People's Republic of China Chris Patten, the last British governor, said of Hong Kong: "I think the British legacy is the rule of law, the lack of corruption, the belief in public civil service, the sense of citizenship the people have" (Patten 2007: 33). Shortly before this article appeared in the *South China Morning Post*, a senior writer for the same newspaper submitted that "[t]he whole world is marching

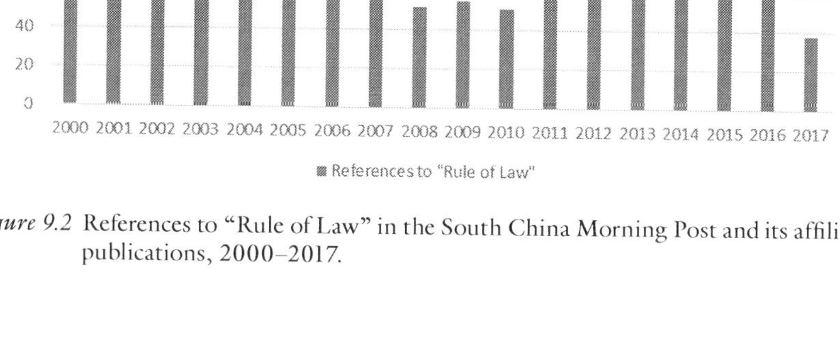

Figure 9.2 References to "Rule of Law" in the South China Morning Post and its affiliate publications, 2000–2017.

towards democracy, human rights and rule of law. I can't see the leaders of China succeeding to block the tide of democracy for long" (Lo 2007: 12). That same reporter, in 2009 stated that

> Hong Kong is one of the few decolonised places in the world where talk of Western imperialism does not automatically inflame the kind of passions it does in many developing countries. One reason is that the British undoubtedly left us – and it may be politically inconvenient to say so – better off than we would have been, left to our own devices.
>
> (Lo 2009: 14)

Another Hong Kong-based writer boldly stated that

> [o]n a larger scale, let Hong Kong be an honest broker between China and the west, emphasizing its rule of law, commitment to the environment and education and low taxes. Hong Kong's success remains the best proof that China is a responsible global citizen. Let Hong Kong tell its story....
>
> (Edith 2013: 12)

In the surveyed media for this chapter reports reflecting Chinese perspectives on Rule of Law discourse were quite uncommon for the period 1905 to approximately 2013. In a news article reporting on China's stance regarding the Rule of Law in 2001, it was stated that former Chinese leader Jiang Zemin (China's president from 1989 to 2003) said in a speech made in Hong Kong that he was determined to "rule by virtue." This pronouncement was later explained by a government official as stemming from a trip he undertook to France in the previous year, and during which scholars had told him that

> their nation was "falling apart," that it had lost direction and citizens were "feeling desperately lonely"...He said it occurred to him that it was not healthy for the country to be solely governed by law. It had to be complemented by moral values, human touch and family concerns. If all aspects of life were governed by law, there would be little need for human contact, resulting in a cold and indifferent society... "We should not repeat the mistakes made by the West. We should not lose the close ties between individuals,"...He praised collectivism, which he regarded as one of the most important features of Chinese culture. "Individualism, if expanded beyond control, is just like cancer to society. [Individualism] is not suitable for China"...
>
> (Li 2001: 8)

However, in January 2013, less than two months after Xi Jinping became party leader, it was reported that he pledged to uphold the Rule of Law and rein in abuses of power (Choi 2013: 6; SCMP 2013a: 12). Since this pronouncement in 2013, a marked increase in reports on Rule of Law discourse in China is notable (e.g. SCMP 2013b: 1; SCMP 2013c: 14).

In addition to its hallmark of "othering" Hong Kong from the People's Republic of China, Rule of Law discourse in Hong Kong is in recent years also used for another purpose: Increasingly, the Rule of Law is invoked and relied upon by local politicians and other stakeholders for the purpose of winning favor among the general public. For example, in the 2000 local elections "[t]op vote-winner in the legal subsector, leading barrister Audrey Eu Yuet-mee SC," polled 961 votes and said "Everybody says I stand for the rule of law. I think the number of votes each candidate gets probably reflects how the voters judge what you have done in the name of the rule of law" (Li 2007: 7). In 2001, both candidates for the chairmanship of the Hong Kong Bar Association said that they saw the "defending [of] the rule of law as one of their foremost duties" (Shamdasani 2001: 6), and in 2014, lawyers who initiated a vote against the then Law Society president, Ambrose Lam San-keung, criticized him for, inter alia, "a lack of comprehension of what the rule of law entails" (Lam 2014: A.4). And, in 2016 the outgoing Chief Executive, Leung Chun-ying, was accused of "obfuscating the city's rule of law with 'Chinese characteristics'" (SCMP 2016: 1).

This "re-purposing" or "multi-purposing" of Rule of Law discourse was also evident in 2012 to 2014, during the time of the so-called "Umbrella," – or "Occupy Central" movement, when thousands of Hong Kong people took to the streets in protest against "Beijing's policy towards, or restrictions on, democratisation in Hong Kong" (Chen 2017: 65–83). While those opposing the movement warned that the "youth's actions" will "damage and trample" on the Rule of Law in Hong Kong and that they should "pursue their admirable ideals through legal avenues" (But & Cheung 2013: 2; SCMP 2014: A.16), the protestors claimed that they were acting in terms of "the spirit of the rule of law" (Cheung 2013a: 5). This ultimately led to a fierce debate of what constitutes the Rule of Law. The then outgoing chairman of the Bar Association criticized the Hong Kong government for overemphasizing the obeying of the law as an element of the Rule of Law, while the Secretary for Justice stated that the Rule of Law is "the bedrock of democracy and universal suffrage," that

> '[c]onstitutional development or universal suffrage without the rule of law is no different to a house without foundations'...[and that] [t]he pursuit of universal suffrage or social justice 'cannot and should not be used' as a justification to act in the detriment of rule of law....
>
> (Lau 2015: A.1)

It is evident from the exposition above on the manner in which Rule of Law discourse in Hong Kong has been invoked in recent years that references to its "thin" or "formal" conceptualization have now completely disappeared. This is true even where reference is made to the Rule of Law in the context of a specific criminal proceeding or other judicial or legal matter (e.g. Cheung 2013b: 1). In terms of its "thick" or more "substantive" meaning, an interesting articulation about the Rule of Law can be found in a 2005 report, in which the then Chief Justice of the Hong Kong Court of Final Appeal likened the Rule of Law to a song, saying that it "survives so long as people are prepared to sing it. [And that] [i]t is hoped the people of Hong Kong will remain in good voice" (SCMP 2005: 12). In 2013, it was reported that Judge Frank Stock said in an appeal case where it was found that a witness had been coached to lie, that

> [d]isdain for the rule of law in a particular case in order to achieve what [the officers] perceive to be the "right" result is to contribute slowly but surely to the destruction of the checks and balances which have been designed over time to provide the public and individuals with a respected system of justice...The rule of law is not a sound bite.
>
> (Chiu 2013: 1)

Yet, it seems as though the Rule of Law discourse in Hong Kong has become a sound bite through which claims are made about core values that represent the "true identity" of Hong Kong and its people. The law is no longer the primary focus being served by Rule of Law discourse, it has now rather become an identity-marker and a divisive tool. Teemu Roskola explains this legal development as follows:

> when the constitutive view is extended beyond law's role in the construction of our social worlds to include its role in the construction of our *selves*, as subjects, then law does not simply mirror "our" pregiven national identity but *enacts* that identity. That is, the legal subject's consciousness is constituted in part by the categories enshrined in law. Therefore, no subject stands outside the law, and interpreting legal categories is not just something that we do to law. In the process, law also aids – and limits – us in our process of "self"-understanding.
>
> (Ruskola 2013: 38)

The Rule of Law as a constitutive ideology in Hong Kong

The identity of Hong Kong and its people are unique in the sense that more than 90 percent of its resident population are of Chinese nationality, yet, and despite Hong Kong being officially under the sovereignty of the People's Republic of China, a notable sector of the population self-identify and regard the city of Hong Kong as being different from the PRC and their fellow Chinese (Hong Kong Census and Statistics Department 2016: 7). This difference and the act of "othering" are closely connected to Hong Kong's colonial past under British rule and its lingering influence in terms of the negotiated truce of the Sino-British Joint Declaration of 1984/1985. In terms of the Rule of Law and its discourse as a legal concept, the prevalence of the British common law legal system in Hong Kong greatly contribute to this constitutive view, whereby the identity of Hong Kong and its people are both socially and legally constructed and maintained. This is because the Rule of Law is generally associated with common law systems: It has been suggested that common law systems "have a competitive edge" over civil law systems in promoting and maintaining the Rule of Law, as the English common law developed mainly to protect the property of individuals and to limit state power, while civil law systems – like that of the PRC – developed more as an instrument for the state to expand its power and to regulate its citizens (Joireman 2001: 573; Møller & Skaaning 2014: 154). Common law systems furthermore emphasize process and legal precedent which allows for a legal system that is more flexible across time and space and lawyers also have a stronger position within common law systems presenting an important alternative power to the state, thereby increasing the chances of an endogenous development of the Rule of Law (Joireman 2001: 573; Møller & Skaaning 2014: 154–155).

This view, that the Rule of Law is generally more closely associated with common law systems, is especially prevalent in the legal and popular discourse of Hong Kong. In fact, the composite and multi-dimensional characteristics of the Rule of Law are no longer reflected in Hong Kong Rule of Law discourse. It has rather developed as an essentially "Western" analytical category, a binary and moralistic divisive tool that is used to separate the Hong Kong people from that of the People's Republic of China. For example, in 2017, the Secretary for Justice stated with regard to the need for improved and closer cooperation on legal matters between the respective agencies and institutions of the People's Republic of China and the Hong Kong Special Administrative Region that

> [t]he importance of preserving the city's common law system, with its well-established principles such as judicial independence, right to a fair trial and judicial review, has long been recognized. The rule of law depends on this separate system being maintained.
>
> (SCMP 2017: 8)

This confrontational dichotomy in terms of Rule of Law discourse in Hong Kong is an example of a constitutive ideology, a rhetoric that

> simultaneously presumes and asserts a fundamental collective identity for its audience, offers a narrative that demonstrates that identity, and issues a call to act to affirm that identity... [it] warrants action in the name of that common identity and the principles for which it stands... It arises as a means to collectivisation, usually in the face of a threat that is itself presented as alien or other.
>
> (Charland 2006; Wong 2012: 12)

The Rule of Law as a constitutive ideology therefore becomes a tool that serves both a collectivizing and a separating function, a tool that presumes and asserts a particular (idealized) collective identity and by doing that, also distinguishes that identity from "the other(s)" that seemingly do not share those principles for which the collective stand. These principles are furthermore usually presented as "pointing to the given, the natural, [and] the already agreed upon," those characteristics that constitute a kind of "'unqualified human good' to which no sane person can object, whether liberal or conservative" (Ruskola 2013: 12; Zumbansen 2017: 5).

Setting aside political differences and ideals, the constitutive ideological turn of the Rule of Law discourse in Hong Kong warrants closer analysis and reflection in terms of its meaning and effect as a legal artifact. For example, while common law systems may "have a competitive edge" over civil law systems in promoting and maintaining the Rule of Law, it can hardly be inferred that the Rule of Law is absent or exist to a limited extent in countries with a civil legal system. Such a narrow conception of the Rule of Law "smacks of the dogmatism of the untraveled" (Damaška 1986: 199). Ruskola explains the prevalence of such a narrow legal conception in terms of our need to "understand ourselves legally against our ideas of others"; a practice through which we "create others as well as ourselves" and in which the law is one "resource of signification" (Ruskola 2013: 59). Yet, given that the Rule of Law has developed into a concept with a global circulation and with global cause and effect, the present confrontational constitutive ideological Rule of Law discourse in Hong Kong must be heeded against as it has the potential of discounting any diversity of opinions, cultures, and (other) legal systems. It ultimately gives way to a "slippery assertion of a value system caught up, endorsed and given validity [to] in the constitution and the execution of an institutionalised legal architecture..." (Zumbansen 2017: 5 & 3).

It is for this reason that Zumbansen advocates for a legal pluralist perspective of the Rule of Law which allows for "a complex and constantly shifting and evolving assemblage of actors, norms and processes" instead of a fixed and institutionalized divisive tool (Zumbansen 2017: 6). He describes such a legal pluralist Rule of Law as

> a living organism, pulsating and shaking, multidimensional and with sensitive nervous fibres, operating at different levels of the political, cultural and socio-economic system. [Such a legal pluralist Rule of Law seeks] to decenter the material infrastructure of the state, its institutions and processes as based on Western analytical categories, and, at least, recognise the existence of other alternatives.
>
> (Zumbansen 2017: 6–7)

The Rule of Law in the People's Republic of China offers one such alternative of which Ruskola states,

> However one defines rule-of-law, whether as an ideal type or a set of historical institutions, it seems beyond argument – tautological, in fact – that China does not have rule-of-law in the Anglo-American sense of the term. The analytical, and political, mistake is to identify rule-of-law as a universal good-in-itself that requires no justification beyond itself. Michael Dowdle

> suggests sensibly that we end our fixation with the metaphysical question that currently dominates the field of study of Chinese law: "Is there rule of law in China?" We would be better off asking: "Should there be rule of law in China as we currently conceive of that concept?" In answering the latter question, we ought to remain realistic about what law can and cannot accomplish. This is not to prejudge the question. Even if law is something less than universal and associated not only with benefits but costs as well, it may in the end still be worth those costs. Yet it is not to anyone's benefit to call universal what is particular, or costless what is not. Even freedom is not free.
> (Ruskola 2013: 58; also see Dowdle 1999: 287)

Conclusion

The Rule of Law has always been a composite concept, containing multiple dimensions, considered by scholars working on vastly different phenomena relating to its conceptual, theoretical, and empirical being, and utilized in equally diverse contexts and settings in achieving an array of objectives. In this chapter, the legalistic, formal, or "thin" conceptualization of the Rule of Law, as well as its "thick," "substantive" or normative conceptualization were considered in the context of the Hong Kong Special Administrative Region. The analysis was based on a survey of popular English news media referring to the concept "Rule of Law" and it was shown that contemporary Rule of Law discourse in Hong Kong reflects a rather careless extension of this concept's original meaning, both in terms of its "thin" and "thick" designators, and also in terms of its purpose for invocation. Contemporary Rule of Law discourse in Hong Kong is increasingly enunciated as a constitutive confrontational rhetoric that not only supposes a particular collective identity but also functions as a divisive measure that separates or "others" Hong Kong from the People's Republic of China.

It was argued that such careless "innovation" in the meaning and purpose of Rule of Law discourse is not only untrue to the original meaning and purpose of the Rule of Law, but it also holds risks in terms of the concept's future development. Burgess warns, for example, that "neglecting the origins of the various frequently cited conceptions of the Rule of Law, has the potential to result in (unintended) conceptual eugenics… [risking the import of] meaning that is fundamentally different to that [originally] intended" (Burgess 2017: 2). Møller and Skaaning, with reference to Raz, voiced the same concern referring to

> an inherent danger in choosing too thick a conception of the rule of law which not only prevents treating some of the defining attributes as potential causes or consequences of the rule of law but may also empty the concept of its distinct meaning, as to become a term which means everything and means nothing… not to mention the possible political (ab)use that an ever more elaborate augmentation of the definition may pave the way for….
> (Møller & Skaaning 2014: 26)

Of such "possible political (ab)use," Teemu Ruskola noted the "identity of the colonial and postcolonial West," as a "rhetorical achievement," in which the English-Euro-American "West" and "the other," which can broadly be defined as the Global South (including China), are continuously produced and reproduced through discourses of law (Ruskola 2013: 4–5). Ruskola explains,

> Who has law? Who gets to decide who has law? And, perhaps most importantly, what is at stake in asking the question? A statement that someone has or does not have law is not only a descriptive claim but also a normative assessment of a particular society. Inevitably, not having law implies missing something that one *should* have.
>
> (Ruskola 2013: 5)

While it is so that the law, including legal discourses like that of the Rule of Law, continue to define, in part, who and what we are as subjects, and becomes part of people's identity as people, the concept of Rule of Law as a legal artifact was never intended to be used as a divisive tool in identity politics, or for prioritizing one legal system, the common law, over that of another, i.e., civil law (Ruskola 2013: 39–40). It is submitted that rather than using Rule of Law discourse as a constitutive rhetoric in "othering" Hong Kong from the People's Republic of China, the intended and unintended universalizing narrative such rhetoric creates, should be unpacked and challenged in order to allow for Hong Kong and its peoples to reflect on their own identity, separate from the fear of risking change through the act of legal interpretation (Ruskola 2013: 59).

Note

1 Multistate systems are defined by Møller and Skaaning as systems consisting of "independent units competing within an integrated whole in the absence of a higher secular authority" (Møller & Skaaning 2014, 132 & 142). The social contexts of these various independent systems are furthermore characterized by "a multiplicity of privileged groups" who exert particular societal demands within the units of each system.

References

Barton, John. 1989. "Right to be optimistic about Hongkong's future." *South China Morning Post* (1946-current). May 6, 1989, p. 14.

Bell, Daniel A. 2017. "Comparing political values in China and the west: What can be learned and why it matters." *Annual Review of Political Science* Vol. 20: 93–110.

Belton, Rachel Kleinfeld. 2005. "Rule of law series: Competing definitions of the rule of law implications for practitioners." *Carnegie Papers: Democracy and Rule of Law Project No. 55 Carnegie Endowment for International Peace*. http://carnegieendowment.org/2005/01/21/competing-definitions-of-rule-of-law-implications-for-practitioners-pub-16405.

Burgess, Paul. 2017. "Neglecting the history of the rule of law: (Unintended) conceptual eugenics." *Hague Journal on the Rule of Law* Vol. 9, No. 2: 195–209.

But, Joshua & Cheung, Tony. 2013. "Mainland official trains sights on occupy central." *South China Morning Post*. Sep. 5, 2013, p. 2.

Charland, Maurice. 2006. "Constitutive rhetoric." In *Encyclopedia of rhetoric*, edited by Thomas O. Sloane. Oxford: Oxford University Press.

Chen, Albert H. Y. 2017. "Chapter 4: The law and politics of constitutional reform and democratization in Hong Kong." In *Law and politics of the Taiwan sunflower and Hong Kong umbrella movements*, edited by Brain C. Jones, 65–83. New York: Routledge.

Cheung, Simpson. 2012. "HK must address handover premise Former chief justice says future of 'one country, two systems' concept must be resolved long before 2047 as he defends city's rule of law." *South China Morning Post*. Nov. 9, 2012, p. 3.

Cheung, Tony. 2013a. "War of words rages over fate of the rule of law silent majority takes self-inflicted blow as it slugs it out against occupy central." *South China Morning Post*. Aug. 11, 2013, p. 5.

Cheung, Chi-Fai. 2013b. "Villagers vow to fight on despite key Legco defeat lawmakers vote down motion to keep enclave out of park; kuk chief says rule of law 'shaken.'" *South China Morning Post*. Dec. 5, 2013, p. 1.

Chiu, Austin. 2013. "Two win appeal due to witness coaching." *South China Morning Post*. Aug. 1, 2013, p. 1.

Choi, Frank. 1985. "Ad says uphold rule of law." *South China Morning Post* (1946-current). Oct. 30, 1985, p. 13.

Choi, Chi-yuk. 2013. "Xi promises to uphold constitution and rule of law." *South China Morning Post*. Feb. 25, 2013, p. 6.

Convention of Peking. 1860. www.chinaforeignrelations.net/treaty_beijing.

Chowdhury, Debasish Roy. 2013. "Democracy Hong Kong may not have universal suffrage but many states that do would kill for its institutions..." *South China Morning Post*. July 6, 2013, p. 4.

Damaška, Mirjan R. 1986. *The faces of justice and state authority: A comparative approach to the legal process*. New Haven, CT: Yale University Press.

Dowdle, Michael W. 1999. "Heretical laments: China and the fallacies of 'Rule of Law.'" *Cultural Dynamics* Vol. 11, No. 3: 287–314.

Edith, Terry. 2013. "What about the next ten years for Hong Kong?" *South China Morning Post*. May 9, 2007, p. 13.

Endacott, George Beer. 1958. *A history of Hong Kong*. Oxford: Oxford University Press.

Garner, Bryan A. 2014. *Black's law dictionary*. 10th ed., St. Paul, MN: Thomson Reuters.

Gilchrist, Jim. 1983. "HK law 'not compatible with China's.'" *South China Morning Post* (1946-current). Apr. 20, 1983, p. 1.

Hartman, Carl. 1978. "When NATO sees red." *South China Morning Post* (1946-current). Feb. 1, 1978, p. 2.

Hong Kong Census and Statistics Department. 2016. "2016 population by-census: Main report." www.bycensus2016.gov.hk/data/16bc-summary-results.pdf.

Hui, Victoria Tin-bor. 2005. *War and state formation in ancient China and early modern Europe*. Cambridge: Cambridge University Press.

Ing, Margaret. 1991. "Hongkong has been cheated over the rule of law after 1997: Viewpoint." *South China Morning Post* (1946-current). Oct. 1, 1991; p. 23.

Joireman, Sandra Fullerton. 2001. "Inherited legal systems and effective rule of law: Africa and the colonial legacy." *Journal of Modern African Studies* Vol. 29, No. 4: 571–596.

Lam, Jeffie. 2014. "Lawyers seeking to oust law society chief Ambrose Lam step up lobbying." *South China Morning Post*. July 17, 2014, p. A.4.

Lau, Stuart. 2015. "HK's legal big guns tussel over rule of law: Bar association head slams Hong Kong officials for feeding public a misleading definition, claiming there is undue emphasis on obeying." *South China Morning Post*. Jan. 13, 2015, p. A.1.

Leung, Oi-sie Elsie. 2003. "Upholding the rule of law." *South China Morning Post*. Sep. 24, 2003, p. 13.

Li, Clara. 2001. "Culture as vital as law, says Jiang aide." *South China Morning Post*. Feb. 13, 2001, p. 8.

Li, Angela. 2007. "Barrister says result a victory for rule of law." *South China Morning Post*. July, 11, 2000, p. 7.

Litton, Henry. 1983. "Chinese sovereignty and the rule of law." *South China Morning Post*. (1946-current). May 2, 1983, p. 2.

Lo, Alex. 2007. "Why 'one country, two systems' is no old hat – Capitalism is narrowing the cross-border divide." *South China Morning Post*. June 25, 2007, p. 12.

———. 2009. "Hong Kong, the post-colonial poster child?" *South China Morning Post*. Aug. 27, 2009, p. 12.

Lococo, Ed. 1995. "Rule of law vital for business." *South China Morning Post* (1946-current). Oct. 14, 1995, p. 26.

MacCallum, I.R.A. 1983. "Disappearance of the rule of law a very real prospect." *South China Morning Post* (1946-current). Sep. 23, 1983, p. 23.

Moir, Jane & Li Angela. 1996. "Human rights group foresees bleak future." *South China Morning Post* (1946-current). Dec. 5, 1996, p. 6.

Møller, Jørgen & Skaaning Svend-Erik. 2014. *The rule of law: Definitions, measures, patterns and causes*. New York, NY: Palgrave Macmillan.

Nachbar, Thomas B. 2009. "Defining the rule of law problem." *The Green Bag* Vol. 6, No. 2D: 303–318.

Ng, Joyce. 2013. "'Rule of law' behind fugitive's choice of HK legal experts say Snowden may have chosen city due to its complex extradition procedures." *South China Morning Post*. June, 11, 2013, p. 4.

Patten, Chris. 2007. "Eyewitness Chris Patten Last governor of Hong Kong." *South China Morning Post*. July 1, 2007, p. 33.

Rawls, John Bordley. 1971. *Theory of justice*. Oxford: Oxford University Press.

Rodrigues, Gustave. 1919. "French journalist on America: 'The people of action.'" *South China Morning Post* (1903–1941). Feb. 7, 1919, p. 11.

Ruskola, Teemu. 2013. *Legal orientalism China, The United States, and modern law*. Cambridge, MA: Harvard University Press.

SCMP. 1916. "False gods and true: 'The weightier matters of the law.'" *South China Morning Post* (1903–1941). Feb. 26, 1916, p. 11.

SCMP. 1918. "Chinas troubles: Canton and the fundamental law of the land, Canton, Sept. 21." *South China Morning Post* (1903–1941). Sep. 24, 1918, p. 6.

SCMP. 1934. "Chinese courts: Criticism in a London paper no rule of law London August 1." *South China Morning Post* (1903–1941). Aug. 28, 1934, p. 15.

SCMP. 1936. "Ruling the colonies: Direct and indirect methods of moulding empire units Lord Lugard as Governor." *South China Morning Post* (1903–1941). July 11, 1936, p. 14.

SCMP. 1949. "'The Rule of Law': Attorney general's talk to past students world systems." *South China Morning Post* (1946-current). Feb. 14, 1949, p. 4.

SCMP. 1965. "Rule of law cannot be achieved here, says barrister." *South China Morning Post* (1946-current). Apr. 23, 1965, p. 6.

SCMP. 2005. "A timely warning from the chief justice." *South China Morning Post*. Feb. 19, 2005, p. 12.

SCMP. 2013a. “Major advance for rule of law.” *South China Morning Post*. Jan. 9, 2013, p. 12.

SCMP. 2013b. “‘Litmus test’ for Xi Jinping’s resolve.” *South China Morning Post*. Jan, 9, 2013, p. 1.

SCMP. 2013c. “A welcome step in legal reform.” *South China Morning Post*. Nov. 29, 2013, p. 14.

SCMP. 2014. “Above all, Hong Kong society must abide by the rule of law.” *South China Morning Post*. Nov. 2, 2014, p. A.16.

SCMP. 2016. “Veteran lawyer vows competitive race for top job: Leader of ProDem21 seeking election committee seats attacks Leung Chun-ying on rule of law.” *South China Morning Post*. Nov. 23, 2016, p. 1.

SCMP. 2017. “It’s time to reconcile one country, to legal systems.” *South China Morning Post*. May 19, 2017, p. 8.

Seawright, Stephen. 2003. “Hong Kong too slow to embrace governance: Values have changed in Asia but domestic reforms are not taking place fast enough.” *South China Morning Post*. Oct. 20, 2003, p. 2.

Shamdasani, Ravina. 2001. “Bar contenders pledge to focus on the rule of law.” *South China Morning Post*. Jan. 13, 2001, p. 6.

Sino-British Joint Declaration of Beijing. 1984. www.gov.cn/english/2007-06/14/content_649468.htm.

Siu, Kwok-kin, Anthony. 1989. “The history of Hong Kong: From a village to a city.” *Journal of the Hong Kong Branch of the Royal Asiatic Society* Vol. 29: 302–375.

Slambrouck, van Paul. 1984. “Blask sash solders on in *South Africa*.” *South China Morning Post* (1946-current). Jan. 27, 1984, p. 2.

Smith, Ewan. 2018. “The rule of law doctrine of the politburo” *The China Journal* Vol. 79: 40–61.

Tamanaha, Brian Z. 2004. *On the rule of law: History, politics, theory*. New York: Cambridge University Press.

Thatcher, Margaret. 1992. “Why we are not going to let Hongkong down.” *South China Morning Post* (1946-current). Dec. 20, 1992, p. 11.

Treaty of Nanking. 1842. www.chinaforeignrelations.net/treaty_nanking.

Tsang, Steve. 2004. *A Modern History of Hong Kong*. London: I.B. Tauris & Co Ltd.

Uys, Stanley. 1972. “South African lawyers urged to end their silence.” *South China Morning Post* (1946-current). Jan. 11, 1972, p. 2.

Von Falkenhausen, Lothar. 2006. *Chinese society in the age of Confucius*. Los Angeles: University of California Press.

Wong, Eric & Chung, Tung. “Rule of law a precious commodity.” *South China Morning Post*. May 30, 2012, p. 12.

Yeung, Chris. 1988. “Rule of law crucial for Hong Kong, says banker.” *South China Morning Post* (1946-current). Jan. 20, 1988, p. 2.

Yuen, Alvin. “South China morning post history.” *South China Morning Post*. Sep. 27, 2009. http://yp.scmp.com/blog/952/south-china-morning-post-history.

Zhang, Xiaodan. 2017. “Rule of law within the Chinese party-state and its recent tendencies.” *Hague Journal on the Rule of Law* Vol. 9, No. 2: 373–400.

Zumbansen, Peer. 2017. “The rule of law, legal pluralism, and challenges to a western-centric view: Some very preliminary observations.” *King’s College London Dickson Poon School of Law, Legal Studies Research Paper Series*. Paper No. 2017-05.

10 Justice in the Ibero-American world in the Enlightenment Era

Andréa Slemian

The idea that historical processes experienced in Latin America may be compared to each other is already quite old, as is the debate over the differences between the Latin-American States and Anglo-America (a discussion that could generate several spatial histories). However, there is widespread agreement about the danger of "globalizing" theses serving as frameworks for explaining the specificities of each process. While commonalities existed, it is crucial to highlight their unique trajectories and influences so that other frameworks and totalities may be inferred from these histories.[1]

From the justice system's perspective, on which I will focus in this chapter, there is no way to deny the inheritance of a shared colonial European juridical culture in the formation of its institutions.[2] There are two reasons for this: one is structural, and the other is based on shared experiences. The former establishes that the re-creation of the Iberian justice system in America worked as an important means of domination among the inhabitants, considering the submission of many thousands of natives and Africans to forced labor. From the colonizer's perspective, the upholding of order was a requirement for maintaining the legitimacy of the colonial enterprise, *and* the reason for weaving their bonds of allegiance as vassals of the king. The latter shows how the merging of the Iberian monarchies during the sixteenth and seventeenth centuries was of fundamental importance to the institutionalization of similar forms of government (Schwartz 1979; Camarinhas 2010).

Shortly after the first reconnaissance trips of the new conquests, and the birth of awareness about a new continent, the Spanish monarchy and Portugal initiated efforts to colonize America. A papal bull of 1494, the Treaty of Tordesillas, divided the new territory between both kingdoms. Nevertheless, colonization in the Spanish and Portuguese Americas proceeded at different paces. On the one hand, the Spanish monarchy invested heavily in the occupation of select spaces beginning in the sixteenth century—financed by precious metals and economic power. On the other hand, Portugal, focused on its "pepper empire" in India, only turned its attention to its American territories with the launch of the sugar industry in the seventeenth century (Monteiro 2009; Slemian 2014). Thus, in the Spanish domains, the establishment of the institutions, which were to determine the course of the colonial administration, occurred in the early decades of the sixteenth century, as evidenced in the case of the *Audiencias* (Appeals Courts).

The *Audiencias* was fundamental to the transference and reproduction of the corporate and jurisdictional societies that were characteristic of the kingdom of Castile, and to key elements of the governance and justice system of the new lands (Brading 1984; Barrios 2004). In the sixteenth century, there were already eleven *Audiencias*, with three more installed by the late eighteenth century.[3] From the beginning, the participation of the Creoles in their posts was common, as was the practice of selling the offices (especially nonjudicial positions).[4] Since the sixteenth century, the existence of universities also played an important role in ensuring the participation of Creoles in the administration. Even if the higher education institutes were founded by religious orders, the most complete universities taught theology as well as arts, law, and medicine.[5]

In Portuguese America, the expansion of European settlements and institutions was more modest. Assigned a function comparable to that of the *Audiencias*, the Portuguese *Tribunais da Relação* initially developed at a slower pace than the Spanish *Audiencias*. The first *Tribunal da Relação* was established in Salvador, Bahia in 1609 when the two monarchies merged under Habsburg rule. The Spanish experience of governing significantly influenced the establishment of the *Tribunal* and its attributes. The *Tribunal* ceased to function in 1626, in part because of the political instability generated by Dutch advances in the region (they occupied Pernambuco, Brazil, in 1630). However, the *Tribunal* was reestablished in 1652 and was the only existing court in Portuguese America until the mid-eighteenth century. At that time, the development of South-Central Brazil, driven by the discovery of gold in the Minas Gerais region, imposed a need for higher levels of control by the monarchy. The *Tribunal da Relação*, established in Rio de Janeiro in 1755, is evidence of this additional need. Unlike in the Spanish territories, Portuguese magistrates known as *Ouvidores* (who were appointed by the crown to keep tabs on the administration of justice) ended up taking charge of complaints and appeal referrals in many parts of the colony (Wehling & Wehling 2004; Mello 2015).

Universities never existed in Portuguese America despite the massive participation of Americans in the administration. The eighteenth century was a time of higher growth of the judicial system, with wide territorial coverage (Camarinhas 2010), as immigrants arrived in far greater numbers from the Portuguese Peninsula than to the Spanish Peninsula. Furthermore, native Portuguese predominantly occupied positions in the New World, a pattern that never occurred in Spanish America.[6] Nonetheless, one must be careful with theses which uphold the idea that, in comparison with Portugal, the Spanish government ran a better-organized and more centralized administration of their American territories. As I will show here, both monarchies followed the same juridical logic that led to impasses of a similar nature.

In this context, it is worth noting the normative dispositions related to Ibero-America, including the debate about the so-called *Indian Law* [*Derecho Indiano*]; from the beginning of colonization until the end of the twentieth century, the *Indian Law* was a set of laws made specifically for the *Indias*, belatedly called *indiano*. This *Law* had two implications: first, to deny that the colonies would really be colonies since their rights were not recognized by the monarchy; second, to draw a distinction between Spanish America and Portuguese America since Portugal did not have a similar law. Recently, there has been a renewal in the historiography, including new approaches to the *Indian Law* that would consider it not as an historical reality (as one organic whole on the then-current legislation), but as a historiographical concept.[7] This change was made possible by the perception that the law was not central in the Old Regime since the rules were developed much more by the act of judging itself than by the legal codes.[8] Taking into account that the act of judging was always a decision for one specific space—a phenomenon now known as "localization of law"—a valid law was always that which could be decoded for one specific situation in this operation, both in the Peninsula and in its dominions. Following this rationale, judging and ruling were not differentiated in Spanish and Portuguese America (Agüero 2016).

Connected or integrated with the processes in Ibero-America, the comparative perspective reveals commonalties and helps identify problems within each of the specific histories.[9] In this sense, "enlightened reforms" constitute a privileged framework for the study of their interconnectedness. Even though they may take apparently disparate measures, they are remarkably close to each other procedurally, as demonstrated by their objectives and even by their reactions.

In this chapter, I raise this issue to provoke further discussion. With respect to the administration of justice in these territories, reform measures were solely aimed at maintaining the operation of the judicial apparatus without implementing any changes as a result either in the nature *or* the legislating of the government. By honing the existing devices for enhanced efficacy *and* promoting a significant expansion of the government's jurisdiction in America, the reform aimed only at maintaining order.

This dynamic may be seen in the Spanish governments of Carlos III and IV (1759–1808) and in the Portuguese governments of D. José and D. Maria (1750–1808). One may see a common process that was only possible by a long legal-policy tradition shared by Iberian monarchies which, with a jurisdictional, corporative, and catholic character, impose some limits on the achievement of the reformist projects looking for a "rational" and more effective implementation of justice.[10] Applying what José Reinaldo de Lima Lopes said about Brazil to Spanish America, this spirit of "reform," as seen from the point of view of the law, made its presence felt through and after the independence revolutions. Although they shared commonalities, they also diverged in their application of justice (Lopes 2013).

The *Audiencias* provide an adequate point of departure for understanding what was at stake. Created with the purpose of preserving order, the *Audiencias* were typical entities in a world where the administration of justice was viewed as an aspect of governance. Contributing to this view was the fact that these courts represented the king; they acted in his name. In this regime, the dispensation of justice was the main form of exerting royal power. Appellate judges and governors sat side by side. In addition to performing the function of an appellate court, the *Audiencias* also filed requests, complaints, and petitions about a wide range of governmental matters. They also ruled on these matters. These activities, separated into the administrative and juridical fields in modern nations, were so enmeshed that jurisdictional conflicts over who had the power to decide on what cases were a constant occurrence. There was also the added complexity implicit in the provisions that allowed parties to challenge political or administrative actions, as long as the challenging party stated that their privileges had been infringed upon. The *Tribunais da Relação* in Portuguese America followed this model where governing and judging were tightly bound to each other (Garriga 2004; Wehling & Wehling 2004; Slemian 2014).

One of the distinguishing characteristics of this society, known as the *Ancien Régime*, was the multiple forms of judicial appeals, a feature that harkened back to a widespread procedural tradition rooted in canon law.[11] In addition to the ordinary judicial appeals, there were extraordinary ones addressed directly to the king, as well as extrajudicial pathways (petitions) for filing complaints against an authority or government office.[12] In comparison to the Spanish, the Portuguese were more generous towards ordinary appeals. Beyond the *apelações*, which involved an appeal to a superior authority in the search for legal support and reparations, and the *embargos*, which were means to appeal against the judge who meted out the sentence, there were also the *agravos*, a Portuguese invention for cases in which no appeal was possible, even in the face of an interlocutory or temporary sentence. Given that the appeal, with its exact rules, is the most formalized of recourses, the use of another form of recourse when its formalities are disregarded goes a long way towards understanding how that world functioned. Perhaps this was an excellent fit given the vast expanses of lands in America, as it provided for the adaptation of the rules as a way to facilitate the acceptance of the king's justice. After all, to give vassals access to the king's court was one of the few available means to keep them loyal and motivated to act in the name of the monarchy (Azevedo 1976; Tucci & Azevedo 2009; Hespanha 2015).

Thus, the "enlightened reforms," far from forsaking this model for the administration of justice, instead proposed solutions meant to contribute to greater efficacy.[13] For this reason, trying to understand the judicial system within the parameters of an increasingly centralizing force is problematic, despite the proposed ways of increasing the populational density of the territory and the number of agents involved in the process. In fact, the "enlightened reforms" focused mostly on repressing deviant conduct, quelling corrupt practices, and putting an end to lengthy court procedures and sluggish decision-making processes.

These aims were quite evident in the case of the enlightened reform in Spain. Some measures would even be taken in the aftermath of *visits* made in the name of the king by authorities—a mechanism used to keep tabs on the activities of the agents when faced with some devastating petition about the absence of justice drafted well-within the enlightened parameters of the times. Among these measures, the one that yielded the greater impact was the crown's policy to curtail the participation of the *creollos* in the government system. So as to give an idea of the dimensions of this issue, one must bear in mind that the *Audiencias* were mostly staffed by these selfsame *creollos*; whether on account of their lineage as the descendants of the Spanish settlers in America and the existence of local universities (as mentioned above), or as a result of the sale of positions, a common practice in the Spanish monarchy relevant to the exercise of a wide variety of offices, and not only judgeships. The fact remains, however, that it was at the time of the enlightened reforms that these sale practices were forbidden both in Spain and its colonies. With respect to the *Audiencias*, the preference for peninsulars, or for *creollos* from other provinces, was blatant, leading the local persons to express their displeasure in very forceful ways. The locals alleged that they were entitled to hold those positions and offices by way of acquired rights (Burkholder 1972; Campbel 2010; Garriga 2014). For this reason, it made sense to politicize the crown's actions to achieve control of these positions in Spanish America.

Taking this action as a basis for comparison, it may be noted that nearly the opposite scenario occurred in Portuguese America. As mentioned, native Portuguese not only emigrated in much greater numbers than the native Spanish but also held, in their majority, a much higher percentage of the positions and offices in comparison with Spanish America. The fact that there was only one university in Coimbra, Portugal, made it more difficult for Americans to obtain these positions. In the case of the *ouvidores*, for instance, the vast majority were from Portugal. It is only in the eighteenth century that historians observe a marked growth in the number of professional judges in the Portuguese territory—a time in which this situation changes with the inauguration of the *Tribunal da Relação* in Rio de Janeiro. This opened the way for locally born descendants of settlers to occupy most of the positions and offices, especially given the increased number of American students who were graduating from the University of Coimbra. In this sense, one could even claim that the Portuguese crown was following the example set by Spain (except for the temporal difference) (Wehling & Wehling 2004; Camarinhas 2010).

Reforms in Spain's colonial possessions also implied an expanded jurisdiction over their territories when three new *Audiencias* were inaugurated. Above all, this was due to an observed effort to reduce the judges' scope by curtailing the extent of their interference in governmental matters. Evidence of that may be observed in the creation of the regime of Hispano-American intendants who were agents with the power to govern over matters under their charge without having to seek the mediation of a court of law. These agents were especially prevalent in cases dealing with the administration of business concerning the economy of the colonial territories, most evidently in smuggling cases. In the eighteenth century, the policy of the Iberian monarchies was to increase their ability to compete in an increasingly competitive international market (Pietschmann 1996; Diego-Fernández, Gutiérrez, Arrioja 2014). The Portuguese availed themselves of a similar logic (although not as intense) as their Iberian neighbors and created *intendencias* in strategic fields such as gold and diamonds. Though it is outside the scope of this paper to evaluate the efficiency of these reforms, the fact remains that the measures led to an increased potential for conflict between the authorities concerned with the administration of the territories, for the reasons mentioned above.[14]

The Iberian monarchies implemented distinct measures to evolve their judicial systems beyond medieval traditions and practices instilled in law school curricula and a system of unchecked magistrates who indulged in abusive and corrupt practices (Araújo 2002; Marcos 2006). Portugal trended towards checking judicial powers, as noted in the emblematic approval of the measure that came to be known as the *Boa Razão* Act. The fact that the Spanish monarchy did not come up with any similar action is noteworthy.

The *Boa Razão* Act reflected the zeitgeist, as it stated the need to fight abusive interpretations that went against the "majesty of the laws" and the good standing of the magistrates. It proposed reducing medieval scholarship (particularly the work of Accursio and Bártolo) and Roman and Canon laws. These were labeled as archaic practices underpinned by the ancient tradition of *interpretatio* in the name of the laws and customs of "enlightened and polite nations" (*usus modernus pandectarum*) (Hespanha 1998; Wehling & Wehling 2012). This practice enabled the practice of Portuguese jurists considering anything filtered by reason as a matter of law, such as using foreign sources when nothing relevant could be found in Portuguese. The *Boa Razão* Act refuted this practice and expressly declared that all sentences had to state the motives (or rationale) of the ruling or judgment (Slemian 2017).

Although this measure contributed to the expansion of the sources of law, I would like to focus on its motives. The conclusion that this rationale could be seen as publicizing the reasons why a particular decision was reached may be misguided. The measure ratified an already existing Portuguese practice that explained the rationale used by magistrates to make decisions in appellate cases. Its practice brought together decisions made in the Portuguese world. Under the form of a unitary monarchy, the Portuguese government employed its jurisprudence as a way of imparting a measure of cohesion for diverse territories under the rule of a single monarch.

Nothing akin to the *Boa Razão* Act ever applied in the territories of the Spanish monarchy, even though the practice of reasoning (motives) was used in some kingdoms such as Catalonia. Even the effort to standardize judicial sentences implemented in Portugal in the same period by means of the decisions (*Assentos*) made by the higher royal court was nothing compared to the *Boa Razão* reforms (Garriga & Lorente 1997). Nonetheless, it should be noted that the Spanish crown had a composite character given the merging of two kingdoms known their distinct laws, including in America. The resulting formation was a complex compilation of laws that were much more systematized in Portugal due to the *Ordenações Filipinas*.

When focusing on the reforms as a whole, it can be observed that the two Iberian monarchies agreed upon the juridical logic of their territorial possessions. Though Portugal's stance was to defend the unity of the monarchy, it felt compelled to prize the actual colonizers of its territories. By contrast, when faced with negative evaluations of the juridical system in place, Spain reacted by reducing the power of the Creoles although it recognized the privileges of each of its viceroyalties.

In conclusion, the period of enlightened reforms allows us to test a perspective of connections or integration of judicial processes in Ibero-America beyond simply offering a comparative perspective. First, the new policies did not drastically change the logic of the justice system although these processes reformed what was already in place in the territory. Second, the measures of both colonial powers responded to the specific needs of their territories despite being evidently different. Finally, their processes were based on a common juridical tradition of a jurisdictional, corporate, and Catholic character—a tradition which allowed the Americans to also distinguish themselves. These comparisons allow us to understand the reform moment, and understand why, decades later, many would once again welcome the same tradition when facing the threat of disorder implicit in independence movements.

Notes

1 For decades, the attempt to make a comparative history of colonial Latin America has provoked discussion among scholars (see Hanke (1964), Genovese (1970), Graham, and Smith (1974)). Of the studies that intend to understand it as integrated or connected, I highlight Gruzinski (2001). In recent years, the Atlantic perspective has been quite productive for this comparative effort, see, e.g., Bailyn, Denault (2009); Greene, Morgan (2009), and Games (2008).

2 On the understanding of the juridical categories, especially in the Iberian spaces, see Garriga (2006), Hespanha (1994), Clavero (2012), Garavaglia, Schaub (2005). Good examples of operation in America are: Agüero (2008), Cardim (2008).

3 They were: Santo Domingo (1526), Nueva España (1527), Panamá (1538, restored in 1563), Guatemala (1542, restored in 1568), Lima (1542), Santa Fé (1547), Nueva Galicia (1548), Charcas (1555–1561), Quito (1563, restored in 1720), Chile (1567, restored in 1605–1609), Manila (1583, restored in 1595), Buenos Aires (1661, restored in 1782), Cuzco (1787) and Caracas (1786). See: Garriga (2009: 236).

4 For a current discussion on the issue of venality, and a comparison between the Americas, see Stumpf & Chaturvedula (2012).

5 The first College was established in Santo Domingo in 1538; in 1551, the University of San Marcos was established in Lima, and in 1553 the Real y Pontificia Universidad de México was established. Subsequently, other universities were founded in Guatemala, New Granada, Cordoba, La Plata, Cuzco, Santiago del Chile, and Quito. See Lafaye(2008).

6 As highlighted by Monteiro (2009), the analysis of the trajectories of Iberian elites to America explains why a correlated identity of *creollo* never existed with the same significance in Portuguese colonies.

7 For an updated discussion, see the latest acts of Congress of the subject: Duve (2017), especially Antonio Hespanha, "O 'direito de Índias' no contexto da historiografia das colonizações ibéricas" (43–83), and Carlo Garriga, "De qué hablamos cuando hablamos de Derecho Indiano?" (223–248). Also see García Pérez (2015).

8 For an interpretation on the subject, specifically for America, see Tau Anzoátegui (1992).

9 See Pimenta (2007) for a thought-provoking analysis of the integrated experiences of the Hispanic and Portuguese although for a later period.

10 This discussion incorporates several ideas outlined by Garriga & Slemian (2013).
11 A fundamental reference for the subject remains Tarello (1976). See also Hespanha (1993), Paz Alonso (2008), and Kagan (1981).
12 A helpful discussion of efficiency in the Ibero-American word may be found in Rojas (2007).
13 There is a large bibliography on this subject including the work of Brading (1984); Lynch (1996); Elliot (2006); Paquette (2009); Ruiz Torres (2011); Garriga (2013); Slemian (2014).
14 For one example, see Chaves (2013).

References

Agüero, Alejandro. "Local law and localization of Law. Hispanic legal tradition and colonial culture (16th–18th)." In *Spatial and Temporal Dimensions for Legal History. Research Experiences and Itineraries*, edited by Massimo Meccarelli and María Julia Solla, 101–129. Berlin: Max Planck Institute, 2016.

———. *Castigar* y perdonar *cuando conviene a la República. La justicia penal de Córdoba del Tucumán, siglos XVII y XVIII*. Madrid: Centro de Estudios Políticos y Constitucionales, 2008.

Anzoátegui, Victor Tau. *Casuismo y Sistema*. Buenos Aires: Instituto de Investigaciones de Historia del Derecho, 1992.

Araújo, Ana Cristina. *O Marquês de Pombal e a Universidade*. Coimbra: Imprensa da Universidade, 2002.

Azevedo, Luiz Carlos. *Origem e introdução da apelação no direito lusitano*. São Paulo: FIEO, 1976.

Bailyn, Bernard and Denault, Patricia, eds. *Soundings in Atlantic History: Latent Structures and Intellectual Currents, 1500–1830*. Cambridge: Harvard University Press, 2009.

Barrios, Feliciano, ed. *El gobierno de un mundo. Virreinatos y Audiencias en la América Hispánica*. Cuenca: Ediciones de la Universidad de Castilla-La Mancha, 2004.

Brading, David. "La España de los Borbones y su imperio americano." In *Historia de América Latina. América Latina colonial: Europa y América en los siglos XVI, XVII y XVIII*, edited by Leslie Bethell, 85–122. Barcelona: Critica, 1984.

Burkholder, Mark. "From creole to *peninsular*: the transformation of the Audiencia of Lima." *Hispanic American Historical Review*, vol. 52, no. 3 (1972): 395–415.

Camarinhas, Nuno. *Juízes e administraçao da justiça no Antigo Regime. Portugal e o império colonial, séculos XVII e XVIII*. Lisboa: Fundação Calouste Gulbenkian, 2010.

Campbel, Leon G. "A colonial establishment: creole domination of the Audiencia of Lima during the late Eighteenth Century." *Hispanic American Historical Review*, vol. 52, no. 1 (2010): 1–25.

Cardim, Pedro. "La jurisdicción real y su afirmación en la corona portuguesa y sus territorios ultramarinos (siglos XVI–XVIII): reflexiones sobre la historiografía." In *De Re Publica Hispaniae. Una vindicación de la cultura política en los reinos ibéricos en la primera modernidad*, edited by Francisco Aranda Pérez and José Damião Rodrigues, 349–388. Madrid: Silex, 2008.

Chaves, Claudia. "A administração fazendária na América portuguesa: a Junta da Real Fazenda e a política fiscal ultramarina nas Minas Gerais." *Almanack*, no. 5 (2013): 81–96. Accessed December 26, 2013. http://www.almanack.unifesp.br/index.php/almanack/article/viewFile/918/pdf.

Clavero, Bartolomé. "Gracia y derecho entre localización, recepción y globalización (lectura coral de *Las Vísperas Constitucionales* de António Hespanha)." *Quaderni fiorentini per la storia del pensiero giuridico moderno*, vol. 41, no. 1 (2012): 675–763.

Diego-Fernández, Rafael, Gutiérrez Lorenzo, María Pilar, and Arrioja Díaz, Luis, eds. *De reinos y subdelegaciones. Nuevos escenarios para un nuevo pedido en América borbónica*. México: El Colegio de Michoacán- Universidad de Guadalajara-El Colegio Mexiquense-Universidad Autónoma de Zacatecas, 2014.

Duve, Thomas, ed. *Actas del XIX Congreso del Instituto Internacional de Historia del Derecho Indiano*. Madrid: Dykinson, 2017.

Elliot, John. *Imperios del mundo atlántico. España y Gran Bretaña en América, 1492–1830*. Madrid: Taurus, 2006.

Games, Alison. *The Web of Empire: English Cosmopolitans in an Age of Expansion, 1560–1660*. Oxford: Oxford University Press, 2008.

Garavaglia, Juan Carlos and Schaub, Jean-Frédéric, eds. *Lois, justice, coutume. Amérique et Europe latines (16e–19e)*. Paris: École des Hautes Études en Sciences Sociales, 2005.

García Pérez, Rafael. "Revisiting the America's colonial status under the Spanish monarchy." In *New Horizons in Spanish Colonial Law*, edited by Thomas Duve and Heikki Pihlajamäki, 29–124. Berlin: Max Planck Institute, 2015.

Garriga, Carlos. "La politización de *la América* criolla (En torno a la Representación mexicana de 1771)." *Actas del XVIII Congreso del Instituto Internacional de Historia del Derecho Indiano*. Cordoba: Universidad Nacional de Córdoba, vol. 2 (2014): 1423–1453.

———. "Os limites do reformismo bourbônico: a propósito da administração da justiça na América espanhola." *Almanack*, no. 6 (2013): 38–60.

———. "Concepción y aparatos de la justicia: las Reales Audiencias de las Indias." *Cadernos de História* (Academia Nacional de Derecho y Ciencias Sociales de Córdoba), no. 19, 2009.

———. "Justicia animada: dispositivos de la justicia en la monarquía católica". In *De justicia de jueces a justicia de leyes: hacia la España de 1870*, edited by Marta Lorente, 61–104. Madrid: Consejo General del Poder Judicial, 2006.

———. "Las Audiencias: la justicia y el gobierno de Indias." In *El gobierno de un mundo. Virreinatos y Audiencias en la América Hispánica*, edited by Feliciano Barrios, 711–793. Cuenca: Ediciones de la Universidad de Castilla-La Mancha, 2004.

——— and Slemian, Andréa. "'Em trajes brasileiros': justiça e constituição na América ibérica (c.1750–1850)." *Revista de História*, no. 169 (julho-dezembro) (2013): 181–221. Accessed on January 24, 2018. http://www.scielo.br/scielo.php?pid=S0034-83092013000200181&script=sci_abstract&tlng=en.

——— and Lorente, Marta. "El juez y la ley: la motivación de las sentencias (Castilla, 1489-España, 1855)." *Anuario de la Facultad de Derecho de la Universidad Autónoma de Madrid*, (1997): 97–142.

Genovese, Eugene. "Comparative focus in Latin America history." *Journal of Inter-American Affairs*, vol. 12, no. 3 (1970): 317–327.

Graham, Richard and Smith, Peter, eds. *New Approaches to Latin American History*. Austin: University of Texas Press, 1974.

Greene, Jack and Morgan, Phillip, eds. *Atlantic History: A Critical Appraisal*. Oxford: Oxford University Press, 2009.

Gruzinski, Serge. "Les mondes mêlés de la Monarchie catholique et autres 'connected histories." *Annales HSS*, vol. 1 (janvier-février) (2001): 85–117.

Hanke, Lewis, ed. *Do the Americas Have a Common History?* New York: Knopf, 1964.

Hespanha, Antonio M. *Como os juristas viam o mundo. 1550–1750. Direitos, estados, pessoas, coisas, contratos, ações e crimes*. Lisboa: Create Space Independent Publishing Platform, 2015.

———. *Panorama histórico da cultura jurídica europeia*. Mem Martins: Publicações Europa-América, 1998.

———. *As vésperas do Leviathan. Instituições e poder político. Portugal séc. XVII*. Coimbra: Almedina, 1994.

———. *La gracia del derecho: economía de la cultura en la Edad Moderna*. Madrid: Centro de Estudios Constitucionales, 1993.

Kagan, Richard. *Lawsuits and Litigants in Castile, 1500–1700*. Chapel Hill: University of North Carolina Press, 1981.

Lafaye, Jacques. "Literature and intellectual life in colonial Spanish America." In *The Cambridge History of Latin America*, edited by Leslie Bethell, 661–704. Cambridge: Cambridge University Press, 2008.

Lopes, José Reinaldo de Lima. "Iluminismo e jusnaturalismo no ideário dos juristas da primeira metade do século XIX." In *Brasil. Formação do Estado e da nação*, edited by István Jancsó, 195–218. São Paulo-Ijuí: Hucitet-Fapesp-Unijuí, 2003.

Lynch, John. "El reformismo borbónico e Hispanoamérica." In *El reformismo borbónico. Una visión multidisciplinar*, edited by Agustín Guimerá, 37–60. Madrid: Alianza, 1996.

Marcos, Rui. *A legislação pombalina. Alguns aspectos fundamentais*. Coimbra: Almedina, 2006.

Mello, Isabelle de Matos. *Magistrados a serviço do rei: os ouvidores-gerais e a administração da justiça na comarca do Rio de Janeiro*. Rio de Janeiro: Arquivo Nacional, 2015.

Monteiro, Nuno. "A circulação das elites no império dos Bragança (1640–1808): algumas notas." *Tempo*, vol. 14, no. 27 (2009): 65–81. Accessed on December 28, 2013. http://www.historia.uff.br/tempo/site/?cat=55.

Paquette, Gabriel, ed. *Enlightened Reform in Southern Europe and its Atlantic Colonies, c. 1750–1830*. Farnham-Burlington: Ashgate, 2009.

Paz, Alonso. *Orden procesal y garantias entre Antiguo Regimén y constitucionalimo gaditano*. Madrid: Centro de Estudios Políticos y Constitucionales, 2008.

Pietschmann, Horst. *Las reformas borbónicas y en el sistema de intendencias en Nueva España. Un estudio político administrativo*. México: FCE, 1996.

Pimenta, João Paulo. *Brasil y las independências de Hispanoamérica*. Castelló de la Plana: Universitat Jaume I, 2007.

Rojas, Beatriz, ed. *Cuerpo político y pluralidad de derechos. Los privilégios de las corporaciones novohispanas*. Mexico: Cide/Instituo Mora, 2007.

Ruiz Torres, Pedro. "Los límites del reformismo del iglo XVIII en España." In *El nacimiento y la construcción del Estado moderno. Homenaje a Jaume Vicens Vives*, edited by Joaquim Albareda Salvadó, 111–150. Valencia: Universitat de València, 2011.

Schwartz, Stuart. *Burocracia e sociedade no Brasil colonial*. São Paulo: Perspectiva, 1979.

Slemian, Andréa. "As monarquias constitucionais e a justiça, de Cádis ao Novo Mundo: o caso da motivação das sentenças no Império do Brasil (c.1822–1850)." *Dimensões. Revista de História da UFES*, no. 39 (2017): 17–51.

———. "A primeira das virtudes: justiça e reformismo ilustrado na América portuguesa face à espanhola." *Revista Complutense de Historia da America*, vol. 40 (2014): 69–92. Accessed on January 24, 2014. https://revistas.ucm.es/index.php/RCHA/article/viewFile/46343/43550

Stumpf, Roberta and Chaturvedula, Nandini, eds. *Cargos e ofícios nas monarquias ibéricas: provimento, controle e venalidade (seculos XVII–XVIII).* Lisboa: Centro de História Além-Mar, 2012.

Tarello, Giovanni. *Storia della cultura giuridica moderna.* Bologna: Il Mulino, 1976.

Tucci, José Rogério Cruz and Azevedo, Luiz Carlos. *Lições de História do Processo Civil lusitano.* São Paulo: Editora Revista dos Tribunais, 2009.

Wehling, Arno and Wehling, Maria J. "*Sem mbargo da ordenação em contrário*: a adaptação da norma portuguesa à circunstância colonial." In *Administrando impérios. Portugal e Brasil nos séculos XVIII e XIX*, edited by Renato Pinto Venancio et al., 45–60. Belo Horizonte: Fino Traço, 2012.

———. *Direito e justiça no Brasil colonial: o Tribunal da Relação do Rio de Janeiro (1751–1808).* Rio de Janeiro-São Paulo-Recife: Renovar, 2004.

11 Family courts and violence against women in Guatemala, 1964–1996

John W. Wertheimer

Introduction

During a single week in 1975, a wife and her husband separately visited a new Guatemalan court. The new tribunal had invited such visits. It was family court.

The husband, Marcelino, visited first. He complained that his wife María had left home, taking their year-old daughter with her. Fearing that María might neglect the baby, Marcelino "urgently" asked the court "to order the mother of my young daughter to appear at a compulsory mediation session before Your Honor, Señor Judge. With your sage advice, we parents will ... find the best way to ... care for our daughter."[1]

Five days later, María visited and told a different story. Marcelino had beaten and expelled her, she said. She asked the court to help her retrieve her possessions and to confirm her custody of her daughter.[2]

The family court judge sprang into action. He immediately ordered the police to help María "get her pertinences ... out of the house that she occupied with her husband." The very next day, with police help, María removed from Marcelino's home a pine armoire, some clothes, a sewing machine, a wooden bed, a straw mattress, two pillows, a transistor radio, an electric iron, and two stones for grinding corn.[3]

The court also summoned the estranged spouses for a mediation session. After hearing both parties' stories, the court granted María the separation and child custody that she requested, along with twenty *quetzales* per month in child support. Marcelino got little: weekly visitation rights, as long as he eschewed alcohol on visitation days.[4]

Although María outdueled Marcelino in family court, the court itself may have been the day's biggest winner. Both spouses resorted to it when their marriage fractured, implicitly recognizing the family court's rightful place as the ultimate arbiter of family disputes in Guatemala. These new tribunals were blind to the widespread problems of domestic abuse and violence against women, but they enabled officials to penetrate the home as never before, impinging, at least to some extent, on traditional patriarchal prerogatives. The courts also accustomed family members to filing legal suits against each other in court, a vital precursor to later attempts to combat domestic violence.

From the start, women were, by a huge margin, the most frequent and effective family court litigants. The feminization of litigation that began in family courts soon spread to other parts of the nation's court system. Subsequent, high-profile, legal reforms, including the Intrafamilial Violence Act of 1996 and the Law against Femicide and other Forms of Violence Against Women (2008), would build on these precedents.

The Family Court Act of 1964

Guatemala's decision to create a system of family courts in 1964 was part of the nation's halting bureaucratic modernization. Decades previously, throughout the industrialized world, urbanization and prosperity had fostered judicial specialization, as seen in the creation of dedicated "juvenile courts" in the United States around the turn of the twentieth century (Rosenheim 2002; Tanenhaus 2004),[5] and in such modernizing Latin American nations as Argentina, Brazil, and Mexico following World War I (Armenta 2014; Beloff 2015).[6] Guatemala was a late adopter of specialized courts. It was an overwhelmingly rural nation. Justices of the peace and other courts of general jurisdiction were the most practical choice for a poor, sparsely populated nation. As Guatemala's population grew and concentrated during the middle third of the century, however, specialized courts became feasible.[7] By the 1960s, Guatemala's population, though still mostly rural, was larger and more concentrated than ever before.[8] Demand for specialized courts grew.

The Family Court Act of 1964 reflected a region-wide belief that the family was in crisis. During the 1950s and early 1960s, the Pan American Child Congress, a multinational group affiliated with the Pan American Union (later the Organization of American States), repeatedly discussed the dangers of family disintegration. Organizers identified several factors that seemed to underlie the breakup of families in the Americas: rural poverty, rapid industrialization, mass migration, political instability, and moral decline. The primary victims of family breakup were easier to identify: single mothers and poor children. This narrative echoed Latin American "maternalist-feminism," a long-standing movement in the region that blended activists' concerns for women's rights with mainstream concerns for "mother-child" issues. To remedy the problem of family disintegration, reformers urged the creation of family courts in countries, such as Guatemala, that did not yet have them (Instituto Interamericano del Niño, 1959: 54; Congresos Panamericanos del Niño, 1965: 251–252).[9]

Reform-minded Guatemalan lawyers proposed the creation of family courts in 1960.[10] Although family law in Guatemala had always been considered a regular sort of private law and had always been handled in the regular courts, these reformers argued that family law was unique, given its broad social ramifications. It deserved special institutions. They argued that regular courts were too formalistic and that regular judges regarded family disputes "not as the ***human*** problems that they are, but rather as routine legal cases." Dedicated family courts and judges were the answer, they insisted.[11] In response, the government appointed a commission of social workers, doctors, and lawyers to study the problem. Women constituted one-third of the commission's members, an unusually high figure for the time. The commission recommended a nationwide network of family courts. The resulting Family Court Act of 1964 established new tribunals with "exclusive jurisdiction over all matters relating to the family."[12]

The Act's blueprints reveal what sort of a court system its architects hoped to build. It started with personnel. Legislators wanted family court judges to be learned in the law but also mature and seasoned in the ways of families. Like all occupants of the Guatemalan bench (other than justices of the peace), family court judges and magistrates had to be trained lawyers.[13] But that was not enough. In addition, they had to be over thirty-five years of age. No other Guatemalan courts required judges or magistrates to satisfy such an age minimum. Judges and magistrates elsewhere merely had to be trained lawyers, a designation that could usually be achieved by twenty-three or twenty-four years of age. Furthermore, the Act specified that preference should be given prospective family court judges and magistrates who were "heads of household."[14] No other provision in Guatemalan law established such a preference for the exercise of a public charge.[15] The ideal family court judge, then, had not only the technical knowledge that comes with legal training and the wisdom that comes with age but also the special insight into family relationships that comes with being a "jefe de hogar," or head of household. The ideal family court judge was also male. The statute explicitly stated a preference for jurists who were not just parents ("*padres de familia*"), but rather heads of household ("*jefes de hogar*"). This wording had gendered implications. Married women with children could have qualified as parents, but, under the day's understanding, they would almost certainly not have been considered "heads of household." Framers clearly envisioned that men, not women, would wield the gavel in family court. Over time, female jurists would become fixtures in family courts. In some areas of the country, women would come to dominate the family court bench entirely.[16] But that was not the original plan.

Another distinctive feature of family court staffing was the required inclusion of social workers. By statute, each family court was to have a judge, appropriate administrative assistance, and "the social workers that shall be necessary."[17] No other Guatemalan court required the employment of social workers.[18]

The reformers' blueprint for family courts also revealed that their primary objective was to address the familial problems of "the lowest social classes."[19] They made sure that the 1964 law guaranteed legal aid to poor litigants whose cases "related to family matters."[20]

Family courts soon opened around the country, beginning in large cities.[21] The new tribunals inevitably fell short of their utopian goal: to resolve all of the nation's family problems. Nevertheless, the brisk business that they did, right from the start, forever changed how families and the state interacted in Guatemala.

The new family courts were places where family members sued each other. Suits between relatives accounted for over 99 percent of their dockets. Of these, about nine in ten cases pitted spouses or ex-spouses (whether formally married or not) against each other.[22] The new court system enabled the government to influence family matters as never before. Both disgruntled husbands and disgruntled wives could now leverage state power. Although wives ultimately proved to be the more active and more successful as litigants, let us begin with husbands.

Men

Men initiated only about 16 percent of sampled cases filed in one Quezaltenango family court in that court's first several decades of the existence. The relative passivity of men in family court contrasted with their relative activity in other sampled courts, where they initiated the majority of cases.[23]

Male litigants tended to use family courts differently than their female counterparts. Typically, women litigants assumed that conjugal bonds had already broken, and went to court seeking favorable breakup settlements, especially child support. By contrast, male litigants hoped that family courts would corral wayward spouses, bolstering male patriarchal authority within ongoing marriages. In doing so, however, these men ceded some authority to the state.[24]

Arturo was one such husband who sought to use family court litigation to rein in a rebellious wife. When his wife Irma left him following what he dismissed as "a little tiff," Arturo resorted to family court. "As my wife's reason for abandoning our home is insignificant," he told a San Marcos family court judge, "I wish to have … a mandatory mediation session with my wife so that … she returns home."[25] A husband named Antonio made a similar request after his wife Rosa left him. He asked a family court to intervene "with the object of making [Rosa] return, for I need her as a companion in our established conjugal home."[26] Another husband, Carlos, went even further. In addition to asking the court to compel his wife Lidia to return, Carlos urged a family court judge to order Lidia to stop working outside the home, apparently believing that Lidia's economic independence had made her difficult to control.[27] Husbands' track record in these cases was mixed. Often, as in the case of Marcelino and María, discussed above in the introduction to this chapter, they lost.[28]

Women

The Family Court Act's framers intended the new courts to provide the greatest benefits to women and children. The cover of a pamphlet that the government produced in 1964 to advertise the existence of the new court system depicted a young mother holding a newborn child.[29] This mother-centered imagery represented a fresh departure for Guatemalan legal culture. Never before had the nation's legal system so explicitly invited women to pursue legal remedies.

The advertising worked. As soon as the new courts opened, women flooded in. In 1965, the family courts' first full year, women initiated 83 percent of cases. This figure deviated little over the next several decades.[30]

Child-support cases dominated the docket from the start. That was by design.[31] "Denial of economic support" was the first cause of action listed in the new courts' founding document. In case after case, family courts ordered deadbeat dads to pay up. Aida Estela Alvarado filed a typical child-support case in family court in 1965. The father of her children had left and refused to pay anything. Despite Aida's poverty, the doors of the family court were open to her. A young institution called the *Bufete Popular* helped. The *Bufete Popular* was a legal-aid clinic for indigent clients run by the law school of the Universidad de San Carlos, Guatemala's major public university. It provided law students with real-world experience while providing poor clients with free legal representation.[32] Represented by the *Bufete Popular*, Aida went to family court, seeking child support. She requested monetary payments of twenty *quetzales* per month. The court awarded her ten *quetzales* per month. The *Bufete Popular* took zero.[33]

In addition to being frequent users of family courts, women were sophisticated users. They and their advocates learned to frame their cases in ways likely to win. The *junta conciliatoria* (mediation session) is a case in point. One of the top goals of Guatemala's Family Court Act of 1964 was to combat the disintegration of the nuclear family. The law deemed the nuclear family to be a "fundamental element of society."[34] The new courts would best be able to provide "effective protection for the nuclear family," the law's framers believed, if they followed "flexible" and "conciliatory" legal processes,[35] rather than rigid, adversarial ones. Mediation sessions were considered to be among the most "flexible" and "conciliatory" of all legal processes. The goal of such sessions was to stitch torn families back together.

To provide this sort of healing justice, the law's framers repurposed a mediation procedure contained in Guatemala's commercial code.[36] The result was the *junta conciliatoria*, or conciliatory mediation session, in family court.

Despite its warm-and-fuzzy exterior, the *junta conciliatoria* was frequently a disaster for abused women. Its goal—family reintegration—was often exactly what abusive men wanted, once they sobered up. Yet female litigants learned to use the procedure to pursue ends other than familial reconciliation. Paula Díaz requested a *junta conciliatoria* in San Marcos's family court in 1966 in order to compel the father of her children to recognize his paternity. Her goal was not to reunite with him. It was to force him to pay child support.[37]

Other women requested "conciliation meetings" in family court, even though their goal was to split, not to reconcile. Lucila sought such a session with her estranged husband Manuel, in 1965. Their marriage had produced zero children and countless fights. "He drinks, comes home drunk, and always mistreats me," Lucila told the judge. After nine years of this, Lucila left home and went to family court. She requested a *junta conciliatoria* not to patch up her marriage, as Family Court Law framers had envisioned, but to negotiate separation terms.[38]

Similarly, a woman name Rosa invoked the conciliation procedure against Mario, the father of her six children. Recently, Mario's "amorous relations" with another woman had destroyed their seventeen-year marriage. Rosa wanted to break free. She asked the judge for a *junta conciliatoria* so that she and Mario could come to an agreement "concerning the terms of separation and especially concerning the financial support that [Mario] shall be obliged to provide."[39] Another woman used a *junta conciliatoria* to demand that her ex-husband's parents return her daughter to her care, and to force her ex-husband pay child support.[40] When women such as these requested "reconciliation meetings," reconciliation was the last thing on their minds.

Domestic violence and family courts

A vanishingly small percentage of the cases in the 1965 sample focused concerted attention on domestic violence. This was entirely consistent with the vision of the Family Court Act's framers. Article I of the 1964 Act purported to give the new tribunals jurisdiction over "all family-related issues." Article 2 itemized the sorts of cases that framers imagined would be arise in family court: economic assistance, paternity disputes, child custody, guardianship, adoption, divorce, separation, and familial patrimony. "As one can see," legal scholar Luisa del Carmen Chinchilla Escobar despairingly wrote in a 2001 study of domestic violence law in Guatemala, "the [1964 Family Court Act] fails to mention anything related to intrafamilial violence" (Chinchilla Escobar 2001: 39–40).

Consequently, although tales of intrafamilial violence abounded in early family court proceedings, neither the courts nor anyone else seemed to care. For example, a woman seeking separation and family support in a mid-1970s family court case testified that her husband had abused her physically. Her husband's response was telling: "It is true what my wife has said, but if I have beaten her a number of times, it is because she has failed to comply with her obligations." To husbands such as this one, wife-beating was fully justified when wives failed to perform their wifely "obligations." The family court judge apparently agreed, treating this as a case of "family reconciliation," not spousal abuse.[41]

Even if these early family court judges had been culturally attuned to the problems of domestic violence and violence against women, as later judges would be, family courts themselves were institutionally ill-equipped to respond. The 1964 Act conceptualized the family as a crime-free zone. Family courts had no criminal jurisdiction. All of the legal issues that they were supposed to handle—economic assistance, paternity, child custody, etc.—came from the Civil Code, not the Penal Code.[42] Family courts employed civil, not criminal, terminology.[43] They followed civil procedures. They dispensed civil remedies.[44] No family court judge, however alert to the problems of domestic abuse, could have sent an abusive spouse to prison.

A troubling case from 1965 illustrates how anemic family courts were during these early years when faced with evidence of spousal abuse. Hilda, a twenty-seven-year-old Quetzaltenango housewife, lived with her husband Benedicto and their two young children. Benedicto was a violent drunk who often abused her physically. One evening, Benedicto came home and attacked her with a screwdriver. Desperate for relief, Hilda summoned the courage to ask the family court for protection. She did not find it. The family court ordered a "conciliation meeting." Hilda showed up at the appointed time, but Benedicto did not, and the case file contains no evidence that he paid any price for flouting the court's order, much less for assaulting his wife. Family court was ill-equipped to provide justice in cases of domestic violence.

Hilda's willingness to blow the whistle on an abusive spouse was rare. More common were indirect mentions of domestic violence designed to strengthen women's claims to other things. Some divorce-seeking women, for example, often hoped that evidence of spousal abuse would convince family courts that their marriages were irretrievably broken. Juana was one such divorce-seeker. Her husband, Higinio, was a heavy drinker. "We have not been able to live in peace," she told a Quetzaltenango family judge in the mid-1960s:

> He has brutally beaten me, to the point where I had to be examined by Dr. José de León, in the city of Coatepeque … Dr. de León confirmed that I had suffered a contusion on my left eye, caused by a blow administered by my husband … He mistreats me, insults me, and beats me.

She supported her divorce petition with a document prepared by Dr. de León of Cuatepeque, testifying to the facial injuries inflicted by Higinio.[45] Many other women also bolstered their requests for divorce by including heartbreaking evidence of domestic abuse.[46]

Other female litigants likewise invoked evidence of domestic violence to buttress their claims to child support. "On the fourteenth of this month [September, 1965]," María Sacalxot explained in a child-support case, "I was subject to mistreatment at the hands of my husband, especially physical blows." María escaped her husband's hands and found refuge for the night, but returned home the next day and "was received anew with another beating and was kicked out of the house." Concluding that no peace was possible with her husband, María planned to move in with her adoptive mother. In family court, she requested child support, nothing more. Tales of physical abuse bolstered her claims to child support, but did not, in themselves, constitute a cause of action.[47]

Other women documented spousal abuse in order to persuade family courts to help them recover personal possessions from marital homes. Juana left an abusive husband and moved in with her mother. She wanted to retrieve clothing and kitchen supplies from her husband's house, but feared his wrath. Her husband's blows were virtually audible in family court when she explained her situation. She and her husband had wed the previous year,

> but owing to … the incompatibility of our characters, we have been fighting almost all of the time since getting married. You see, my husband drinks liquor every weekend, and that's when he hits me. Yes, every Saturday he treats me very badly.

Juana told this story not because she expected the family court to do anything about the physical abuse. She simply wanted the court to protect her so that she could get her stuff back.[48]

Evidence of domestic violence, thus, could bolster women's claims to divorce, child support, and the like. In itself, however, such evidence elicited little response. This was not a case of judicial negligence. Indeed, the most responsible judges—the ones most scrupulous in their application of the law—may have been the most likely to overlook evidence of domestic violence. After all, Article 11 of the Family Court Act instructed judges to respond to family discord by employing "whatever means of persuasion they deem appropriate to achieve compromise."[49] Reconciliation, not punishment, was the goal.

Judges followed this script. Marta returned to her mother's home after seven years of marriage to an abusive husband named Lauro. About a week after moving out, Marta found Lauro waiting for her outside her place of employment. He hurled insults and "attacked her physically." The ensuing medical report that Marta filed in family court estimated that the injuries to her face would take seven days to heal, would cause her to miss four days of work, and would leave visible scars. Marta implored the judge to "prevent her husband from treating her badly."[50] Instead, the judge "proposed equitable formulas of compromise," trying his best, as the law instructed, to convince the family to reunite. Marta objected, explaining that she was "unwilling to return to her husband, in view of his bad treatment of her." What Marta wanted was safe separation and divorce. Lauro, by contrast, wanted reconciliation, and so did the court. Seemingly oblivious to the dangers involved, the judge, to the very end of the case file, continued to urge Marta and Lauro to keep "trying to resolve their problems."[51]

Criminal law

Guatemala's new family courts, thus, did little to combat domestic violence. But they did set in motion multiple trends that would facilitate future action. They dramatically increased women's comfort with litigation, as mentioned above. They demonstrated that Guatemalan households were no longer law-free zones. And they built institutional muscle that later anti-domestic-violence campaigners would flex.

The first sort of institutional muscle that family courts developed related to the criminal law. Family courts had civil jurisdiction only, but their users eventually learned to leverage the power of the nearby criminal courts. Most importantly, mothers seeking child support from deadbeat dads learned to bolster their family court claims with associated criminal prosecutions.[52] Many fathers simply ignored family court orders to pay child support. In many such instances, women who had won child-support awards in soft-and-cuddly family courts subsequently pursued their children's fathers with snarling criminal prosecutions. Their goal was not to jail the men, only to scare them into paying what they owed. "Nothing will be solved by throwing him in jail," noted María Yax while filing criminal charges for "family endangerment" against Trinidad Estrada in 1970. María cared only that he "pay up." The moment Trinidad honored his child-support commitments, María dropped the criminal charges.[53]

By the mid-1980s, child-support cases accounted the majority of all cases heard in Quetzaltenango's family court. They also constituted an impressive 9.5 percent of the cases heard in Quetzaltenango's criminal court.[54] All of these criminal child-support cases originated in family court.

Once child-support claimants had worn a path from family court to criminal court, other family court litigants followed. In 1970, a man sought to avoid paying child support by testifying that he was not the father. The mother knew better, however, and successfully pressed criminal charges against him for perjury.[55] Criminal law similarly got involved when an angry ex-husband sought to take his two-year-old daughter away from his estranged ex-wife. The ex-wife secured a family court order granting custody to her. She also threatened the ex-husband with criminal prosecution for "disobedience" if he refused to hand over the child.[56] More and more, family disputes appeared on criminal dockets. Domestic abuse cases subsequently would build on this trend.

Social workers

The reformers who devised the Family Court Act of 1964 had great faith in social workers. As mentioned above, each family court was to employ judges, administrative personnel, and "the social workers that shall be necessary."[57] One of the most important tasks of social workers was determining how much child support deadbeat dads could pay. This involved an invasive, formidable procedure. A social worker in a typical case from 1980 gave absentee father José the full-body, ability-to-pay treatment. Some components were obvious: income, assets, expenses, and debts. Others were less obvious, but understandable: José's health; whether he smoked, drank, did drugs, or gambled. The cavity search continued: José "does not frequent brothels." "He is not a member of any political party." "He professes the Catholic religion." "He does not play any sports." The level of detail was especially impressive given the José's modest status. He was an assistant construction worker who had been out of work for months.[58] The legal system's power to reach so far into the private lives of even the most non-elite people predicted future increases in the legal system's power, increases that would facilitate future anti-domestic-violence campaigns.

Many credentialed social workers were women.[59] This, too, presaged subsequent trends. In future years, more and more women, including prosecutors, police officers, and judges, would staff offices that dealt with family law in general and violence against women in particular. Indeed, some future governmental offices that worked with victims of domestic violence would, by design, be staffed entirely by women.

New protections

The third main institutional trend initiated by family courts was the development of new protections for vulnerable family members. Article 12 of the Family Court Act laid out the mission: "Whenever the family judge considers it necessary to protect the rights of any family member," the judge may immediately dictate "any and all precautionary measures."[60] In such cases of imminent threat, family courts could not play offence. That is, they could not capture, detain, or punish abusers. Article 12, however, enabled them to play strong defense.

Olimpia's story shows Article 12 in action. She married René in 1970 and soon had three children. But René was violently jealous. He did not permit Olimpia to go out alone. He also beat her, making her life "unbearable." Finally, after suffering a beating in 1975, Olimpia fled to her cousin's house. The cousin accompanied her to family court. Olimpia's statements in family court reveal an impressive, surely excessive, faith in that court's ability to help. "I have come," Olimpia told the judge, "... where I shall be protected from mistreatment and where I can express myself freely, recurring to this tribunal for these effects."[61] Olimpia's trust in the court's protective powers, though exaggerated, is nonetheless revealing. Many future women would likewise look to courts for protection against abusive men.

Other courts

The creation of family courts in the mid-1960s should, in theory, have siphoned all domestic disputes away from Guatemala's other courts. After all, the 1964 Act gave the new tribunals "exclusive jurisdiction over all matters relating to the family."[62] Family disputes, however, did not disappear from Guatemala's other courts. Indeed, they increased.

Family courts stimulated case-loads in other courts by cultivating the habit of intrafamilial litigation. Family court advocates worked hard to convince Guatemalans that domestic disputes were legitimate causes of legal action, rather than the secretive, private affairs that Guatemalan society had traditionally considered them to be. That message got through. Family litigation increased in Guatemala, even beyond family courts.[63]

In large part, family courts failed to monopolize family-related litigation because they lacked criminal jurisdiction. Guatemalans who sought to file criminal charges against family members had to look elsewhere, such as to low-level justice-of-the-peace courts. In these tribunals, as in family courts themselves, women would come to outpace men in filing cases. The 1964 Act seems to have been a turning point. A sample of criminal cases filed in a Totonicapán justice-of-the-peace court reveals this trend. In the decade and a half preceding the 1964 Act, women filed 44 percent of the victim-initiated criminal cases in that court. In the decade-and-a-half following the Act, the proportion of cases filed by women increased to two-thirds of the total.[64] As whistle-blowing in the justice-of-the peace courts feminized, the incidence of domestic-violence cases filed in those courts increased. In the fifteen years before the 1964 act, domestic-violence cases accounted for less than 6 percent of sampled criminal cases filed in Totonicapán's justice-of-the-peace courts. In the fifteen years after the 1964 act, domestic-violence cases in those same courts doubled, rising to 12 percent of the total sample.[65]

Conclusion

The Family Court Act opened a new phase in Guatemala's treatment of families. The law empowered the state to breach the domestic sphere as never before. Guatemalans, including poor Guatemalans, could now sue relatives more easily than ever. By a wide margin, women took fullest advantage of the new law. They initiated the vast majority of family court cases, almost always against current or former domestic partners. The increases in spousal litigation and female-initiated litigation that began in family courts soon spread from to other Guatemalan courts. The overall result was at least a modest decrease in male prerogatives and corresponding increases in state power and women's power. Prior to the family court era, Guatemala's legal system had reliably buttressed traditional marriage and other patriarchal family arrangements. During the family court era (1964–1996), that was less so. Defenders of machismo noticed. They regarded women's increased legal resources as an emerging threat. One unfaithful and abusive Guatemalan husband lashed out revealingly when his wife sued for divorce in family court in 1994. He accused her of being "the lover of all the lawyers to whom she resorts in search of protection and justice."[66]

The many changes initiated by the Family Court Act of 1964 set the stage for future advances in Guatemala's treatment of domestic violence. During the three-decade family court era itself, however, intrafamilial abuse remained largely a nonissue. Family courts were not designed to punish violent spouses. Just as significantly, few people at the time seemed to have considered domestic abuse or violence against women to be much of a problem. It did not help that family courts, which were supposed to have jurisdiction over "all matters relating to the family," were civil courts, ill-equipped to respond to crimes committed by some family members against others.

A 1993 United Nations survey revealed how un-attuned most Guatemalans remained to domestic abuse. Researchers interviewed a series of Guatemalan professionals whose work routinely brought them into contact with domestic violence. Interviewees included police officers, lawyers, doctors, nurses, and social workers. Their responses revealed widespread support for traditional patriarchal assumptions, such as "Women must obey men." When asked under what circumstances men were justified in beating women, about a third of the interviewees listed women's infidelity, drinking, jealousy, and like factors. Most respondents considered domestic violence to be a private family affair without broader social implications (Menjívar 2011: 46–47, 2012: 223).

Three decades into the family court era, thus, Guatemalan opponents of intrafamilial violence faced a daunting challenge. They had to change not just their nation's laws and courts but also its hearts and minds. That process soon began with the passage of two new statutes: the Law to Prevent, Punish, and Eradicate Family Violence (1996), and the Law against Femicide and other Forms of Violence Against Women (2008). These measures would open new chapters in Guatemala's far-from-finished struggle against domestic abuse and violence against women. The Family Court Act of 1964 remains substantially unchanged and is still in effect as of this writing,[67] but it has ceded its position on the leading edge of Guatemala's institutional response to domestic abuse.

Notes

1 Quetzaltenango, Juzgado de Familia [hereinafter QJF] (1975), case #20, recorded in notebook 2011-01, 96–98, in author's possession.
2 QJF (1975), case # 32, recorded in notebook 2011-01, 91–93, in author's possession.
3 QJF (1975), case # 32, recorded in notebook 2011-01, 91–93, in author's possession.
4 Although Marcelino lost on just about all counts, he promised to respect the family court's ruling. QJF (1975), case #20, recorded in notebook 2011-01, 96–98, in author's possession.
5 For more on this general trend in the North Atlantic world, see Rothman (1980), Skowronek (1982), Rodgers (2000), Keller (1977; 1990), and North (1985).
6 Also discussed in e-mail correspondence from Nara Milanich to John Wertheimer, July 27, 2018.
7 See Decreto Gubernative 2043 (1937), Ley de tribunales para menores.
8 Between 1940 and 1964, Guatemala's population density virtually doubled, from twenty-two inhabitants per square kilometer to thirty-nine (Departamento de Censos y Encuestas 1966: 11, 20). The urban population rose from 25 to 34 percent of the national total between 1950 and 1964. *Ibid.*, 20.
9 Participants struggled to agree on the principal causes of familial breakdown. For discussion of the broader "maternalist-feminist" movement in the Americas, see Guy (1998: 449–469) and Molyneux (2000: 49).
10 Guatemalan reformers had pushed for family courts as early as 1943. See Barrios Castillo (1943), discussed in Alburez Escobar (1964: 49). For more on these matters, see Wertheimer (2006: 407–410).
11 Molyneux (2000: 48–49).
12 Family Court Act of 1964 ("Ley de Tribunales de Familia," Decreto Ley No. 206, Guatemala, 1964), Arts. 1–2.
13 Decreto Ley Número 206 (1964), Artículo 5. At the time, Guatemalan justices of the peace did not need to be lawyers. Today, they do. Allan Amilkar Estrada Morales to John Wertheimer, July 23, 2018. The author thanks Allan deeply for all of his help over the years.
14 Decreto Ley Número 206 (1964), Artículo 5.
15 "En cuanto al requisito de jejes de hogar, no hay en la legislación guatemalteca otro precedente sobre esta condición para optar a un cargo público." Allan Amilkar Estrada Morales to John Wertheimer, July 23, 2018.
16 From 2000 to 2016, according to one lawyer, each and every judge and magistrate in the family courts of the nation's second-largest city, Quezaltenango, was a woman. In 2017, four new positions opened up on the family court bench in that city, and two of those four new posts went to men. Allan Amilkar Estrada Morales to John Wertheimer, July 30, 2018. Nationally, the family-court bench is more evenly divided than this between male and female jurists, but Estrada Morales, the Quetzaltenango attorney, estimates that women are slightly more numerous than men. Ibid.
17 Art. 7, "Ley de Tribunales de Familia," Decreto Ley No. 206 (Guatemala, 1964). http://www.forodderechoguatemala.org/wp-content/uploads/2011/07/priva013.pdf.
18 Allan Amilkar Estrada Morales to John Wertheimer, July 30, 2018.
19 This quotation comes from Supreme Court President Romeo Augusto de León, in his formal acceptance of the new law, quoted on page one of "Ley de Tribunales de Familia," Decreto Ley No. 206 (Guatemala, 1964).
20 "Ley de Tribunales de Familia," Decreto Ley No. 206 (Guatemala, 1964), Art. 15.
21 Ibid., Arts. 3–7.
22 One group that hardly ever filed cases was the government. The contrast with the justice-of-the-peace courts was stark. The Guatemalan government initiated over 40 percent of the sampled criminal cases taken from a justice of the peace courts in the

1950s. By contrast, government-initiated cases accounted for less than 1 percent of the cases in the family court sample, in the 1960s and thereafter. The government brought cases to family court only in highly unusual circumstances, such as when an abandoned minor child was found and turned over to the authorities. QJF (1975), case # 231. The statistical data in this paragraph and throughout the chapter come from sampling research conducted in Quetzaltenango legal archives. Research notes in author's possession and available upon request.

23 For example, as discussed below, men filed the majority of privately initiated criminal cases filed in a Totonicapán Justice of the Peace Court in the years leading up to the passage of the Family Court Act. Totonicapán Justice of the Peace Criminal Cases, 1952–2007, table compiled by author and in author's possession.

24 Note that men occasionally did seek family-court help when seeking divorce or otherwise navigating break-ups, though male-initiated cases of this sort were outnumbered by female-initiated cases of this sort. The men who initiated such cases tended to offer justifications that reinforced patriarchal norms. For example, Sebastian Otuc testified, when seeking to divorce Tomasa Coyoy de Otuc, "From the beginning of our marriage, my wife refused to perform her obligations." San Marcos, Juzgado de Familia [hereinafter SMJF] (1966), case #12, research notebook 2010-01, 16–17.

25 San Marcos, Juzgado 2[ndo] de 1[era] Instancia y Tribunal de Familia (1982), case #26/82, research notebook 2010-01, 28–29. My late father-in-law, Ezequiel Samayoa Sandoval, worked for a time as a lawyer in San Marcos. He represented the woman in this case, Irma Estela Cardona Vásquez de González.

26 QJF (1975), case #229/75, research notebook 2011-01, 106.

27 "I seek to reconcile with her and to reestablish our conjugal home," Carlos told the court, "with the single and strict condition that she stop working outside the home and dedicate herself exclusively to her domestic duties." QJF (1965), case #506, research notebook 2011-01, 79–80. Lidia was open to the idea of moving back in with Carlos, but she refused to give up working outside the home. She needed to work in order to pay off a debt. Carlos argued that he could cover the debt with his earnings, but Lidia would not budge. The case ended with Lidia suggesting that she would begin a family court case of her own: for alimony.

28 QJF (1975), case #20, recorded in notebook 2011-01, 96–98, in author's possession.

29 "Ley de Tribunales de Familia," Decreto Ley No. 206 (Guatemala, 1964).

30 In samples taken about once every six years between 1965 and 2003, women filed 83.3 percent of all cases in the QJF. Samples taken from 1965 (95 cases), 1975 (124 cases), 1985 (125 cases), 1994 (140 cases), 1998 (74 cases) and 2003 (179 cases). The total number of cases in the sample is 737, of which 614 (83 percent) were filed by women. Figures in author's possession.

31 The 1964 Act expressly targeted the needs of "abandoned mothers and destitute children." Ibid., 1. Quotation from Guatemalan Supreme Court President Romeo Augusto de León.

32 For background on the Bufete Popular program in general in Guatemala, see: http://www.estuderecho.com/estudiantes/bufete/index.html.

33 QJF (1965), case #112, research notebook 2011-01, 64. Similar examples abound. See the following cases from the Family Court of San Marcos in 1966: case numbers 6, 161, 156, 152, 141 and 111, research notebook 2010-01, 18–22.

34 Ley de Tribunales de Familia, Decreto-Ley Número 206 (1964), first "Considerando" ("Whereas") clause. http://www.foroderechoguatemala.org/wp-content/uploads/2011/07/priva013.pdf.

35 Ley de Tribunales de Familia, Decreto-Ley Número 206 (1964), second "Considerando" ("Whereas") clause. http://www.foroderechoguatemala.org/wp-content/uploads/2011/07/priva013.pdf.

36 Art. 203, *Código Procesal Civil y Mercantil.*

37 SMJF (1966), case #92, research notebook 2010-01, 8.

38 QJF (1965), case # 485, research notebook 2011-01, 81–82. The nature of the risks that Lucila faced came clear with her additional request: that the family court direct the police to provide her with protection as she removed her personal belongings from Manuel's house. Ibid.

39 QJF (1965), case #620, research notebook 2011-01, 72.

40 QJF (1965): case #491, research notebook 201-01, 80.

41 QJF (1975), case #335/75, research notebook 2011-01, p. 102.

42 Art. 2, "Ley de Tribunales de Familia," Decreto Ley No. 206 (Guatemala, 1964). http://www.foroderechoguatemala.org/wp-content/uploads/2011/07/priva013.pdf.

43 Family court cases were categorized according "juicio" (type of civil action) not "delito" (type of crime), and parties to the cases were labeled "actor and "demandado" (civil law terms) not "ofendido and "reo" (penal law terms).

44 Articles 8, 9 and 11, "Ley de Tribunales de Familia," Decreto Ley No. 206 (Guatemala, 1964). http://www.foroderechoguatemala.org/wp-content/uploads/2011/07/priva013.pdf.

45 QJF (1965), case #47, research notebook 2011-01, 64–66.

46 A twenty-one-year-old newlywed named María bolstered her family-court divorce petition by explaining that her young husband Agustín was drunk and abusive the point of threatening her life. QJF (1975), case #346/75, research notebook 2011-01, 99–100. See also SMJF (1966), case #17, research notebook 2010-01, 13–14; and San Marcos, Juzgado de Familia (1966), case # 15, research notebook 2010-01, 15.

47 QJF (1965), case #443, legajo #3, research notebook 2011-01, 84. Ana's family court case was similar. She and David were married in March of 1975, and the beating started almost immediately. By May, she was pregnant, disillusioned, separated, and in family court. "It is the case that my husband has treated me plenty bad since we got married, to the point of beating me," she stated. "I find myself with child, and, having been examined by a doctor, my desire is not to lose the baby." The court ordered David to pay alimony to her and, when the time came, child support to the baby. Ana asked for and received financial support in the context of a petition for a *junta conciliatoria*. The *junta* did not result in the couple reuniting, but did result in an arrangement whereby David would pay alimony and, ultimately, child support. QJF (1975), case #249/75, research notebook 2011-01, 104–105.

48 "What I ask for is that he hand over the rest of my clothes and my kitchen things," she told the court. QJF (1965), case #510, legajo #3, research notebook 2011-01, 74–75.

49 Art. 11, "Ley de Tribunales de Familia," Decreto Ley No. 206 (Guatemala, 1964). http://www.foroderechoguatemala.org/wp-content/uploads/2011/07/priva013.pdf.

50 QJF (1965), case #225, legajo #2, research notebook 2011-01, 66–67.

51 Ibid, 68–69. For another case in which a family court appears to have papered over a wife's concern about her mistreatment at her husband's hands, see the case of Marta and her husband Agustín. Agustín Coyoy's abuse caused María to flee to her parents' house. Agustín went to family court and requested a *junta conciliatoria*. The judge worked hard to persuade María to return to her husband. Agustín promised "not to treat María badly" in the future, to "behave himself" with her, and in general to "treat her well." María agreed to return, to carry out her homemaking obligations, to present herself and the children well, and in general to behave herself. The court-brokered deal appears to have papered over María's concerns about mistreatment to achieve a reconciliation. QJF (1965), case #152, legajo 2, research notebook 2001-01, 70–71.

52 Maximiliano was one such dad. Three months after marrying Juana, Maximiliano flew off with another woman, leaving Juana alone and pregnant. Juana then gave birth to María. When Maximiliano, an illiterate day laborer, refused to provide any support to his newborn daughter, Juana took him to family court. He "doesn't even know if it's a boy or a girl," she complained. The family court ordered Maximiliano to pay six *quetzales* per month—three each for Juana and her daughter. These were modest amounts, but more than Maximiliano wanted to pay. So he paid nothing. A

year later, Juana persuaded the family court to issue a more menacing order, but again Maximiliano ignored it. Out of patience, the family court set a criminal case in motion. Capture orders went out for Maximiliano. A month and a half later, he was arrested, charged with family endangerment, and thrown in jail. A subsequent criminal trial resulted in his being convicted and sentenced to a year in prison, commutable at least in part as long as he paid what he owed. Quetzaltenango, Tribunal de Sentencia [hereinafter QTS] (1970), case #8776, research notebook 2011-01, 8–11.

53 QTS (1970), case #8558, research notebook 2011-01, 12. A sampling of over 4,000 criminal cases filed in one Guatemalan criminal court between the 1920s and the 1980s illustrates the dramatic impact of family court on criminal court dockets. Prior to the Family Court Act of 1964, obviously family-related criminal charges (e.g., adultery, infanticide, abandonment of minor children, family endangerment) constituted less than two percent of all criminal cases. After the passage of that act, the incidence of such charges more than doubled, to over four percent of all criminal cases. Child-support cases filed by women in family court spearheaded this change. Such cases accounted for just 14 percent of family-related criminal cases prior to the creation of family courts, but 66 percent of family-related criminal cases thereafter (Wertheimer 2006: 401–406).

54 "Negación de Asistencia Económica" cases accounted for 122 of 1281 criminal cases heard in 1984 in Quetzaltenango's Juzgado de Primera Instancia criminal court [hereafter QJPI].

55 QTS (1970), case #8094, research notebook 2011-01, 55–56.

56 QJPI (1994), case # 538/94, legajo 14, research notebook 2011-02, 6–7.

57 Art. 7, "Ley de Tribunales de Familia," Decreto Ley No. 206 (Guatemala, 1964). http://www.foroderechoguatemala.org/wp-content/uploads/2011/07/priva013.pdf.

58 QTS (1980), case #2888, research notebook 2011-01, 27–28.

59 Apparently, university degrees in social work have existed in Guatemala since the 1940s and Guatemalan family courts have required these degrees of their social workers since the 1970s. Allan Amilkar Estrada Morales to John Wertheimer, July 30, 2018.

60 Art. 12, "Ley de Tribunales de Familia," Decreto Ley No. 206 (Guatemala, 1964). http://www.foroderechoguatemala.org/wp-content/uploads/2011/07/priva013.pdf.

61 QJF (1975), case # 42, research notebook 2011-01, 90–91.

62 Family Court Act of 1964 ("Ley de Tribunales de Familia," Decreto Ley No. 206, Guatemala, 1964), Arts. 1–2.

63 For a discussion of this phenomenon in the context of Quetzaltenango criminal courts, see Wertheimer (2006: 401–406).

64 Totonicapán Justice of the Peace Criminal Cases, 1952–2007, table compiled by author and in author's possession.

65 Domestic Abuse Cases in Totonicapán Justice of the Peace Courts, 1952–1980, a sample of 384 cases. Notes in author's possession. The upward trend in justice-of-the-peace courts would continue in subsequent years.

66 QJPI (1994), case #568–594, research notebook 2011-02, p. 5.

67 Allan Amilkar Estrada Morales to John Wertheimer, July 23, 2018.

References

Alburez Escobar, César Eduardo. 1964. *El derecho y los tribunales privativos de familia en la legislación guatemalteca.* Tesis: Facultad de Ciencias Juridicas y Sociales de la Universidad de San Carlos.

Armenta, Martha Frías and Livier Gómez Martínez. 2014. "Juvenile Justice in Mexico." *Laws* 3: 580–597.

Barrios Castillo, Oscar. 1943. "El juez de familia." Tesis.

Beloff, Mary and Máximo Langer. 2015. "Myths and Realities of Juvenile Justice in Latin America." In *Juvenile Justice in Global Perspective*, by Maximo Langer and David S. Tanenhaus, eds. Franklin E. Zimring, 248. New York: NYU Press.

Chinchilla Escobar, Luisa del Carmen. May 2001. *Violencia Intrafamiliar: Aplicación legal en el juzgado de primera instancia de familia del Municipio de Quetzaltenango*. Quetzaltenango, Guatemala: Facultades de Quetzaltenango Universidad Rafael Landívar, Facultad de Ciencias Jurídicas y Sociales.

Congresos Panamericanos del Niño. 1965. *Ordenación sistemática de sus recomendaciones, 1916–1963*. Montevideo, Uruguay: Impresora Liga.

Departamento de Censos y Encuestas. 1966. *Censo de población 1964: Resultados de tabulación por muestreo*. Guatemala: Ministerio de Economía.

Guy, Donna J. 1998. "The Politics of Pan-American Cooperation: Maternalist Feminism and the Child Rights Movement, 1913–1960." *Gender & History* 10 (3): 449–470.

Instituto Interamericano del Niño. 1959. *XI congreso panamericano del niño, Bogotá, Colombia*. Montevideo, Uruguay: Impresa LIGU.

Keller, Morton. 1977. *Affairs of State: Public Life in Late Nineteenth Century America*. Cambridge, MA: Harvard University Press.

———. 1990. *Regulating a New Economy: Public Policy and Economic Change in America, 1900–1933*. Cambridge, MA: Harvard University Press.

Menjívar, Cecilia. 2011. *Enduring Violence: Ladina Women's Lives in Guatemala*. Berkeley, CA: University of California Press.

———. 2012. "Violencias en la vida de las mujeres en Guatemala." In *Diálogos interdisciplinarios sobre violencia sexual: Antologia*, by Patricia Ravelo Blancas and Héctor Domínguez Ruvalcaba, eds. México, DF: Fondo Nacional para la Cultura y las Artes FONCA 449–470.

Molyneux, Maxine. 2000. "Twentieth-Century State Formations in Latin America." In *Hidden Histories of Gender and the State in Latin America*, by Elizabeth Dore and Maxine Molyneux, 33–82. Durham, NC: Duke University Press.

North, Douglass C. 1985. "The Growth of Government in the United States: An Economic Historian's Perspective." *Journal of Public Economics* 28 (3): 383–399.

Rodgers, Daniel T. 2000. *Atlantic Crossings: Social Politics in a Progressive Age*. New York: Cambridge University Press.

Rosenheim, Margaret K., Franklin E. Zimring, David S. Tanenhaus and Bernardine Dohrn, eds. 2002. *A Century of Juvenile Justice*. Chicago, IL: The University of Chicago Press.

Rothman, David J. 1980. *Conscience and Convenience: The Asylum and its Alternatives in Progressive America*. Boston, MA: Little, Brown and Co.

Skowronek, Stephen. 1982. *Building a New American State: the Expansion of National Administrative Capacities, 1877–1920*. New York: Cambridge University Press.

Tanenhaus, David S. 2004. *Juvenile Justice in the Making*. New York: Oxford Univeristy Press.

Wertheimer, John. 2006. "Gloria's Story: Adulterous Concubinage and the Law in Twentieth-Century Guatemala." *Law and History Review* 24 (2): 375–421.

Index

Note: Boldface page numbers refer to tables; italic page numbers refer to figures and page numbers followed by "n" denote endnotes.

About Philosophy in Havana (Mestre) 57
accusations, impeachment 130–4, 135n3, 136n17
Act Concerning Paths through Vines (1788) 148
"act of constituent power" 91
Adame Goddard, Jorge 107
Adams v *Lindsell* (1818) 42–3
Ahrens, Heinrich 57
Alcibiades (Plato) 24–6, 28, 32, 32n6, 33n27
Alcibiades, Socrates and 24–6, 32n6
Allison, John W.F. 37
Altamira, Rafael 57
Alvarado, Salvador 110
American Bar Association 75, 77
American codification 8
American common law 40, 48
American legal scholars 6
"American model" 90
amparo **114–16,** 114–17
Analects 21, 25, 26, 28, 31, 34n38, 35n62; proper relationship in 30–1; reverence in 29–30; sincerity in 28–30; trustworthiness 29; wholeheartedness 29
Ancien Régime 8, 179
Anglo-American law 163; impeachments in 123–5
Antiquitates 2
Apology (Plato) 22, 23
Appadurai, Arjun 4
Argentinian bar associations 70, 73, 74, 79
Argentinian–Brazilian legal exchange 12–13, 67–79
Argentinian Civil Code 71
Argentinian Federation of Bar Associations (FACA) 69, 70, 72, 76
Argentinian Institute for Legislative Studies 70
Argentinian jurists 69, 70
Argentinian lawyers 67, 68, 70–4, 76, 78
Association of American Law Schools 6
Audiencias 176–80
Audren, Frédéric 3–4, 80n4
Audrey Eu Yuet-mee SC 167
Augustine 15n2
Austin, John 11
Austrian ABGB (1811) 55
Austrian Kelsenian model 93
Azcárate, Gumersindo de 56–7
Azevedo, Filadelfo 76

Bachiller y Morales, Antonio 57
Baggio, Kátia Gerab 78
Baker, John Hamilton 38
bar associations 67–79
Barroso, Luís Roberto 138n43
Basic Structure Doctrine of India 88
Batiza, Rodolfo 150
Bello, Andrés 8
Benedict, Michael Les 136n15
benevolence 30–1
Benjamin, Judah Philip 12; biographies of 48n1; correspondence and consent 42–5; doctrine of mistake 45–8; early legal career 39; English law of contract 39–40; and legal change 38; nature of consent 40–2; reasoning 45, 46; reliance upon Louisianan Code 41–3, 48; resolution of difficulty 42; A Treatise

on the Law of Sale of Personal Property 39, 40, 44
Berger, Raoul 126, 134n2, 135n9
Berghmans Doncel, Carlos A. 74, 76
Beranger Law of Jalisco (1916) 110–11
Bevilaqua, Clovis 71
Bicudo, Hélio 137n41
Bildungsreise 78
Blackburn J 41, 45, 46
Black Codes 57
Boa Razão Act 181
Bojórquez, Djed 106
Book of Song 30, 35n61
Bourbonis reforms 15n9
Bracton 6
Bramwell J.A. 42
Brazil: and Argentina 67, 68, 71–2, 76–9;constitutional impeachments in 133–4; Constitution of 1824 127–8, 136n23; Constitution of 1891 128; Constitution of 1946 129; Constitution of 1988 130–31, 134, 137n34, 137n35; Decree 27 of 1892 137; Decree 30 of 1892 129–30; Federal Law 1079/1950 129; First Brazilian Juridical Conference 69; House of Representatives in 131–2; impeachments in 127–30; Law of 1827 127; law schools in 74; Proclamation of the Republic (1889) 68; re-democratization 130; Supreme Court 130–2
Brazilian Academy of Letters 73
Brazilian bar associations 70, 71, 74, 79
Brazilian Intellectual Embassy 74
Brazilian jurists 70, 134
Brazilian lawyers 67, 69, 71–3, 77, 78
Brazilian public law 127
Brazilian scholars 129, 130
"bribery" 124, 125, 135n9
British common law system 39, 125, 168
British New Liberalism 107
British rule, Hong Kong under 160–1
Brossard, Paulo 127, 129, 135n12, 136n20, 137n29
Brown, Eric 28
Buen, Néstor de 109
Buenos Aires Bar Association (CABA) 67–70, 72, 80n8; Franco's speech at 71, 78
Buenos Aires Jockey Club 72
Bufete Popular 191
Bulletin of the Pan-American Union 76
Byrne & Co v *Leon van Tienhoven & Co* (1880) 44
CA *see* Constituent Assembly (CA)
CABA *see* Buenos Aires Bar Association (CABA)
Cabral, Antonio Vanguerve 15n4
Cabrera case (1918) 112–13
Caenegem, Raoul van 7
Cajas-Sarria, Mario Alberto 13
Calasso, Francesco 4
Callicles 21, 23, 27–8, 33n32
canon law 3, 9, 179, 181
Canovas del Castillo, Antonio 107
Carranza, Venustiano 106, 111
Carrera Jústiz, Francisco 61–2
Carreras, Julio 63
Carvalho, José Murilo de 136n25
"catching up" ideology 6
Center for Latin American and Latino Studies (CLALS) 134n1
Centrality and Commonality 21, 26
Céspedes y Orellano, José María 57–9
Chaco War 74, 80n9
Charmides (Plato) 22, 28, 31
Chaves, Raul 130
Chen, Chi-Shing 12
child-support cases 191, 195, 201n53
Chilean lawyers 69–70
Chilean "social issue" 108
China, Rule of Law and 159, 162–3, 166
Chinchilla Escobar, Luisa del Carmen 192
circulation of legal knowledge 67–79
Civil Code of Lower Canada (C.C.L.C.): article 528 148; article 532 151; articles 510–527 146
Civil Code of the Canton of Fribourg (C.C.C.F.): article 471 147; article 477 145; article 490 149; article 491 150; article 492 150
Civil Code of the Canton of Valais (C.C.C.Vs.) 145–6, 148, 149, 153
Civil Code of the Canton of Vaud (C.C.C.Vd.) 149; article 441 145; article 458 147, 148; article 459 147; article 462–465 149; article 470 152
Civil Code of the Kingdom of Sardinia (C.C.K.S.) 146, 148
Civil Code of the Republic and the Canton of Neuchâtel (C.C.R.C.N.) 146, 147; article 522 148; articles 531–533 153
Civil Code of the State of Louisiana (C.C.S.L.): article 671 146; article 687 148–9; articles 689–691 150
civil law system 7, 39, 42–4, 48, 144, 155, 169, 170, 172
Code Napoléon (C.N.) 13, 143, 145–7, 151; article 653 145; article 674

150; articles 676 and 677 152, 153; promulgation of 55
codification 6, 8, 55, 71, 144, 155
Coing, Helmut 4, 5
Collor, Fernando 123, 130, 131
Colombia 13, 101, 102n2, 102n6; comparative legal history 87–9; Congress of Colombia 89–101, 102n8; constitutional amendment of 1968 93–4; Constitution of 1886 89–97, 101; Constitution of 1991 88, 89, 95–8; decision C-379/2016 99; decision C-551/2003 97; decision C-630/2017 100; decision C-674/2017 101; decision C-699/2016 99; decision C-1040/2005 98; Decree 927 of 1990 96; Decree 1926 of 1990 96; Federal Law 1354/2009 98; during military rule 90–2; *see also* Constitutional Court of Colombia; Supreme Court of Colombia
Colunga, Enrique 113
common law system 2, 168–70; American 40, 48; civil law and 7, 44; concept of estoppel 46; England 39, 125, 168; legal change in 38
"common walls and ditches" 145–6
comparative law, legal history and 2, 7–8, 11, 56–7
"competence vices" 97
Comte, Auguste 58
The Concept of Law (Hart) 1
Conciliation and Arbitration Board 111–12, 115
Confucius 12, 32, 35n77; *Analects see Analects*; *Centrality and Commonality* 21, 26; "ren," notion of 21
Congress of Colombia 89–101, 102n8
Conseil d'État 153
consent: correspondence and 42–5; nature of 40–2
Conservative and Liberal factions 89–91
Constituent Assembly (CA): Colombian context 94, 96; Mexican context 106–7, 113, 117
"constituted power" 91
Constitutional Affairs Chamber 92
Constitutional Court of Colombia 87–9, 93, 97; peace process with Farc 98–101; President Uribe and 97–8
"constitutional guarantees" 13
constitutional impeachments, in Brazil 133–4
constitutional judges 87, 88, 101
constitutional replacement doctrine 13, 97
"container society" 3
Conte, Emanuele 4
contemporary legal history 12
contract, Pothier's conception of 40
Contrat de Vente 43
Cooke v *Oxley* (1790) 43
Corpus Iuris Civilis (Justinian) 62
Cortina, José Manuel 76
courts, role of 87–8
Creoles 177, 182
creollos 179–80, 182n6
crimes de responsabilidade 128, 129, 136n17, 136n20
criminal law, in Guatemala's family courts 194–5
Crown Colony of Hong Kong 161
Cuba 12; comparative legal history 54–9; History of the State and Law 63; legal-historical analysis 59–62; revolutionary period 62–3; Spanish colonial domination on 54, 59
Cuban jurists 55, 60
Cuban War of Independence 58
Cueva, Mario de la 111
cultural history 5–6
Culture and imperialism (Said) 5
Cundy v *Lindsay* 47
Custom of Grandson (1703) 152
Custom of Orleans 146
Custom of Paris 148, 150–1

Dauchay, Serge 4
De doctrina Christiana (Augustine) 15n2
denationalizing legal history 3–6
Department of Press and Propaganda (DIP) 70
"*derecho indiano*" 8, 61
Derisi, Domingo A. 74
"development politics" 4
Digest of Civil laws (1808) 154
direct amparo system 113, 114 *see also* amparo
Dogmengeschichte 4
Dolz y Arango, Ricardo 60
domestic violence 14; and family courts 192–4
Duhamel, Vincent 165
Duve, Thomas 4

Ehrlich, Eugen 6
Eighth American Scientific Congress (1940) 75
El Brasil Intelectual 78
Elements of Commercial Law (Riesgo) 60
El Independiente 108

El País 107, 108
El Pueblo 111
Emperor 127–8
England 12; *Bracton* 6; common law 39, 125, 168; impeachments 123–5
English contract law 12, 39–40, 48 *see also* Benjamin, Judah Philip
English jurists 40, 46
English lawyers 40, 48
English news media 160, 161; in Hong Kong 162–8
"enlightened reforms" 178
Escobar, Arturo 4
Escobar, Pablo 95
"*esprit de corps*" 94
Europe: "catching up" ideology 6; codification paradigm 55; comparative legal history in 53; legal scholarship in 4, 6; legal tradition 4; social issue concept 107
European Middle Ages, law in 2
European model 93
Euthydemus (Plato) 22–3, 34n36

FA *see* Final Agreement (FA)
FACA *see* Argentinian Federation of Bar Associations (FACA)
Failures of the Legal Imagination (Watson) 49n2
"False Gods and True: 'The weightier matters of the law'" 162
family court: in Guatemala *see* Guatemala's family court system; in Quezaltenango 190
Family Court Act (1964) 188–90, 197; article 11 194; article 12 195–6
family law, in Guatemala 188
Farc, peace process with 98–101
Federal Board of Conciliation and Arbitration 116
The Federalist 126
Federal Labor Law (1931) 111, 116
Ferejohn, Michael 22
Ferguson, James 4
Fernández Bulté, Julio 63
feudal law 9
Final Agreement (FA) 87, 99, 100
First Anglo-Chinese War (1839–1842) 160
Florentine center 5
Flores Magón, Ricardo 110
Fonseca, Deodoro da 129
formants 7, 8
France 3; anti-formalists in 10; national law 15n9; political arrangement in 8; Society for Comparative Legislation in 56
Franco, Afrânio de Melo 67, 71–2, 77
Francophone Switzerland 143–4
Franklin, Benjamin 125
frankness, of interlocutors 25
Freitas, Augusto Teixeira de 72
French Civil Code *see* Code Napoléon (C.N.)
French Code of Property and the Different Modifications of Ownership 143
French law on neighboring plots of land 13–14, 143–4, 154–5; common walls and ditches 145–6, 155n5; distance and the intermediate works required for certain structures 149–52; plants bordering neighboring estates 146–9; right of view over neighboring property 152–4
"from soul to soul" 22, 25

Galuppo, Marcelo Campos 137n36
García Mérou, Martín 77–8
Gaviria, César 96
General History of the State and Law 63
Génesis de los Artículos (Rouaix) 111
Gény, François 6, 56
Genzner, Eric 4
Gerhardt, Michael J. 137n31
German Civil Laws 55
Germany: anti-formalists in 10; civil codification in 55; Historical School 3, 55; legal tradition 5; private law in 5
Gil, Enrique 76–7
Gill, Christopher 33n25
globalization 1, 7, 12; mondialization *vs.* 6, 15n6
Gómez, Laureano 90–1
Góngora, Victorio 107
Gonnet, Manuel B. 72
González, Alberto M. 113
González Lanuza, José Antonio 60
Gordley, James 38
Gorgias (Plato) 21, 23, 26, 28
Great Learning 21
Grossi, Paolo 5, 15n5, 53
Grotius, Hugo 11
Gruzinski, Serge 5–6
Guatemalan lawyers 188
Guatemala's family court system 14, 187–8, 196, 198n22; child-support

cases in 191, 195, 201n53; criminal law 194–5; domestic violence 192–4; Family Court Act (1964) 188–90, 194–6; *junta conciliatoria* 191–2; male litigants 190; new protections 195–6; social workers 195; women litigants 190–2
Guignard, Pierre-Henri 152

Halpérin, Jean-Louis 3
Hamilton, Alexander 125
Hannen J 45, 46
Hans, Valerie 15
Hart, H.L.A. 1
Hastings, Warren 124, 135n4
Havana conference 80n10
hermeneutic method 55
Hernández Corujo, Enrique 61
Hernández Más, Orestes 63
Herrera, Domingo 62
"high crimes and misdemeanors" 124, 125, 130
Hispanic America 5, 78
Historical Fundaments of Merchant Law (Infiesta) 62
historical method of interpretation 15n2
Historical School 3, 55
History of Private Law in Europe (Wieacker) 61
History of State and Law in Ancient Times (Fernández Bulté) 63
History of the State and Law in Cuba 63
Hoffer, Peter C. 124
Holston, James 4
Hong Kong News 162
Hong Kong, Rule of Law discourse in 159–62, 171–2; common law systems 168–9; as constitutive ideology 169–71; in English news media *see South China Morning Post*; legal pluralist perspective 170
The Household Fire and Carriage Accident Insurance Company (Limited) v *Grant* 44
House of Commons 123
House of Lords 41, 42, 123, 126
House of Representatives 126, 127, 129, 130; in Brazil 131–2; Caribbean island 76; legitimacy of 125; in United States 132
Huerta, Victoriano 110
Hull, Natalie E. H. 124

IAB *see* Institute of Brazilian Lawyers (IAB)
IABA *see* Inter-American Bar Association (IABA)
Ibero-American justice system 14, 176–82
Ibero-American lawyers 67
impeachment(s) 122 *see also* presidential impeachments
implied assent 42
India: Basic Structure Doctrine 88; "pepper empire" in 176
Indian Law 177–8
indiano 177
Infiesta, Ramón 61, 62
Institute of Brazilian Lawyers (IAB) 67–70, 72–4, 80n7
Inter-American Bar Association (IABA) 13, 67, 70, 75–8
International Federation of Lawyers 76
international law 9
Ion (Plato) 32n7
Islamic world, legal history 5
Italian Unitary Code (1865) 55
ius civile 2
ius commune 3
ius gentium 2
ius patrium 3, 7, 15n9
ius quiritium 2

Jacottet, Henri-Pierre 148
James, Timothy 113
Jiang Zemin 166
Johnson, Andrew 133
Jordão, Edmundo de Miranda 76, 77
Jornal do Comércio 70, 72
José Varona, Enrique 60
Judges, Legislators & Professors (Caenegem) 7
Judicial Committee 132
judicial review of constitutional amendments 88
judicium accusationes 131
junta conciliatoria 191–2
Juntas de Conciliación (1926) 112
jurisprudential thesis 37
justice-of-the peace courts 196
Justo, Agustín P. 74

Kennedy v *The Panama, New Zealand and Australian Royal Mail Company* 48
Krause, Karl Christian Friedrich 57

Labor Law of Bernardo Reyes 111
Labor Laws of Cándido Aguilar 110
Labovitz, John R. 135n4

Labra, Rafael María de 57
Laches (Plato) 34n36
La Corona factory case (1924) 112, 113
La Cuestión Social (Méndez Medina) 118n4
Lagos, Ricardo A. 74
La Madre Patria 55
Lambert, Édouard 7, 10, 56
Lam San-keung, Ambrose 167
La Nación 107
L'Ancien régime et la revolution (Tocqueville) 8
La Novísima Recopilación 109
La Prensa 70, 73
Larceny Act (1861) 47
Latin America 176; comparative legal history of 63; legal history 53, 63–4; legal system 10; maternalist-feminism in 188; presidential impeachments in 133
Lau, Dim C 34n37, 34n46, 34n47
La Violencia 90
Law against Femicide and other Forms of Violence Against Women (2008) 197
law books 2, 73
law of nature 33n24
Law on Workers of 1865 (articles 58–60) 109
law professors 1
law schools 1, 63; in Brazil 74; in European tradition 7
law-shaping lawyers 38
Law to Prevent, Punish, and Eradicate Family Violence (1996) 197
lawyers 3; in Argentina 67, 68, 70–4, 76, 78; in Brazil 67, 69, 71–3, 77, 78; in Chile 69–70; delegations of 72–5; in England 40, 48; in Guatemala 188; and legal change 38, 39
legal change, dynamics of 37–9
legal doctrine 1, 11, 88, 101
legal historians 3–4, 67
legal institutions 38
legal irritant 38
legal knowledge transmission 10, 67–79
legal philosophy *see* Confucius; Plato; Socrates
legal positivism 12, 56, 58, 60
legal scholars(hip) 2–3, 6, 11, 88
legal transplants *see* transplants
Legislative Act (LA): LA 01 of 1952 91; LA 01 of 1953 91; LA 01 of 1954 91; LA 01 of 1968 93–4; LA 01 of 1979 95; LA 01 of 2016 99; LA 01 of 2017 101; LA 02 of 1977 94–5; LA 02 of 2004 98; LA 02 of 2017 100; LA 03 of 1910 90; unconstitutionality of 91–2
Legislative Decrees No. 0247 and 0251 92
Le Roux-Kemp, Andra 14
Leo XIII, encyclical of (1891) 107
Leung Chun-ying 167
Leung Oi-sie, Elsie 165
Levene, Ricardo 61
Lewis v *M'Kee* 41
lex 3
Liberal and Conservative factions 89–91
Liberal Party 89, 90
Lima, Oliveira 79
Lindley J 44–5
Lin, Yü-Sheng 35n61
Litton, Henry 164
Lleras, Carlos 102n8
"localization of law" 178
local law *see ius patrium*
Loix et Statuts du Pays de Vaud (1616) 152
Lopes, José Reinaldo de Lima 178
Louderback, Harold 133
Louisiana 143–4; codifiers 154
Louisiana Civil Code 40, 42–3, 45–8 *see also* Civil Code of the State of Louisiana (C.C.S.L.)
Lower Canada, Civil Code *see* Civil Code of Lower Canada (C.C.L.C.)
Lysis (Plato) 24

Macias, José Natividad 106, 110, 111
McCarty, Philip C. 6
MacMillan, Catharine 12
Madison, James 127
magnum opus 5
Maine, Henry Sumner 56
Maine, Sumner 7
manner-related virtues 29
María Truchuelo, José 113
Martinez de Escobar 106
Martínez Pastor, Manuel 113
Martínez Paz, Enrique 74
Mason, George 135n4
Mattei, Ugo 7
Max Planck Institute for European Legal History 4–5
Mazatlán District Court 115
mediation session *see junta conciliatoria*
Mellish L.J. 42
Memorabilia (Xenophon) 23, 33n27
Méndez Medina, Alfredo 118n4
Meno (Plato) 34n36

"Mérou formula" 78
Mestre Domínguez, José Manuel 57
Mexican Liberal party 110
Mexican Revolution 106
Mexican revolutionary constitution of 1917 13; amparo **114–16,** 114–17; article 1 106; article 27 106, 107; article 123 106, 107, 111–13, 115, 116
Mexico: Catholic newspapers of 107; Constitution of 1857 109; Constitution of 1917 106–17; National Railways of Mexico 116; National Supreme Court of Justice *see Suprema Corte de Justicia de la Nación* (SCJN); in nineteenth-century 109
Milsom, Stroud Francis Charles 38
Minimum Wage Law and Board of Agreements 111
Mittermeier, Carl Anton Joseph 7
M-19 guerrilla group 96, 102n9
moderation 21
Møller, Jørgen 158, 159, 171, 172n1
mondialization 6, 15n6
Monteiro, Nuno 182n6
Montevideo 71
Morales Moreno, Humberto 13
Morris, Gouverneur 126, 133
Mulet Martínez, Fabricio 12
"multidirectional exchange" process 8
multistate systems 172n1
mutual assent 40, 43, 46

nación 8
Nam Ching Jo Bo 161
Napoleonic Code *see* Code Napoléon (C.N.)
National Conferences of Lawyers (1924) 69
National Constituent Assembly (ANAC) 90–1
National Front (NF) 92–4
"national law" 9–11, 15n9
National People's Congress Standing Committee (NPCSC) 164
nation-state, global legal history and 3–6
natural law 9, 38, 118n1
Natural Law Course (Bachiller) 57
Netherlands Civil Code 55
Neuchâtel: Civil Code *see* Civil Code of the Republic and the Canton of Neuchâtel (C.C.R.C.N.); *Conseil d'État* 153
"new man" 63
Nixon, Richard 122
Nogueira, Lauro 129
North Atlantic model, of law and politics 8
Nuevo León 111
Nuñez, Rafael 89

OAB *see* Order of Attorneys of Brazil (OAB)
Oakeshott, Michael 4
Obregón, Álvaro 106
"Occupy Central" movement 167
Octavio, Rodrigo 73, 74
O'Farrill, Juan Francisco 59
O impeachment (Brossard) 129
"An opinion on American solidarity" (Gil) 77
Opium War 160
Ordenações 15n4, 181
Order of Attorneys of Brazil (OAB) 69, 70, 80n7
Ordonnance des Ligues of 1523 148
Orientalism (Said) 5
Ostroukh, Asya 13–14
ouvidores 177, 180

Palavicini, Carrancista Félix 106
Pan American Child Congress 188
Pan-Americanism 67, 76
parapolitics 98
Paris: Custom of Paris 148, 150–1; Universal Exhibition in 68–9
Parker v *The South Eastern Railway Co.* 41
Paschoal, Janaína 137n41
Patten, Chris 166
PAU *see* Public Action of Unconstitutionality (PAU)
peace agreements 87, 96, 99
Peace Special Jurisdiction 101
People's Republic of China (PRC) 168, 172; and Britain 161; Rule of Law in 162, 165, 170
Petit, Carlos 56
Philadelphian delegates 124
Pihlajamäki, Heikki 54
Piqueras Arenas, José A. 54
"plan for cultural and juridical exchange" 72–5
plantocracia 55
Plato: *Alcibiades* 24–6, 28, 32, 32n6; *Apology* 22, 23; *Charmides* 22, 28, 31; *Euthydemus* 22–3, 34n36; *Gorgias* 21, 23, 26, 28; *Ion* 32n7; *Laches* 34n36; *Lysis* 24; *Meno* 34n36; *Protagoras*

34n36; *Republic I* 24; self-knowledge, notion of 21; writings 32n1
plebiscitary amendment of 1957 92–3
Poder Moderador 127, 136n23
Political Constitution of the Brazilian Empire 136n16, 136n18
political philosophy 126–7
Pollock, Frederick 44, 49n22, 50n38
Polus 23
Pomeroy, J. N. 137n29
Porfirian period 111
Portugal 180–1; Spanish monarchy and 176
Portuguese America 176–80
Portuguese Civil Code (1867) 55
Posada, Adolfo 57
Pothier, Robert Joseph 39–41, 43–6
pozole 109
praticas 3
presidential impeachments 13, 122–3; accusation 130–4, 135n3, 136n17; in Anglo-American law 123–5; in Brazil 127–30; Senate as a tribunal 126–7; trial of 130–3
"primary constituent power" 96
private international law 10, 57
Program of Political and Administrative Law 60
proper relationship 12, 21; in *Analects* 30–1; Socratic concept of 26–8
Protagoras (Plato) 34n36
Prussia 162
Prussian Empire of Bismarck 107
Public Action of Unconstitutionality (PAU) 87–90
Pym, John 135n3

quasi-contracts 43
Quebec 143–4; codifiers 145, 148, 150–1; French provisions in 154
Queiroz, Rafael Mafei Rabelo 13
Queretaro, Constituent Assembly of 117
Quesada, Ernesto 79
Quezaltenango family court 190, 198n16

Rabban, David 6
Ramírez, Ignacio 109
Raz, Joseph 15n1
reciprocal assent 43
Recopilación de Leyes de Indias of 1593 109
"Regeneration" 89
"*ren*" 21; rites and 30
Renner, Karl 8
representative democracy 10
Republican Union movement 90
Republic I (Plato) 24
Rerum Novarum 107
reverence, in *Analects* 29–30
Revista 70, 76
Reyes, Rafael 89–90
Riesgo, Bernardo del 60
Rio de Janeiro 70–3, 77; *Tribunal da Relação* in 177, 180
rites and *ren* 30
Rivarola, Rodolfo 74
Rodríguez Saráchaga, Oscar 71, 74
Rodríguez, Zorobabel 108
Rojas, Luis Manuel 106, 111
Rojas Pinilla, Gustavo 90–2
Roman law 2–4, 164
Romero del Prado, Víctor N. 74
Romilly MR 44
Rouaix, Pastor 106–7, 111, 117
Rousseff, Dilma 122, 123, 131–3, 138n42
Royal and Pontifical University (of Saint Jerome) of Havana 54
Rule of Law 14, 92, 108; bottom-up approach 159; and China 159, 162–3, 166; definitions of 158–9; discourse in Hong Kong *see* Hong Kong, Rule of Law discourse in
Ruskola, Teemu 168, 170–2

Sacco, Rodolfo 7–8
sacrocracia 55
Said, Edward 5
Saint-Joseph, Antoine Fortuné de 150
Saint Thomas University 58
Sakrani, Raja 5
Salamanca school 5
Saleilles, Raymond 56
Sánchez de Bustamante y Sirvén, Antonio 60
Santamaría García, Antonio 54
Santiago 71
Santos, Juan Manuel 98, 99
São Paulo 74
Sarmiento, Domingo Faustino 74–5
Savigny, Friedrich Karl von 3–5, 11–12, 55–6
SCJN *see Suprema Corte de Justicia de la Nación* (SCJN)
self-knowledge, Plato's notion of 21
Senate 122–3, 130–1; impeachment committee in 132–3; "tribunal" for impeachments 126–7; United States 127, 133

Seventh Ballot proposal 96
Silgueira, J. Honorio 70, 72, 77; "plan for cultural and juridical exchange" 72–5
Silveira, Mariana de Moraes 12–13
Simpson, Alfred William Brian 38
Simpson, Cheung 165
sincerity 12, 33n23; in *Analects* 28–30; Socratic concept of 24–6
sincerity-based proper relationship 12, 21–32
Sino-British Joint Declaration (1984/1985) 161, 164, 168
Skaaning Svend-Erik 158, 159, 171, 172n1
Slemian, Andréa 14
Smith v *Hughes* 41, 45
Snowden, Edward 165
Soares, Gabriela Pellegrino 79n1
social constitutionalism 110, 117
social guarantees 13, 106, 111–13; ambiguities and protection of 114–17
social issue: Chilean 108; European concept of 107
social rights 106
Social Rule of Law model 98
Society for Comparative Legislation 56
Socrates 12, 21, 32, 32n1, 35n77; and Alcibiades 24–6, 32n6; and Callicles 23, 27–8, 33n32; idea of soul 22–4; idea of virtue 22; proper relationship 26–8; *Republic I* 24; sincerity 24–6; wisdom, notion of 34n36
Socratic elenctic practice 21, 24, 33n1, 33n23
Sorá, Gustavo 78
soul, Socratic idea of 22–4
South Africa 164
South America: bar associations 71; legal scholars 6
South-Central Brazil, development of 177
South China Morning Post 161; post-handover on July 1, 1997 164–8, *165*; prior to July 1, 1997 162–4, *163*
Spain: civil codification in 55; comparative legal studies 55
Spanish America 176–8, 180
Spanish monarchy 180; and Portugal 176
Spanish reform 54
specialized courts, in Guatemala 188
Special Legislative Act for Peace 99
State, law and 9–11
"state of siege" 92, 93
"state-of-soul" 22
Stock, Frank 168
Story, J. 137n29
"The Student Movement of the Seventh Ballot" 96
"Substitution of the Constitution Doctrine" 89, 97
Sunstein, Cass 124
Supervielle, Manuel Fernández 76
Suprema Corte de Justicia de la Nación (SCJN) 111–17, **114–16**
Supreme Court of Brazil 130–2
Supreme Court of Colombia 13, 88, 89, 92–7, 101
Supreme Court of Mexico 13, 112–15
Swiss Civil Code 155n7 *see also* Civil Code of the Canton of Fribourg (C.C.C.F.); Civil Code of the Canton of Valais (C.C.C.Vs.); Civil Code of the Canton of Vaud (C.C.C.Vd.); Civil Code of the Republic and the Canton of Neuchâtel (C.C.R.C.N.)

Tarello, Giovanni 15n7
Tayloe v *Merchants' Fire Insurance Company* 43–5
Teixeira de Freitas 8
Teubner, Gunther 38
Theiler, Eduardo 73
The nature of the judicial process (Cardozo) 6
Thesiger LJ 44
Thibaut, Anton Friedrich Justus 55–6
Thousand Days War 89
Totonicapán justice-of-the-peace court 196
Traité des Obligations (Pothier) 40
transplants 7, 8; Watson's thesis of 37–8
"treason" 123–5
Treatise of International Private Law (Sánchez de Bustamante y Sirvén) 60
A Treatise on the Law of Sale of Personal Property (Benjamin) 39, 40, 44
Treaty of Tordesillas 176
Tribunal da Relação 177, 180
Trigo, Octavio 113
trustworthiness, in *Analects* 29
Truth 163
Tsang, Steve 160–1

"Umbrella" movement 167
unconstitutional constitutional amendments 88–9; Constitutional Court and 97–101; LA 01 of 1979 95;

LA 02 of 1977 94–5; during military rule 90–2
United States 75–6; comparative legal history in 53; House of Representatives 132; juvenile courts in 188; Senate 127, 133
United States Constitution 123–6; art. I, §2, 5 135n13; art. I, §3, 7 135n11; art. I, §9, 8 135n6; art. I, §3, 6 135n14; art. II, § 4 135n5; art. III, § 3, 1 135n8
University of Cordoba 74
University of São Paulo 15, 79n1
Uprimny, Leopoldo 92
upside down parliamentarianism 128
Urdaneta, Roberto 90
Uribe Vélez, Álvaro 97–8, 102n11
Uriburu, José Félix 74

Valladão, Haroldo 73
Vallance, William Roy 75
Vargas, Getúlio 70, 74–5, 77, 129
Vassalli, Filippo 53
Vélez Sarsfield, Dalmacio 71–2
Veracruz: District Court in 115; Labor Laws of Cándido Aguilar 110
virtue(s): of manner 29; Socratic idea of 22
Vlastos, Gregory 32n1

Walton, Frederic 144
Washington, George 127
Watson, Alan 37, 49n2
Wertheimer, John 14
Western legal tradition 7
wholeheartedness, in *Analects* 29
Wieacker, Franz 4, 5, 61
Willes J 41
will theory of contract 40, 41
wisdom, Socratic notion of 34n36
work accidents, compensation criteria for 111
"The Workers Question" 108

Xalapa, Central Board of Conciliation and Arbitration 115
Xenophon 23, 33n27
Xi Jinping 166

Yan, Shi-an 35n61
Yiannopoulos, Athanassios N. 146
"*yi*," idea of 31
Yucatan: Board of Conciliation and Arbitration 112; law of Salvador Alvarado 110

Zachariae, Karl S. 7
Zambrana, Antonio 58
Zeballos, Estanislao 79
Zumbansen, Peer 158, 170